The Sky's the Limit

THE JOE DIAL STORY

DOUG EATON with JOE DIAL

WITH FOREWORDS BY

Garth Brooks

Sergey Bubka

Steve Patterson

"You have only one chance to be the best and that's to dedicate yourself to one thing. You can't spread yourself too thin. People say I'm dumb to put all my eggs in one basket, but I'm going to give it my very best. I'm giving it everything I've got."

> — **Joe Dial** after setting a new American record in the pole vault as he cleared 19 feet, 1½ inches at the Big Eight Conference meet at Manhattan, Kansas; May 12, 1985.

Gold Medal Publishing, LLC
10329 South Granite Avenue
Tulsa, OK 74137

GoldMedalPublishingLLC.com

First Edition: January 2018

ISBN 978-0-09994607-2-6 (paperback)

ISBN 978-0-09994607-0-2 (hardcover)

ISBN 978-0-9994607-1-9 (ebook)

Printed in Canada

TO THE MEMORY OF DEAN DIAL ("DAD")

Thanks for not only being my coach from age 5–34, but for being the best example and role model possible for me.

TO THE MEMORY OF TIM SKITT

From the first day I saw you as a seventh grader to the last day I talked and prayed with you, one word comes to my mind when I think of you—"Champ."

— JOE DIAL

TO THE MEMORY OF THOMAS LIGON

A rising decathlete who loved track and field with a passion and whose favorite saying was "Never Stop."

— DOUG EATON

"Be passionate, be daring, be courageous, all while being true to yourself."

— THOMAS LIGON

CONTENTS

FOREWORD

Garth Brooks

Joe's teammate on the Oklahoma State University track team

We've all been there . . . seeing the surface of the water from underneath, battling to get there with little or no breath left, trying not to think about what happens if you don't get there, while the whole time, that exact thought is what is driving you to get there. That was Joe Dial and his sports journey throughout the many different levels of his career. You could see he had goals, dreams and a vision, but only Joe could see what they were and you believed he would get there or die trying.

I believe all dreams start casually and then progress to become what drives you. Joe would joke about going to meets and passing under the bridges and each bridge had a height on it and he would say to himself, "I'm going to clear that height today." But at some point, those heights turned from bridges to world records. It was cool to be friends with someone who dreamed and competed on a "global" level. I have to say I truly believe getting to be a part of that is what made me not afraid to compete on a global level with music. Joe is the most down to earth guy there is, so if he can come from a small town with big dreams, then all of us can. All you have to do is trade your days, work your ass off and believe.

For me, the actual "doing" of something is not the greatest talent. What value is a gift if you cannot pass it on? This is where Joe Dial became a hero to me. Joe has to be one of the greatest teachers of the sport. I watch him, all the time, take what gifts God has given an individual and he goes to work making those gifts the best they can be. He will not try to change you; he will try to make what you believe in stronger. That is a true gift, one very few people possess. I know I do not. He also applies that "teaching" in life. As a friend, a teammate, dad, and husband, I truly feel blessed to have Joe Dial in my life and believe with all my heart, there are a lot of people who would say the same.

Sergey Bubka

Arguably the world's best pole vaulter in track & field history; Set world
records in the pole vault 35 times (17 outdoor, 18 indoor); Gold medal
winner in pole vault at 1988 Seoul Olympic Games; Won six consecutive
IAAF World Championships, 1983–1997; Currently Senior Vice President
of the IAAF and President of the National Olympic Committee of Ukraine;
Joe's friend and respected competitor

I competed together with Joe Dial in the 1980's. There are many
memorable moments from that time – we both were young and
optimistic - and it was really nice to perform and spend time together.

Joe was fond of pole vault, thirsty for jumping but I remember him
not only as a perspective pole-vaulter that he proved winning the bronze
medal at the 1989 World Indoor Championships in Budapest. I remember
Joe as a positive and open person who was always very enthusiastic.

The 1980's was a difficult time, taking in account the special political
situation. Nevertheless, we (the athletes from USA and USSR) competed
together, communicated and were friends. That once again reflects the power
of sport.

I have heard that Joe has dedicated his life to sport as a coach. I would like
to wish him success in implementing all initiatives and inspiration in his
daily challenging activities!

Steve Patterson

Joe's childhood friend, teammate at Marlow High School
and on the Oklahoma State University track team

No one could outwork Joe. It just wasn't possible. Joe and his dad would go out and vault eight to ten hours a day in the summer. Sometimes they would turn the headlights on their car so Joe could still jump after dusk. They weren't going to lose any opportunity to practice. It was almost that Joe willed himself to be good. He simply outworked everyone.

The times that they weren't out actually practicing, they spent time watching film of other vaulters. They would look at what made other vaulters successful and constantly look for ways for Joe to improve.

Joe would often vault some 100 to 120 times a day in the summer, which is an unbelievable number considering the amount of effort and strength required and the degree of stress and tension placed on one's body. Joe wanted to be great and Joe's dad wanted him to be great. They wanted him (Joe) to succeed and were going to do whatever it took to make that happen. They left it all on the runway.

He still practiced in college more than anybody I've ever seen. There were probably some people who may have had as much or more athletic ability than Joe, but they didn't have the same passion, the same work ethic, the same desire to be great as Joe. He structured his life to be great in the pole vault. His whole life was built around pole vaulting.

PREFACE

Having been a life-long track and field fan, I enjoy attending track meets and reading about track and field athletes. Unlike the gigantic revenue-producing sports of college and professional football and basketball, the sport of track and field is often an overlooked, or even forgotten, sport.

While football, basketball and baseball players often receive the publicity, adulation and endorsement deals, track and field athletes often fly under the radar. They may go unnoticed by the fans, except by parents or friends, and are often underappreciated by sports fans in general, with the possible exception of every four years when the Summer Olympic Games roll around.

When our American athletes are running, jumping and throwing against the best the world has to offer, Americans often take notice during those ten days that track and field is highlighted during the Olympic Games. But with the method the USA Olympic Track & Field Team is selected — i.e., based on how well an athlete performs on a single day during the Olympic Trials determines if he or she makes the USA team — many otherwise deserving and accomplished athletes may not make the USA Olympic team for various reasons.

Such was Joe Dial's experience.

Despite setting the indoor pole vault World Record; despite setting the American Record in the pole vault nine times; despite being a four-time NCAA pole vault champion and despite being a four-time Oklahoma high school state champion, Joe never enjoyed the honor of representing his country at the Summer Olympic Games. But qualifying for the Olympic Trials a record-tying five times, is a remarkable accomplishment itself.

But at each of those five Olympic Trials, fate intervened in a number of ways, sometimes just enough to nudge Joe out of the three qualifying spots. Youthfulness (Joe was just 17 years old at his first Olympic Trials), injuries, the death of a close family member, and just plain bad luck all seemed to take turns to prevent Joe from making the USA Olympic team.

But don't feel sorry for Joe.

Born and raised in the small southern Oklahoma town of Marlow (population 4,662), Joe enjoyed the advantages and benefits of small town living as he established the foundation for what would become his life's occupation and dedicated his life to the sport of pole vaulting.

From the age of five when his father, Dean Dial, a former pole vaulter himself, started teaching Joe the finer points of vaulting in the family's front yard, until Joe retired from the sport at age 34, Joe experienced one of the most remarkable and enviable careers in the sport. Going on to serve as a head coach of track and field for 24 years (and still going strong) at the collegiate Division I level enables Joe the opportunity to pass on his wisdom and insight to the next several generations.

Owing to his incredible work ethic, his fearless attitude and an insatiable desire to succeed, Joe traveled the world many times over to compete against the world's best vaulters. Many times, events off the track proved to be as exciting and memorable as the competition on the track and runway.

In writing this book, I have attempted to capture the essence of the remarkable story of this unassuming, humble, God-fearing individual. More people need to know who Joe Dial is, learn of his accomplishments, share in his lighter moments and appreciate his efforts, not only in the sport of pole vaulting, but also in shaping and molding the lives of young student-athletes in his role as a collegiate coach.

— DOUG EATON

As I reflect on my pole vaulting and coaching career, I realize how fortunate and blessed I have been. I have traveled to places, experienced and seen things, and met people through the sport of track and field on more occasions than I had ever imagined I would be able.

I have become friends with so many people — from around the country and the world — that it is hard to comprehend what my life would be without the experiences I was able to enjoy thanks to my pole vaulting.

For all this, I have many people to thank.

First, I want to thank God. Looking back, I can easily see how things could have turned out in so many different paths. I want to thank my parents, Dean and Lena Dial. My parents sacrificed much in order to provide me the opportunity to participate in sports while growing up. It was a team effort from my parents as my Dad coached me my whole career in vaulting and my Mom would video me.

I also owe a lot to my immediate family. My wife Shawna has always been there for me through the good times as well as the challenging times. She has, and is, serving many roles — wife, mother, grandmother and assistant coach. My three sons, Tim, Tommy and Tyler, have been a real joy as we witnessed their growth and watched them excel in athletics in their own right. Now with our family growing and the addition of our daughter-in-law Kristen, granddaughter Leighton and grandson Graham, we hope to keep the Dial pole vault tradition rolling!

While I may have incurred my share of injuries and unfortunate turn of events at times, I refused to give up and always tried to fight the good fight. Every time I ran down the pole vault runway, whether it was in high school, college or as a professional, I was confident that I was going to clear that height. The power of positive thinking is a remarkable thing. Being prepared was the product of my working hard at it. I felt that no one could outwork me. I made sure I was as prepared as much as possible and I have tried to instill those qualities in the young men and women I am coaching.

I have more people to thank for helping me along the way. My high school coaches, Darvis Cole and Gary Boxley; and my college coach, Ralph Tate, all showed me how to motivate athletes and taught me how important it is to respect individuals regardless of ability. I was also fortunate to serve under the tutelage of J.D. Martin, Bob Brooks, Mike Carter and many others. I tried to take bits and pieces of their collective wisdom and leadership traits and incorporate those qualities into my personal coaching philosophy.

I have also been fortunate to have great teammates through the years. Even though the pole vault event is an individual event, being a part of a high school, college or national-level track team was always a thrill which I enjoyed.

So many individuals have had a positive influence on my life and contributed to my success. I hope to pay it forward by touching and influencing many young lives and serving as a positive role model.

While world records, American records, meet records, college records, and high school records are all nice, the simple ability to compete in a sport I truly love is what I cherish the most.

— JOE DIAL

The World Record

February 1, 1986 » Hearnes Center » University of Missouri » Columbia, Missouri

On a cold, blustery winter day in the central Missouri college town of Columbia, a young, aspiring athlete set his sights on clearing the highest obstacle he had ever faced.

Joe Dial, at twenty-three and a half years old, had spent practically his entire life perfecting the art of pole vaulting. Starting at age five, thanks to his father who was an outstanding pole vaulter in his own right, Joe had sprinted down a pole vault runway carrying a carbon fiberglass spear literally thousands of times.

A little background: the year 1986 started with the world indoor record set at 19 feet, 2¾ inches by Joe's long-time rival Billy Olson on December 28, 1985, in Saskatoon, Canada. Olson's jump broke the previous mark that had stood for over a year and a half of 19-2 set by Thierry Vigneron of France.

"In early January, I jumped 19 feet in practice one day and came back and jumped 19-1 the next day. I then tried 19-8 but I hit the light (the ceiling light in the practice facility but more on that later). Based on those practices, I had lots of confidence and was sure the record would soon be mine.

"There was no doubt in my mind that I was going to break the world record in my first meet of the year. No doubt about it," Joe said.

Joe's first meet of 1986 was on January 15 at Osaka, Japan, where Joe would go head-to-head against Soviet pole vaulter Sergey Bubka, who had already broken the world indoor record three other times, all back in 1984.

Joe recalls his last practice just prior to flying to Japan was probably the "best practice I've ever had."

At the last minute, one of Joe's friends decided to accompany him on the trip. The only trouble was this friend was coming down with a case of the flu, unbeknownst to Joe.

Being in close quarters with someone already bitten by the flu bug, by the time the 13 hour flight to Japan had landed at Osaka, Joe discovered he had also come down with the flu.

"I went from one extreme to another. I went from feeling the greatest I ever felt and looking forward to competing to suddenly being down with the flu. I stayed in bed for three days before that meet," Joe said.

Still feeling bad and definitely less than 100%, Joe nevertheless made a valiant attempt in his efforts in battling Bubka.

"I made 18 feet and then tried 18-8 but tweaked my hamstring, I think from being so dehydrated from the flight and fighting off the flu."

Bubka went on to break the world record at the meet with a vault of 19-3.

Two days after Bubka's record, Olson regained the record at a meet in Inglewood, California, as he cleared the bar at a half inch higher to up the world record to 19-3½.

Eight days later, Olson is on a tear as he improved his indoor record a fraction of an inch higher to 19-3¾ competing in a meet at Albuquerque, New Mexico.

In the meantime, Joe sat on the sidelines nursing his tender hamstring, watching the world record gradually inching upward, but anxious to get back in action and make his run at the record. But Joe had some particular limitations in mind.

Returning from the injury, Joe was seeking a relatively smaller meet in which he could test his hamstring. Competing in a larger meet not knowing exactly how his hamstring would hold up in the heat of competition might risk further injury.

Originally planning to travel to Dallas to participate in the Dallas Times-Herald Invitational Meet, Joe then became aware of a smaller meet to be held in Columbia, Missouri, home of the University of Missouri.

Joe's mindset was: "I'm going to go jump next week, but I don't want to go to a big meet and take a chance of blowing my leg out. The meet at Columbia will be perfect."

The meet, held on Saturday, February 1, 1986, in the Hearnes Center on the University of Missouri campus had an unusually early start.

Joe started his personal preparations early in order to get in all his warm-ups. Especially with the sensitive hamstring, he wanted to take his time and not rush his routine that he had grown accustomed to over the hundreds of meets in which he had participated over the years.

Being hypoglycemic, Joe could sense his blood sugar was getting low after his warm-up and felt a "case of the shakes" coming on. Eating cheese and crackers in an attempt to get his blood sugar stabilized, Joe got to feeling a little better.

Joe, not wishing to waste any attempts, waited to take his first jump until the bar was raised to 18 feet. By this time, there were no other competitors left in the field. Only Joe remained.

"I jumped 18 feet real easy, then 18-6 real easy, and then I switched to a bigger pole. I knew I could jump to a new world record with it," Joe explained.

"I then made 19 feet real easy. I just blew over it."

Joe then requested the crossbar be raised to 19-4¼.

Joe, small in stature, unassuming in build, and likely among the last person one would recognize in a crowd as a world-class athlete, stood at the end of the pole vault runway in the Hearnes Center.

The Oklahoma native held in his hands a 16 foot, 6 inch fiberglass pole vaulting pole.

At the other end of the runway stood the pole vault standards with the bar set at 19 feet, 4¼ inches. The height, when cleared, would establish a new world record.

"My first jump I came up a little short, but I grabbed the bar and amazingly the bar stayed up," Joe said. "That wasn't even my best jump. I didn't have a good take-off and came up a little bit short."

But even with that self-critique, that height had topped Billy Olson's existing world indoor record by a half inch — a NEW WORLD INDOOR RECORD!

Protocol for establishing world records calls for the official measurement utilizing a steel tape measure. Once the landing mats were pulled back, a ladder was brought out for the meet official to climb with the steel tape. The official measurement was determined to be 19-4¾.

Joe's record-breaking jump had gained a half-inch with the official measurement!

"A world record! Man, oh, man," said Joe, a six-time Big Eight Conference champion in the indoor and outdoor pole vault while competing for Oklahoma State University. He was also the NCAA pole vault indoor and outdoor national champion for 1984 and 1985.

"This is a dream come true," said Joe, who did not attempt another vault after setting his new mark.

"All my life I've wanted a world record. I knew I had a world record in me," Joe added.

"My phone at home (this was prior to cell phones) would ring off the hook. It would start really early in the morning getting calls from all over — New York, Chicago, Los Angeles — from sports writers wanting to talk about the record. After awhile, it got to where the calls would come in too early in the morning, so I got to where I would just leave my phone off the hook until I got up in the morning and then I would put it back on."

A few days later while preparing to travel to a meet in the Myriad Convention Center in Oklahoma City, Joe received some rather unwelcome news.

Exactly one week after Joe had set the new indoor record, Sergey Bubka, in a meet in Moscow, had broken Joe's world record — by a mere quarter inch — as the Soviet vaulter cleared 19 feet, 5 inches.

"Well, at least I got to enjoy the world record for a week," lamented Joe.

Actually, none of the athletes involved in chasing the world record at that time enjoyed the luxury of resting on their laurels very long once they broke the existing record.

It was one of the most amazing streaks of establishing world records in track and field — or in any sport for that matter. From December 28, 1985, when Billy Olson set the record at Saskatoon, Canada, through February 28, 1986, the world indoor record was broken nine times by three different athletes. Bubka and Olson each broke it four times and Joe broke it once.

It was an amazing, unbelievable, inexplicable nine record-breaking efforts in nine weeks. The progression was as follows:

DATE	HEIGHT	METRIC	VAULTER	LOCATION
Dec. 28, 1985	19-2.75	5.86	Billy Olson	Saskatoon, Canada
Jan. 15, 1986	19-3	5.87	Sergey Bubka	Osaka, Japan
Jan. 17, 1986	19-3.5	5.88	Billy Olson	Inglewood, California
Jan. 25, 1986	19-3.75	5.89	Billy Olson	Albuquerque, New Mexico
Feb. 1, 1986	19-4.75	5.91	Joe Dial	Columbia, Missouri
Feb. 8, 1986	19-5	5.92	Sergey Bubka	Moscow, Russia
Feb. 8, 1986	19-5.5	5.93	Billy Olson	East Rutherford, New Jersey
Feb. 21, 1986	19-5.75	5.94	Sergey Bubka	Inglewood, California
Feb. 28, 1986	19-6.25	5.95	Sergey Bubka	New York City, New York

Another interesting side note on Joe's indoor world record: sometime later after his record-breaking vault, Joe learned that one of the photographers at the meet was paid $5,000 by one of the major television networks for the video of Joe's world record vault which later appeared on ABC's "World Wide Sports."

In addition to holding the world indoor record, Dial also held the U.S. outdoor pole vault record at that time of 19-2¼. The world outdoor record of 19-8¼ at that time was set in Paris in July 1985 by one of Joe's chief rivals, Sergey Bubka of the Soviet Union.

The following is a report that appeared in the *Marlow Review,* Joe's hometown newspaper, on February 5, 1986, five days after Joe set the new World Record. It is reprinted with permission from the *Marlow Review.*

Dial Soars To New Heights

As the sports world watched in amazement, Marlow's Joe Dial took his latest accomplishment in humble stride.

The former Marlow High School and Oklahoma State track star cleared 19 feet, 4¾ inches last Saturday, to set a new world record in the pole vault. Dial's effort broke the old record, set only one week earlier, by one inch.

Although elated with his personal accomplishment, Dial's attitude continues to epitomize his small town background and his natural, friendly nature.

The new record was set during a college track meet held in the Hearnes Center at the University of Missouri in Columbia. The record came on Dial's second attempt at the height.

"The first thing I said when I made it was, "hey, they're going to have to change the sign in Marlow," Dial said.

Dial entered the Missouri meet primarily as a practice session, rather than competing in one of the several larger meets scheduled last weekend.

"I hadn't jumped since Jan. 15 when I pulled a hamstring in Osaka, Japan. In fact, I hadn't even taken my pole out of the packing since then, Dial said this week.

He said because of his inability to practice, he decided to skip several larger meets and use Columbia as sort of a "practice session."

Dial indicated he started vaulting at a lower height because of the nearly three-week layoff. "I began at 18-0 for my first jump, sailed right over it, then went to 18-6, 18-8, 19-0 and 19-4¼ and the shot for the record."

He said he could not explain why he had so much success, but added, "I just felt good and my jumping proved it."

Dial said setting a new world record may accord him the respect he has been missing. 'it really doesn't bother me that I don't get the recognition other vaulters get. I simply want to be known as one of the best vaulters in the world today, whether anyone recognizes me or not."

He said he actually never wants to get so popular he cannot walk out his door without retaining some privacy.

"It really doesn't matter whether anyone knows me outside the state of Oklahoma, because this is where I want to live, and these are the people I want to be proud of me."

When questioned about future records, Dial said the world outdoor record of 19 feet, 8¾ inches, held by Soviet vaulter Sergey Bubka, is within reach and felt he would vault 20 feet within a year. "I just need to keep working out with weights to get stronger. The stronger I get, the higher I can hold the pole. I know I can jump 20 feet. I don't think I can right now, but in six months to a year, I think I can."

He said he honestly feels he and Bubka are presently the two best vaulters in the world today. "We're friends, I like him and he is always telling me, 'Joe, my friend.' He speaks a little English, but I don't speak any Russian."

To Dial, Bubka is the best athlete in the world. "He's great, but he knows I'm right behind him."

Dial is not cocky about his ability. "Believe me, Joe Dial is nothing special. I'm fortunate to have the ability, but someone with a lot more authority and ability than me made it all possible."

Dial speaks very candidly about his religious beliefs. 'I'm still just Joe Dial from Marlow. I love what is happening in my life, but someone else made it all possible. You have to remember that."

Dial will take his world-class talents to the Myriad Convention Center in Oklahoma City this weekend to compete in the Oklahoma City track Classic. Dial is scheduled to vault on Saturday night beginning at 7:30 p.m.

"I would love to break the record in Oklahoma City before the home folk," Dial said.

National and world attention sometimes has a way of changing a person's personality. Fortunately for track and field, Oklahoma and yes, Marlow, that has not happened to Joe Dial.

PART I

A "FAMILY AFFAIR"

E very sport seems to have a natural "first family." But just what is a "first family in sports?" In sports parlance it's commonly known as a family consisting of at least two generations whose members have achieved levels of greatness to the extent that the mere mention of the surname causes an instant connection to that particular sport.

For football it could be the Mannings. Father Archie and sons, Peyton and Eli, all played quarterback at major colleges and then later in the National Football League. The three well-known and well-respected men have collected a total of four Super Bowl championships. And among the three, they have combined to be named to the NFL All-Pro team a total of 20 times. Recently retired, Peyton was honored 14 times, while his younger brother Eli was named four times and Archie achieved All-Pro status twice with the New Orleans Saints.

In baseball, a viable argument can be made that the Bell family qualifies as baseball's "first family." Grandfather Gus Bell, played most of his 15 year major league career with the Cincinnati Reds, while his son Buddy Bell played third base, coached and managed in the big leagues for a combined 27 years and currently works in the Chicago White Sox front office. Buddy's sons (and Gus' grandsons) David and Mike Bell, both followed in their father's footsteps and played in the majors as third basemen.

The "First Family" of pole vaulting

In track and field, specifically pole vaulting, there is no doubt as to who best represents the sport's first family.

The Dial family, originally from southern Oklahoma, is hands down the most logical claimant of the title "first family of pole vaulting."

Four generations — and counting — of the Dials and their collective pole vaulting accomplishments reverberate across the state, nation and, thanks to Joe's world record, even across the globe.

Joe Dial's bloodlines in track and field run deep in southern Oklahoma.

Joe's grandfather, Earl C. Dial, was the original track patriarch of the Dial clan as he blazed the path for the family in the world of track and field. Mr. Dial attended Duncan High School and starred on the Demons' track teams during the early 1920's. He was the first in the family to be recognized for his track prowess as he was honored by being named the "All Around Stephens County Track Athlete" in 1924. That title was commemorated by Mr. Dial being presented with a solid gold medal in recognition of the honor.

At the time of Mr. Dial's death, Joe's grandmother, Zelma Dial, known to many as "Momma Zel," presented Joe with five gold medals that his grandfather had won at the Stephens County Track Meet.

"I remember coming home from eighth grade football practice. I would walk to his house because that's where my parents usually were since he was sick and they were helping to care for him," Joe said.

"On the day that that my grandfather passed, my grandmother came up to me with the medals in hand," explained Joe.

"Here, I'd like for you to have your grandfather's medals," she quietly whispered to Joe.

"Why she picked me over everyone else in the family — my brothers, my cousins — I don't really know," Joe added.

There were five gold medals — one each for the shot put, discus, broad jump and high jump. The fifth medal was for being named the All-Around Athlete for Stephens County at the Stephens County Track meet during his senior year at Duncan High School in 1924.

"I still have those medals and I treasure them very much. My grandmother and I were very close," Joe explains.

Joe's father, Earl Dean Dial, represented the second generation of the

Dial family in the track and field world and is actually the source of the Dial Family pole vaulting tradition that is still prevalent today.

Going by "Dean," Joe's father competed on the Marlow High School track teams during the late 1940's and into the early 1950's and competed in what else — the pole vault.

Mr. Dial, in an 1999 interview, noted that the early pole vaulters used very rudimentary bamboo poles. Those poles were rigid and did not flex, unlike today's fiberglass and graphite high-tech poles.

"They were pretty brittle and would break very easily. They weren't anything like today's poles," he said.

In 1946, Mr. Dial went to the state meet as only a freshman after he qualified at the regional meet with a vault of nine feet. His best year as a vaulter was the 1950 season during which he topped out with a vault of 12 feet, 6 inches during a regular season meet at Ardmore.

"Times have certainly changed," Mr. Dial later said.

Despite not claiming a state title, the elder Dial still excelled in the event. Even encountering a strange bit of misfortune couldn't totally sideline Dean Dial, but it only served to exhibit his degree of toughness and fortitude.

Joe explains the weird circumstance involving his father.

"Dad would probably have won the state meet easily, but he had some bad luck. He was driving to the regional track meet and a cow jumped out in the middle of the road in front of him. He ran off the road, the car flipped over and he broke his wrist. Of course, he couldn't pole vault with the broken wrist, so he didn't get the chance to win the state title in pole vault. He was still able to long jump and he won the state title. It was either in 1949 or 1950. He might have been the best in the state in the pole vault, but unfortunately, he didn't get the opportunity."

Dean Dial served as Joe's coach and mentor virtually all of Joe's extensive career in the sport. He passed in 2006 in Marlow, Oklahoma.

Dean's sister, Joe's aunt Delores Dial Renfro, was an accomplished athlete in her own right.

"People around Marlow always said she could out-vault Dean. But unfortunately, that was before females were permitted to participate in the event," Joe explained.

Dean and Lena Dial were married in 1950 in Marlow, but not without a slight detour.

While both attended Marlow High School, Dean left school after his junior year (1948) to enter the military. Assigned to boot camp at Ft. Benning, Georgia, Dean had his sights set on becoming a paratrooper but injured his back while training.

After about a year, at his mother's urging, Dean joined the Oklahoma National Guard Reserves.

Returning to Marlow High School for his senior year (1949-50), the young couple tied the knot in January 1950 and Dean went on to graduate later that spring. Mrs. Dial had graduated in 1949.

Called back into active duty, Dean was stationed in Ft. Hood, Texas, where he competed in track and field on the base. Later, he served tours of duty in Korea and Japan.

After five years of military service, Dean left the military in 1955 with the rank of Sergeant First Class. His name is among those inscribed on a monument in Marlow saluting the local Korean War veterans.

Dean and Lena Dial had four children — Rex, Jimmy, Sue and Joe. They each competed in the pole vault to some degree while growing up.

The oldest son, Rex Dial, is eleven years older than Joe, who is the youngest of the four.

Rex actually started the chain of claiming championships by winning the 1969 Oklahoma Class B state title for the Marlow Outlaws. Rex's winning height of 13 feet was just an inch and half shy of the being the highest vault among all four classes (2A, A, B and C) at the state meet that year. Later that same year, he won the Oklahoma Coaches "Meet of Champions" that brought together the champions from all classes to compete.

Jimmy Dial, who is ten years older than Joe, pole vaulted early on but was involved in an unfortunate accident early in his career that changed his course in athletics.

"I remember he tried to vault over a barbed wire fence, but got his ear caught on a barb and almost ripped it off," Joe recalled.

That was it for Jimmy as far as active vaulting was concerned.

After that, Jimmy still competed in track and field, mainly concentrating on running the 880 yard run. Ironically, heights still played a prominent role in his later life, as he worked as a lineman. His job responsibilities included climbing poles for the local electric company in Marlow and later in Duncan.

Jimmy kept his involvement in the sport of track and field on the front burner for over 20 years as he served as a volunteer pole vaulting coach with stints at both Marlow and Duncan High Schools. As a matter of fact, his sphere of influence extends even beyond the borders of Stephens County as young pole vaulters from a wide area in that part of the state come to Jimmy seeking his guidance and advice in the sport.

"He would coach anyone in the area who wanted help in pole vaulting who didn't already have a coach," explained Shawna Dial, Joe's wife and Jimmy's sister-in-law.

As a testament to Jimmy's teaching ability and dedication, two of his students, Dean Howard and Ashley Waller, both of Marlow, were each three-time state champions. Ashley was the Class 3A champ in 2003-2005 while Dean captured the Class 3A state pole vaulting title at the state meet 2014-2016.

In addition, Jimmy's students from Marlow finished 1-2-4 in the 2016 Class 3A state meet to narrowly miss a sweep in the pole vaulting event. Besides Howard, who cleared 14-6 for the title, Marcus Mercer soared 14 feet for second place and J.D. Howard cleared 13-6 for fourth place.

Sue Dial was the lone daughter of Dean and Lena and is just three years older than Joe. Following her older brothers' examples, she tried her hand at pole vaulting as a young lady, but again pole vaulting as a competitive event for females had not yet been approved.

Joe, born in 1962 in Marlow, received his introduction to his sport just as most standouts do — at a very young age.

"I was five and Rex broke one of his poles in half at school. His high school coach, Carl Melson, gave me one of the halves of the broken pole. I started right there in the front yard. I dug a little hole. My dad was a welder and he welded the standards. He then took a tire and he welded a metal pole in the center and then poured in concrete to provide weight and stability. He then welded pins every three inches or so where the crossbar would set," Joe recalls with fondness.

"Joe was a little, bitty fellow five or six years old when he first started to vault. At first, he would just land on the bare ground. Later on, when he was about in the fifth grade, we had some old mattresses and stuff in the backyard and he would jump on that for his pit," Joe's father said in an newspaper interview.

Joe would go down to the family pond to collect "cattails" (a long and thin

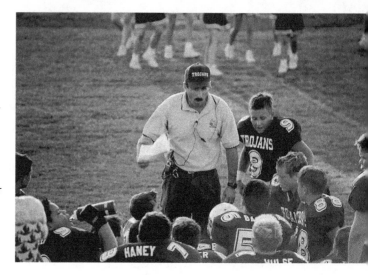

reed-like plant often found on pond banks) which he would utilize as the crossbar.

The young Dial soon became fascinated by the thrill of running with the remnants of the pole, planting it and then attempting to clear the cattail (crossbar), which couldn't have been more than five or six feet high at the time.

"I remember being out there for hours by myself trying to clear the bar. I'd make that height and then put the bar up on the next notch and try to make that height," Joe says.

Dean Dial attributed son Joe's success and rapid development in the art of pole vaulting to Marlow High School track coach Darvis Cole.

"He takes video-tape films of Joe in practice and just plugs it in and watches Joe in slow motion. He's helped Joe a lot on his form, " Joe's father explained.

However, Coach Cole has always been hesitant to take any credit for Joe's success.

"Joe's dad is the one that works with Joe. I just take him (Joe) to the meets and we have some pretty good vaulting facilities at Marlow," Cole said.

The fourth generation

The fourth generation of the "Vaulting Dial Family" can also claim their fair share of success as well as several state titles in pole vaulting.

Bruce Dial, Rex's son, was an accomplished athlete and vaulter in his own right. During the 1992 and 1993 seasons, Bruce was ranked among the best high school pole vaulters in the nation with his best jump at 17 feet, 2 inches.

"Bruce was one of the main reasons why I ended up coaching at Oral Roberts University," Joe recalls.

Joe had retired from the sport, at least for the time being, in 1992 after the Olympic Trials for the Barcelona Olympics. "I had just finished my vaulting career and had moved to Tulsa and was helping to coach at Union High School. I also had a pretty good-sized lawn care company that kept me busy."

It was Bruce's desire to take advantage of his Uncle Joe's skills and technical know-how and have his Uncle Joe coach him in college.

The head track and field coach at ORU at the time was Claude Roumain who decided to hire Joe as an assistant coach for the south Tulsa university.

"Bruce vaulted here (at ORU) for me one year and he performed really well. He ultimately vaulted 17-6¾," Joe explained.

However, after completing his freshman year at ORU, Bruce decided to drop out of the sport.

"I really never liked vaulting," Bruce admitted to Joe at the time. "I was just good at it, but actually I'd just rather go to work," Bruce said.

Jimmy's son, Josh Dial from Duncan, was perhaps the most successful of the fourth generation of the Dial clan along with Tommy Dial, Joe's son.

Josh was a three-time Oklahoma Class 4A state champion for the Duncan Demons, capturing the title in 1997, 1998 and 1999. In each of those three title years, Josh's winning heights were higher than the winning heights of all other classes.

In the state track meet during Josh's senior year, he was so dominant that his winning height of 17-2 was more than two and half feet better than the next best class winning height.

Josh's best overall mark of was 17 feet, 6½ inches.

"He tried to break my high school record and he gave it an awful good shot, but he didn't quite make it," Joe explains.

Josh went on to attend junior college in Kansas. After being on the juco campus just a few months, Joe recalls that as Josh was attempting a dead lift during a weightlifting workout, he tore most of the muscles in one shoulder and was unable to ever vault again.

Dena Dial, Jimmy's daughter, was likewise an accomplished athlete in high school track and field and possessed the talents to do well in many events. After graduating from Marlow High School, she also enrolled at ORU in order to take advantage of her Uncle Joe's track and field coaching expertise.

However, during her freshmen year, pole vaulting was not yet available to women as a competitive intercollegiate sport.

It was not until Dena's sophomore year at ORU that the NCAA sanctioned pole vaulting as a women's sport.

Lacking a background in vaulting, Dena was somewhat apprehensive in her approach to the event. However, others apparently did not possess that same level of apprehension.

Joe recalls the level of confidence that others expressed on behalf of Dena.

"You are a Dial. You can pole vault," her friends bluntly encouraged her.

Those words were somewhat prophetic as Dena went on to be a four-time conference champion and five-time All-Conference selection. She was named a two-time NCAA All-American and finished fifth one year and seventh another year at the NCAA national meet. Her all-time best was an impressive 13 feet, 2 inches. She was inducted into the ORU Athletics Hall of Fame with the Class of 2013.

Joe's sister Sue's son, Karry Joe Phillips (Joe's nephew) was another outstanding pole vaulter on the high school level. His all-time best was 15 feet, 10 inches as he represented Duncan High School.

Lastly, the three sons of Joe and his wife Shawna have all shared in the pole vault experience.

Their oldest son, Tim, was an impressive athlete as a youngster starring in both football and track. During his freshman year at Tulsa Union High School, he showed tremendous skill as he cleared 14 feet in the pole vault, earning fifth place in the Class 6A state track meet as well as the school record, which still stands today. His athletic achievements were recognized as he was named the Ninth Grade Athlete of the Year by *The Oklahoman*.

Joe's and Shawna's middle son, Tommy Dial, enjoyed a very successful high school career representing the Jenks Trojans in the sport as he placed in the Oklahoma Class 6A (the largest class) state meet during all four years, winning the state title in 2014, his junior year at 17 feet, one inch and again in 2015, his senior year with a jump of 17-2.

Tommy even made a close run at his father's Kansas Relay's meet record. Tommy cleared 17 feet, 1½ inch at the 2014 Relays at the Jayhawks' brand new world-class track and field facility, Rock Chalk Park, in Lawrence, Kansas.

Tommy had the bar raised to 17 feet, 5¼ inches in an attempt to tie his father's 34 year-old Kansas Relays record but fell just short in clearing that height.

Tommy currently attends Oral Roberts University and is on the Golden Eagles track team continuing his vaulting career.

Youngest son, Tyler, currently a freshman at Jenks High School, has expressed interest in vaulting and is looking forward to participating in the sport under the watchful eyes of his father.

When Thanksgiving Day rolls around, some families often look forward to a touch football game in the back yard after the big meal.

To illustrate how much the entire Dial family enjoyed the sport of pole vaulting, they had a little different spin to that tradition.

"We would often go to Joe's parents' house for Thanksgiving and if it was nice out, everybody would go out in the front yard and some would hold up crossbars so the kids could get a broomstick and try to vault," Shawna explained. "Vaulting is just something that everyone in our family does."

"Yes, there was a lot of pole vaulting going on," chuckled Joe.

Joe's early years

Joe came from a family of modest means. As he looks back on that part of his life, he realizes that in today's terms, they would be considered poor. There was not much money available for candy, Cokes, eating out, new clothes or other such luxuries. As one might expect, with two older brothers, Joe often wore hand-me-downs. But like many other families in Marlow and the surrounding area of that era, times were often tough, money was sometimes short, but the six-member Dial family was able to get along just fine and survive.

Joe started school when his family lived in Gatlin, Oklahoma, a very small town located between Marlow and Duncan in Stephens County in southern Oklahoma. The school was likewise small in size as Joe recalls that there were only about eight to ten students in his class.

The Dial family moved to Texas City, Texas, when Joe was in the third grade.

"We moved to Texas City for my dad's job. He worked as a pipefitter for the Monsanto Company. We stayed there part of my third grade year and during my fourth grade year."

Joe had not yet developed an interest in pole vaulting, but being in Texas, where football seems to be king at all levels, he did enjoy playing football for his elementary school team, the Texas City Rebels.

"At the start of my fifth grade year, my dad became disabled and couldn't work anymore," Joe said, "so the family moved back to Marlow.

"When we moved back to Marlow, I actually started vaulting and competing against other kids. I went to a track meet and we started warming up and just practicing. I remember doing really well. The officials running the meet said I couldn't participate because I was beating the older kids.

"Luckily my dad was there. He had made it a point to attend just about all of my brothers' and my games and sporting events," Joe recalls.

"My dad came to my defense and responded to the officials, "'Hey, that doesn't make any difference. He should still be able to jump.'"

The track meet was actually for sixth and seventh graders.

"I was only in the fifth grade, but I could still beat the sixth and seventh

LEFT : THE DIAL FAMILY OFTEN SPENT FAMILY GATHERINGS WITH AN INFORMAL POLE VAULT COMPETITION IN THE FRONT YARD.

RIGHT : A YOUNG JOE DIAL RIDING A PONY AT HOME. WHO KNEW HE WOULD BE A FUTURE COWBOY?

graders. They didn't think it was fair for a younger kid to beat kids a year or two older. The good news was they ended up letting me jump and I won," Joe laughed.

"My dad was retired and he started coaching me. When I started bending the pole during my eighth grade year, that's when it started getting really fun. There was something new to learn every single time I vaulted. Once you start bending the pole, it's a whole new realm of technique. That's what was really fun. We would spend hours and hours practicing. We had a little video camera. We would spend hours watching video of good guys vaulting and then video me," recalled Joe.

Hunting and learning how to drive

Living in southern Oklahoma, fishing and hunting were a favorite pasttime for many residents. The Dial family was no different. Joe's mother can attest to that fact.

"Our whole family liked to hunt. They liked to hunt coyotes and deer. And most of them could shoot a bow and arrow, too," according to Mrs. Dial.

Joe and his father both loved to go hunting together with one of their favorite targets being coyotes.

Joe recalls he and his dad traveling the back roads out in the country in their pickup truck, constantly scanning the horizon for any glimpse of the elusive animal. If one was spotted running through a distant field or grassy pasture, the truck was quickly stopped with both men hurriedly exiting the vehicle.

Time was of the essence before the fast-moving coyote disappeared from sight.

Joe's dad would pull out his favorite rifle, a .264 Winchester Magnum, and take aim.

"My dad was a remarkable shot," Joe said. "I've seen him shoot coyotes on the run from about 300 yards away. The coyotes would be on a full sprint. It was amazing."

If Mr. Dial's shot was successful, and it was more times than not, once the coyote was down, it was Joe's duty to retrieve the animal and bring the carcass back to the truck.

When the target was a deer during these hunting excursions, Joe also learned to how to field dress the deer carcass quickly and return it to the truck.

Perhaps those hunting sessions with his dad had another unforeseeable benefit.

"I look back at those days and think sometimes running out and back to get the coyotes and deer may have helped me to get faster," Joe said.

Besides the thrill of hunting, the ventures could be profitable, as Joe recalls that the coyote hides could be sold for anywhere from $30–$40 each.

Besides learning the finer aspects of hunting, Joe also learned to drive on some of those hunting trips out in the country. Many times after Joe and his dad had finished hunting for the day, Mr. Dial would allow Joe to get in the driver's seat and drive. Since Joe was just a fifth-grader at the time, his father would still closely monitor his driving and instruct exactly what he needed to do.

"Slow down. Turn left. Stop here," his dad would often instruct Joe from the passenger seat.

JOE VAULTING AS AN EIGHTH GRADER WITH OLDER BROTHER REX READY TO CATCH HIS POLE.

PART II

HIGH SCHOOL PRODIGY

Early start

Even prior to entering Marlow High School, Joe was well on his way to becoming a prodigious pole vaulter.

In the eighth grade, Joe set new meet records at five different meets: the Healdton Relays, the Marlow Invitational, the Washita Valley Conference Meet at Pauls Valley, the Duncan Invitational, and the Stephens County Junior High School Meet.

His best jump of the year was at Pauls Valley where he soared 12 feet, 2 inches.

At the Stephens County Junior High Meet, Joe led his Marlow Junior High Outlaws squad to the team title as he set a new county record in addition to the meet record in the pole vault by clearing 12 feet. For good measure, Joe also captured second place in the low hurdles and third place in the high jump at the meet.

At age 14, Joe broke the Amateur Athletic Union (AAU) record for the state of Oklahoma for the Intermediate Division (14 and 15 year olds) at Jacobs Field in Norman, Oklahoma, when he pole vaulted 12 feet, 7 inches.

Joe's first high school track coach, Darvis Cole

Joe's first high school track coach, Darvis Cole, coached Joe's older brother, Rex, in junior high school, so he was fully aware of the Dial family and their deep affinity for the sport of pole vaulting.

Cole left for another coaching assignment but later returned to Marlow in time to also coach Joe.

"Joe's dad, Dean, really loved pole vaulting and would do about anything to help Joe in the sport. Pole vaulting was something he really got into," Cole recalls about Joe's father. "He really helped the boys."

Coach Cole related the impact Joe had on the younger athletes in Marlow.

"Joe left a legacy at Marlow when he graduated. His level of success influenced other kids to take up pole vaulting as well. There's been a number of pole vaulting champions come out of Marlow since Joe left. I don't know how many have been state champions, but there's been quite a number," Cole explained.

Studying video tape

Joe fondly recalls that he and his father constantly studied all aspects of pole vaulting. While track and field was not a widely televised sport at the time when Joe was growing up — there was no ESPN, no Fox Sports, no 24 hour cable — anytime that the sport of track and field would come on television, whether it was via ABC's popular series "Wide World of Sports," the Summer Olympic Games, or perhaps just an occasional televised track meet, Joe and his father would intently concentrate on watching the pole vault competition.

Joe recalls that he and his father would often video tape competitors like Mike Tully, Earl Bell and others when they appeared on television in order to go back and study the tape and analyze every move in their vaults. Joe was always looking to learn from other vaulters and found one who shared a talent for vaulting that Joe admired.

"Jeff Buckingham from Kansas was a vaulter I really admired when I was in the eighth grade and he was a junior in high school. We would video-tape him and at that time he was jumping almost 17 feet," Joe said. Buckingham and Joe were both rather small in stature for elite vaulters as both stood about 5 foot, 10 inches with a slight build. Another factor they shared was the fact that both young vaulters were coached by their fathers.

"I also remember watching Brian Shaw, former state pole vault champion from nearby Duncan, as he vaulted 16 feet in Oklahoma. We really watched what he did. We studied the way he vaulted," Dial recalls. "But we kept going back to check out Buckingham because he was built more like me. Shorter in stature, but with speed," Joe explained.

Buckingham's father had even formed a vaulting team for Jeff and some of his vaulting friends.

The club was called "Lakeside Vaulters" because their practice facility was located next to a small lake in the Kansas City, Kansas, area where the Buckinghams resided. The club even had their own jerseys, with "Lakeside Vaulters" emblazoned across the chest.

As a matter of fact, Joe even vaulted for the Lakeside Vaulters during one meet and recalled a rather unpleasant memory that involved Jeff's younger brother, George Buckingham.

"At one of the meets that I participated in for their club team, I vaulted with my ball cap on. I didn't think anything about it. I had worn a cap many times when vaulting. One time when I came running down the runway and planted the pole, it knocked my hat off. I'm sure it was pretty funny," Joe said.

George Buckingham saw the hat fly off Joe's head and remarked, while laughing at Joe, "What a country hick."

While Joe clearly remembers the sting caused by the remark, the insult didn't upset him. It merely stoked the fires to improve and gave him more incentive to become a better pole vaulter.

Father knows best

Joe recalled an incident during his eighth grade year in which he and his father had a disagreement concerning pole vaulting.

"But after that, all through high school, there was never, ever an argument. A lot of times, a father-son's relationship may not go well. But after that one time, we never had any problems," Joe explained.

Joe and his father had a great coaching-working relationship, as evidenced by the obvious level of success Joe achieved.

"We kind of figured out what roles we would each need to play. I wanted him to set my standards. He would stand off to the side as I warmed up and see where my peak was, and make sure where my steps were. He would give me that information. Then I would make any adjustments based on the information he gave me," said Joe.

Let there be light

"I came home one day and dad had a light, a long penlight, with an extension cord, and he had it down inside my pole vaulting pole. He was studying how the poles were designed and made. This was before computers so you couldn't read anything about how poles were made like you can today. He was wanting to know how each one was built," Joe recalled.

"It was so much fun learning something completely new. All my dad knew about pole vaulting was in regard to a bamboo pole like he used back in the day when he vaulted. Studying the poles was a challenge for him. He always had the mindset of accepting challenges like that. He was really good at analyzing stuff. He would always tell me, 'Let's try this, let's try that,'" Joe recalled.

Joe sometimes considered himself as somewhat of a guinea pig. "Whatever he would tell me to try, I would do it. I always said it was a good thing I was a good athlete or else things would not have gone very well."

Joe eventually followed his father's example of analyzing the poles and soon Joe started studying the poles in detail, becoming acquainted with the various companies that manufactured vaulting poles, investigating the processes of how they were developed and manufactured, as well as the strengths and weaknesses of each.

"I always found that aspect of vaulting fascinating," Joe said.

Custom poles for the asking

"My dad was just way ahead of his time. He knew as much about pole vaulting technique and training as anyone, anywhere, including college coaches. He knew exactly what size pole I would need to maximize my potential, " Joe related about his father.

JOE AND
HIS FATHER
ROOFING
JOE'S CABIN
IN SOUTHEAST
OKLAHOMA.

Joe recalls a conversation his father had on the phone with a representative of a vaulting pole manufacturer that illustrates the level of expertise his father possessed when it came to the finer points of vaulting.

"My dad told the company rep that we would like a 15-115 pole (i.e., a pole 15 feet long with a suggested capacity of 115 pounds). The company representative curtly replied, "No one could jump on that pole."

Dean Dial countered back to the company rep that "my son can do it. The 14 foot pole is just too short. My son is gripping on the end of all of them."

"Why don't you just go to a stiffer 14 foot pole?" asked the company rep.

"Well, so he can raise his grip," Dean Dial replied.

The company rep then relented, "That makes sense. Ok, we'll make it."

The company (AMF) came through as promised and made the Pacer-3 pole to the requested specifications and sent it to Joe and his father. Best of all, due to Joe's rising prominence in the pole vaulting world, the company said it would be complimentary.

"They sent it and it came at no charge. Oh, my goodness!" Joe exclaimed.

"I started going through that pole and after many jumps, it became too soft. My dad called the company again and asked if we could get a 15-9; 120 pole. That particular request got the pole company people to chuckle. They told my dad there is no way a pole of that size can be used," Joe recalled.

The issue of the cost of the pole arose in Joe's mind since Joe often described his family as having modest means. But Joe's dad told Joe not to worry. The family would do whatever they have to do in order to get that pole, no matter what it costs.

"We didn't have much money, but dad could hock a gun or something to get the money. He had done that a few times before," Joe said.

George Moore — a savior

Joe cites George Moore, an executive with AMF Pacer, a vaulting pole manufacturer, for also playing a critical support role in his development in the sport of pole vaulting.

"I wouldn't be here in the position I am in the sport without him," Joe declares.

"At really the most crucial time in my pole vaulting career, during my ninth grade year, I didn't have the right poles. They were either too short or they didn't make them light enough. The smallest 15 foot pole they made was for 140 pounds, but we needed a 15 foot for 115 pounds. They never even thought about making a pole of that size. I was so little but I could jump with that size of pole.

"My dad asked what would it cost and said that we will pay for it. But when the pole came, it said 'No Charge."

Recognizing Joe's obvious talent and need, George Moore had the pole manufactured just like Joe and his dad had requested at no charge.

Joe recalls that as a major point in his upward move in the sport.

"Getting the new pole was huge. I made 14-1 on that pole. Then later my dad called and asked for a 15-9, 120 pole. I used that pole to jump 14-9 and set the 15 year-old national record," Joe said.

Moore was inducted into the National Pole Vaulting Hall of Fame in 2010 as he is cited for being instrumental in the development of the fiberglass vaulting pole.

Joe followed him in to that Hall of Fame in 2011.

Local support

Being the top high school vaulter in the state of Oklahoma and one of the best in the nation often did have its benefits. As just mentioned, Joe frequently received new poles from the various pole manufacturers.

"I often got free poles. Occasionally some companies would charge a little, but often someone in town would help take care of it," Joe explained.

Dial recalls specifically how some of the local townspeople would assist him.

"I remember one guy in town had a little bit of money. Not many people in Marlow had much money back then, but this one guy did.

"In high school I needed some new poles to vault. Of course, we couldn't afford to buy them. But sure enough, I would soon get some new poles at school. I remember my dad pointing out this one guy later at a track meet," Dial said.

"See that guy standing over there?" he asked Joe. "He's the one who bought these two new poles for you."

"I quickly went over and thanked him for buying the poles for me," Dial recalled.

"Later, that man was working as a toll collector on the Turner Turnpike at the Cushing exit. Whenever I would come through to Cushing and see him working, we would talk about vaulting," Joe said.

Even Phyllis Cole, the wife of the high school track coach, Darvis Cole, got into the act. She often traveled to area towns to exchange pole vaulting poles with other high school athletes.

Coach Cole explains how she got involved.

"Joe knew a lot of high school pole vaulters from around the state. Joe would talk to them and then perhaps work out to trade poles from other boys. Poles were very expensive back then and the school couldn't afford many new poles. My wife made a lot of trips going around over the state exchanging poles."

Another example of local assistance involved former NFL player Terry Brown, who was born in Walters, Oklahoma. Brown played football for Marlow High School and collegiately at Oklahoma State University. He then went on to play in the NFL for seven years for three different teams. His career highlight occurred while playing for the Minnesota Vikings in the 1975 Super Bowl versus the Pittsburgh Steelers. Brown recovered a blocked punt in the end zone for the Vikings' only touchdown of the game as the Steelers defeated the Vikings 16-6.

After his NFL career, Brown returned to Marlow and opened up a sporting goods store.

"He paid for a couple of my poles. He was really a great guy. I really appreciated everything the people of Marlow did for me," Joe explained.

These were just a few of many such instances of the generosity of the community. Whether it was someone helping out on travel expenses, entry fees, purchasing other equipment, or whatever, Joe would always make a point to personally thank these benefactors.

Gas money

Early in Joe's high school career, he remembers getting ready to go to a meet one time when his parents delivered some unpleasant news. Joe's parents, who very rarely missed any of Joe's meets or other athletic events, were not going to be able to attend the meet.

"Dad came up to me that morning and told me that they were not going to this track meet. I didn't know why at the time. I found out later the problem was they didn't have the money to buy gas to drive to the meet.

"Later that day I got to the meet, warmed-up, and I was all ready to compete. Right before I started vaulting, my mom and dad suddenly showed up," Joe said.

Joe's dad simply smiled at him and said, "We got it worked out."

"Years later my mom told me that he hocked his rifle in order to get gas money. He probably got $20 or maybe $30 for pawning his rifle and then later he went back and got his rifle out of hock," Joe explained.

First broken pole

The first pole Joe ever broke was when he and his father were experimenting. Joe was gripping at the end of the pole and told his dad that he could grip higher, and vault higher, if the pole was just a little longer.

"My dad went to the machine shop and got somebody to make a dowel to fit inside one pole and then the other pole and we glued an extra foot on that pole. It worked great for six or seven jumps then it just broke at the end," Joe grinned.

FRESHMEN YEAR

MARLOW HIGH SCHOOL (1977–78)

At the Cowboy Relays in Stillwater, Joe won with a vault of 14 feet while only just a freshman, setting a new Marlow High School record in the process. With this effort, Joe distinguished himself as one of the state's top five vaulters and earned recognition as the best freshmen in the state regardless of classification of school.

It quickly became the consensus of most state track experts that if Joe continued to improve, he should enjoy an excellent chance at the Regional and State Championships, discounting the fact that he was only a freshman.

At the Bi-State Classic Track Meet at Lawton MacArthur, Joe was Marlow High School's lone representative, but he made the most of it as he cleared the bar at 13 feet, 2¾ inches in the pole vault to claim the best field events performance of the meet.

At the regional meet at Marlow, Joe set his personal best mark on his vault at 14-1. After starting at 11-0, Joe missed on only a total of three attempts at seven different heights.

May 15, 1979 » Class 2A State Track Meet » Midwest City, Oklahoma

A week later at the Class 2A state track meet in Midwest City, Joe claimed the gold medal, his first of four consecutive state titles. Even though only a freshman, Joe was considered the favorite going into the state meet.

Despite it being his first state meet, Joe didn't appear to be nervous and showed no signs of being apprehensive. Once the competition commenced, Joe's skill level become obvious as he cleared each height on his first attempt.

Taking no chances, Joe decided to enter the competition at 11 feet as his first jump.

"Just to be safe," he thought to himself.

As the bar rose to 12 feet, 6 inches, there were only five vaulters left. When the bar was raised to 13 feet, only three competitors remained.

One vaulter dropped out at 13 feet, leaving only David Thrift of Purcell and Joe vying for the gold medal. The bar was then set at 13 feet, 6 inches. When Joe's name was called, he confidently strode down the runway and easily cleared the height — some say by at least six inches — thereby putting the pressure on Thrift.

Joe then watched as Thrift failed to clear the bar on three straight attempts. Then the stage was Joe's.

With his first state meet gold medal safely his, Joe had two alternatives. He could pack up his poles and go home with his gold medal. Or he could continue vaulting and attempt a new Class 2A state meet record.

Being the competitor he is, there was really no choice. Joe requested that the bar be set at 14 feet, one inch. Joe attempted the vault first with his "old" pole but missed.

Then came the "moment of truth."

Joe pulled out a brand new pole, one that he had never used previously in competition.

"If he hits it right, there's no telling where he'll come down," Dean Dial, his father and coach, shared with friends and coaches within earshot.

On his first attempt with his new pole, Joe was well over the bar, but barely caught it with his left arm. He missed on his second attempt. On his third, and final, attempt, he was off to the side and really didn't have an opportunity to clear the bar.

"I had the standards back just a little too much," he recalls.

"I thought I had it for a moment, but I caught in on the way down. I wasn't even close the third time." Joe related afterwards.

After the competition, Joe did confess that he was a tad nervous going into the competition. But he also added any nervousness left "as soon as I made my first vault.

"I was afraid I wouldn't sleep much last night, but I did. When I first woke up I was nervous, but I got over it, " Joe admitted.

Practice makes perfect — four practices in three towns in one day

Joe and his father were not hesitant about traveling to different practice locations depending upon the wind direction and weather conditions.

"If the wind is out of the east, we would go down to Duncan," Dean Dial explained. "If it's out of the west, we'll go to Chickasha because they have an east-west runway.

"When you get the wind to your back, it's a big help. Joe likes a little tailwind."

Joe relates the time he was breaking in a new pole but was having trouble finding a practice location with favorable wind conditions.

The pole manufacturer delivered the new pole as promised. Father and son anxiously went to the track at Marlow High School to check out the new pole, but on each attempt, the pole kept throwing Joe back on the runway. So they decided to go to Duncan (about 11 miles away) but again, the pole kept throwing Joe off the runway. He couldn't even get to the landing pit. They then returned back to Marlow to try to practice once again, but they noticed the wind had switched direction and was coming out of the west which was unusual for that part of the state.

Joe and his dad knew that Chickasha had a pole vault pit that was set up for the runway to go from west to east so the two of them hopped back in their car and drove down to Chickasha. Once they arrived, Joe was finally able to get on the pole. And this time, the wind was at Joe's back- just like he preferred.

It was indeed a full day. Four practices in three towns in one day. No doubt that had to be another record!

But the extra effort eventually paid off. When Joe was finally able to vault at Chickasha, the bar was raised to 15 feet, which Joe cleared. It was the first time ever he had made 15 feet.

"I ended up going to the next meet and jumping 14-9 which broke the national age group record for 15 year olds. That was my first age-group record," Joe said.

Joe would later go on to set similar national age group records for 16, 17 and 18 year olds.

Everyone gets involved

As previously explained, Joe's father played an integral role in Joe's success in pole vaulting as his coach and mentor. Joe benefited in numerous ways from the experience and expertise his father offered.

But Joe's father was not the only Dial family member to contribute to Joe's immense improvement in pole vaulting. Other members of his immediate played critical roles in his climb to world prominence.

Ten years prior to Joe winning his first state championship, Joe's older brother Rex claimed the Oklahoma Class B state championship with a vault of 13 feet.

JOE ON THE RUNWAY
PREPARING TO
VAULT RECEIVING
LAST MINUTE
ADVICE FROM OLDER
BROTHER REX AND
FATHER DEAN.

The year was 1969 and Rex's winning height was the best among all classes at the state meet with the exception of the Class A champion —Dewayne Smith of Ada — who cleared just an inch and a half higher at 13-1½.

Rex had a role to play in Joe's success as well. He assisted in setting the standards as Joe desired depending on the height of the bar, the wind direction, which pole is being used and other factors. Rex also served as the pole-catcher, protecting the most important tool of a pole vaulter.

Even Joe's mother, Lena, got in on the action.

"What I usually did was to drive to the meets and then I would film," Mrs. Dial explained. "We each had a job we did. My job was to drive and film. It was definitely a family affair."

She filmed practically every one of Joe's vaults on the family's movie camera. Father and son would later review and re-review time and time again such films in order to catch any small flaw in Joe's technique and to improve future performances. Every little bit of information was important; every tiny advantage mattered. Oftentimes, Dean Dial could pinpoint some small nuance that perhaps Joe was not aware of that could potentially add inches to the height that Joe clears at his next meet.

Joe's mother explained how the family's teamwork was coordinated.

"Most of the meets were on a Friday or Saturday. I would usually end up using a roll of film at each meet. I would send the film off on a Monday morning to be processed and then get it back on Wednesday. Joe and his dad would then spend a couple of days looking at the film to see what could be done to improve or what he was doing wrong. Then they would be ready for the next meet," she explained.

Even back at that early date, Joe proved to be a good prognosticator in regard to his long-term goals. Just after claiming his first state title his freshman year at Marlow High School, Joe made it fairly clear of his intentions.

"I want to be a four-time state champion. That's what I'm really hoping to do," he declared.

Joe was the first high school freshmen in state history to clear 14 feet in the pole vault.

Track was not Joe's only athletic endeavor in which he was an accomplished athlete. He was a major contributor to both his freshmen football and basketball teams.

Joe was an outstanding football player as his Marlow freshmen team enjoyed an undefeated season, their first since 1968. Head coach of the freshmen team was Bob Patterson.

Joe also excelled in basketball. He tallied 15 points in one game versus Bray in the Stephens County Junior High School basketball tournament and also scored 12 points against Pauls Valley. The freshmen basketball team finished the season with an impressive 19-1 record and were Stephens County champions as well as being crowned champions of the Walters Invitational Tournament. The basketball team was also coached by Bob Patterson.

Budding decathlon star

Being a natural athlete with blazing speed and enjoying an abundance of inherent talent, a deep love for track and field and, perhaps most importantly of all, possessing a great work ethic, Joe was a prime candidate for the decathlon — a grueling competition of ten different track and field events held over a two-day period.

At a summer track meet, Joe took on the challenge of the decathlon. He proceeded to break the state age-group record for 15 year olds in the decathlon, which qualified him to advance to the next level — Region 9 level.

"I was just 120 points from the national age-group record. I thought I could just work on my shot put a little or maybe on the javelin or something in order to make up those 120 points," Joe said.

At the Region 9 meet, Joe ran a good 100 meter dash and the hurdles. He won the pole vault at 13-6. It wasn't his best, but it was still good for a decathlon competition. He did well in the long jump and high jump.

"When the final results were tabulated, I had broken the U.S. national age-group record for 15 year olds alright, but I only finished sixth overall in the meet.

"After that, I realized that I would be better off to concentrate in just one event, the pole vault, than trying to master ten different events," Joe explained.

SOPHOMORE YEAR
MARLOW HIGH SCHOOL (1978-79)

As in many smaller high schools, most of the boys who participated in athletics would play more than one sport. Often, they might participate in three different sports in a single school year- one sport for each season: football in the fall; basketball in the winter and track or perhaps baseball in the spring.

Joe was no different. Despite his lack of size, he excelled in football, primarily due to his impressive quickness and blazing speed.

"My sophomore year, I initially thought about not going out for football, but our coach, Darvis Cole, who was a great guy, kind of talked me into coming out to play. I didn't think there was any way that I could start. His pitch to me was simple: He said, 'Why don't you come out and give it a try?'"

Joe was always on the small side. He began his sophomore year in school weighing in the neighborhood of only about 120 pounds. But what he lacked in size, he more than made up for it with his speed.

"I remember thinking that I probably wouldn't get the chance to play much as a sophomore on the varsity because the guy that I had to beat out for a starting position at wide receiver was a tall guy, about 6-3 or 6-4, and he was a great athlete, later being drafted right out of high school to the pros to play baseball."

Another sophomore, Scott Hall, played quarterback. He and Joe were among the reserves who played on the "scout team," consisting of the younger players who practiced against the varsity and often in the role of the varsity team's upcoming opponent.

With Joe playing wide receiver, his key asset was his speed. He could manage to get open and would simply outrun anyone on the team, including most members of the varsity first-string.

With Scott Hall playing quarterback and Joe at wide receiver for the scout team, they combined for some long pass completions in practice. Scott would simply heave the ball down the field and Joe would just run under it, catch it and often go in untouched for a touchdown. The first team defense was virtually helpless in stopping the long-pass combination of Hall to Dial.

This big-play action quickly caught the coach's eye that ultimately resulted in a lineup change.

"One day in practice we did it (make a long pass completion) three times in a row. After a couple of days, the coach told me that I would be moving up to starting split end and they would be moving the big guy from split end to tight end," Joe recalled.

"I could tell that Joe was really talented, but we had a senior that was starting at wide receiver in front of Joe. But it didn't take long to figure out that Joe needed to be out on the field. We moved the senior to tight end and Joe to split end. That move really helped us out. It gave us two great receivers," Cole related.

Joe recalls how the level of chemistry worked between him and the team's quarterback.

"That year, my sophomore year, we had a really good team. Our varsity quarterback, Bobby Shannon, was a great player. Often on pass plays, we would break the huddle and I would simply tell him to throw outside or low or wherever, and he would literally put the ball just where I wanted it. I was so little at the time that I hated going over the middle and risk the chance to get hit by the bigger guys. I preferred to play on the outside where I could utilize my speed to my advantage."

The Marlow Outlaws went on to a successful season and advanced to the state football playoffs where they faced the Clinton Red Tornadoes.

With Clinton leading 13-7 and with the clock winding down to its last few ticks, there was just enough time for one last play. Marlow had possession of the ball with the opportunity to tie, or possibly win, the game. The Marlow coach called Joe's number and told him simply to just go straight downfield and Bobby would get the ball to him.

"I sprinted down the field and looking back, I saw the ball coming in my direction and I thought, 'Oh, man.' I jumped as high as I could and the ball just barely skimmed off my finger tips," Joe lamented.

Despite the loss in the championship game, Joe enjoyed a successful sophomore campaign as he scored seven touchdowns during the season. That total would have likely been more but once opposing teams became aware of Joe's speed, he faced more double-teams by the opponent's secondary, which in turn resulted in fewer passes coming Joe's way. It eventually got to the point that Marlow's quarterbacks would not throw as often to Joe since with a double-team, the likelihood of a completion was lower and the possibility of an interception was greater.

That sophomore year was Joe's last season to play football.

"I really don't have any regrets, but sometimes I kind of wish I played my senior year. It would have been fun to play my senior year of football with all my friends," he said.

Commitment

As much as Joe loved to play football and as good as he was in the sport, Joe made, what in hindsight could be argued a life-changing decision, his sophomore year. He would no longer play football in order to fully concentrate on his pole vaulting.

"He didn't get the state record in the pole vault when he was a sophomore so he said, 'No, I'm not going out for football anymore. I'm just going to pole vault,'" Mrs. Dial recalls her conversation with Joe.

"Joe just wanted to do track year-round. He was a little upset since he didn't set the state record as a sophomore," his mother explained.

Cut down to size

Joe recalls one specific time when he father was working with him during the warm-ups at a track meet in an effort to obtain the maximum performance from his poles.

"My sophomore year, one of the pole manufacturing companies sent me a new pole, but it was way too stiff. I would plant it and it would shoot me off the runway, not even close to the landing pit. I would try it again and plant it and it would shoot me off the runway again. The pole would simply throw me off. I never even hit the mats," Joe explained.

With the starting time of the meet growing closer, Joe still had little success with the new pole and time was rapidly growing short.

"Where are you gripping?" Joe's father asked, seeking any possible solution to their dilemma.

Joe told his father exactly where he was gripping the pole and then would relate to him how the pole felt during a vault.

"He took my pole out to his car and sawed part of the pole off the bottom. When he returned to the field with the shorter pole, he said, 'I think it's going to work now,'" Joe said.

Dean Dial had cut approximately 11 inches from the bottom of the pole.

He had cut down Joe's poles previously, but never to that extent. Cutting 11 inches off a pole vaulting pole was a fairly drastic alteration.

By cutting off a portion of the pole, Joe's dad had effectively lowered the point of the pole's stiffness, resulting in less pushback from the pole.

"I went in and planted it and it worked. I really didn't know what happened except it worked. I went on the make 15-7 that day at Marlow," Joe recalls.

Joe later went on to attempt 16-2 that day, which would have established a new state high school record, but he barely missed at that height. But not getting a state record that day didn't really matter. What was much more important to Joe and his father was simply the success from making such a critical improvement.

As in many sports, improvement in pole vaulting often came in small increments.

Icy roads in Kansas

In his first appearance of the track season, Joe vaulted 14-6 at an indoor meet at the University of Kansas in Lawrence, Kansas.

Joe's best memory from that meet didn't actually occur on the track or runway, but on the way home back to Marlow from Lawrence.

"The roads were really icy. I was lying down in the back seat with my poles loaded across the roof of the car. My mom is driving our Chevy Chevette when suddenly we hit this patch of black ice. I hopped up as we are twisting in the middle of the road, spinning around several times. When we stopped, we ended up pointing in the right direction. We then we were able to continue on home," Joe remembered.

February 3, 1979 » Albuquerque, New Mexico

Joe won the pole vault event at the National Junior Chamber of Commerce Track Meet at Albuquerque, New Mexico. Joe cleared 15-3 feet as he set a new meet record that had been in place for ten years.

In the process of winning, Joe had requested the bar be set at 15 feet, but for some unknown reason, it was actually set at 16 feet, which Joe barely missed. Once he discovered he had nearly cleared 16 feet, his confidence reached new levels.

"I really got excited. That meet was a breakthrough on that single jump when I thought it was 15 feet, but it was actually 16 feet."

Joe's performance earned him the honor of being named the "Most Outstanding High School Athlete" of the meet.

A new vaulting pit

When Joe was in junior high and as a freshman, Marlow High School's track facilities, at least for jumping, were pretty poor, according to Coach Cole.

"All we had were those old mesh bags filled with foam rubber blocks," Cole explained. We had four of five of those bags, and they were okay for going about 10 feet high. But with Joe going higher and higher, they were not enough. It was getting dangerous to go as high as he was and landing in the foam rubber," Coach Cole said.

Realizing that something had to be done before someone, namely Joe, got hurt, Cole took to action and requested improvements.

"I had to go to the school officials and tell them that what we had was not safe anymore. I told them we needed to get a better pit. They didn't really understand what this meant. I told them we have a world-class pole vaulter and we have terrible facilities. We need to get up to date on this and get something safe for him because he's getting up there now where it's dangerous," Coach Cole explained.

Fortunately, Coach Cole's efforts paid off.

"We finally got the new pits but it wasn't easy," Cole added.

March 14, 1979 » Konawa Relays » Konawa, Oklahoma

Joe turned in his usual winning performance in the pole vault competition, as he captured first place with a 14 foot vault, and he also ran legs on both the 440 yard and mile relay teams.

Joe's friend and teammate, Steve Patterson, turned in a super performance as he finished first in the 220 yard dash, second in the 100 yard dash and ran anchor on both relay teams which placed fourth.

State of Oklahoma Proclamation

After Joe was ranked fifth in the nation among high school pole vaulters, he received a citation from the State of Oklahoma. On March 22, 1979, Joe received an official proclamation of congratulations from the Oklahoma Senate that was sponsored by State Senator Kenneth Landis.

March 17, 1979 » Tishimingo Relays » Tishimingo, Oklahoma

Joe placed first in the pole vault.

March 24, 1979 » Eastern Oklahoma State College Invitational Meet » Wilburton, Oklahoma

Joe captured first place with a vault of 15 feet, 7 inches and then went for a state record of 16-2. He cleared the record height on his first attempt, but he grazed the crossbar on the way down and knocked it off. Joe then banged into the bar on his way on his final two attempts. However, the 15-7 successful effort did break the Class 2A-1A state record.

"He just did nick the bar," said Sulphur coach Jim Dixon, who as a Marlow native had followed Joe's brief but amazing career closely. "A lot of times the bar would have stayed up since it was touched so slightly. He'll get the record pretty soon."

March 31, 1979 » Southern Oklahoma Invitational Meet » Duncan, Oklahoma

Joe's 15 feet, 2 inch vault was one of the top performances of the meet, but he wasn't satisfied with that height. He had the bar raised to 15-10 in an attempt to break the existing national record for high school sophomores. His first attempt was under the bar, and on his second attempt he hit the bar going up. His third attempt came even closer, but he kicked the bar off with his heel as he went over.

April 13, 1979 » OSU Cowboy Relays » Stillwater, Oklahoma

Joe placed first in the Class 2A division as he cleared 14 feet, 3 inches.

The case of the missing pit

Phyllis Cole, wife of Coach Darvis Cole, recalled an incident involving Joe and the new pole vault pit at Marlow High School.

"Marlow was under a tornado warning, and Darvis and I were down in our storm cellar waiting for the storm to blow over. When the winds finally calmed down and we were ready to come out, all of a sudden we heard this pounding on our cellar door. It was Joe and some of the other track boys. They were all in a panic and Joe was almost in tears," Mrs. Cole said.

In a breathless, excited state, Joe tried to explain why he and his track teammates were so upset.

"Coach, coach, the pole vault pit has blown away! The tornado took our pit! The pit is gone!" screamed Joe.

The strong winds that hit Marlow that evening had blown away the pole vault pit as the track boys had discovered. Not knowing what else to do, the group rushed over to their coach's house to inform him.

Luckily, after searching the town's streets, the pit was located about a half-mile away from the track.

Joe remembers one section of the pit was found at one of his classmates' parent's house.

"One section of the pit went right through their roof and landed in their bedroom," Joe recalled.

"It was torn up some, but we could still use it. But Joe was so panicky. He knew how hard it was to get that new pit, and he didn't want to have to go through that again," Coach Cole added.

April 24, 1979 » Stephens County Track and Field Meet » Marlow, Oklahoma

Joe set a new meet record of 16-0 as he captured first place. The Marlow sophomore went on to clear 16-2 twice, but caught the bar on his descent both times in his attempt to better the current state record of 16-1 set by Brian Shaw of Duncan in 1977.

A penchant for helping others

As strong a competitor as Joe was in his sport of pole vaulting, his passion for the event was evident in a little known scenario that epitomizes not only Dial's love for the sport, but also illustrates his unselfish willingness to help others in the sport.

During his sophomore year at Marlow, Joe often worked out with a fellow vaulter from Duncan High School, David Jones.

Both Jones and Joe had their sights set on breaking the state record of 16 feet, 1 inch that was held by another Duncan High School pole vaulter, Brian Shaw.

At the Western Heights Track and Field Championship Meet, David Jones became only the sixth high school competitor in Oklahoma history to clear 15 feet. This came amazingly just one week after he cleared 14 feet for the first time at the Southern Oklahoma Invitational Track and Field Meet.

Jones was quick to pass on the credit for his success and rapid improvement to Joe and his father.

"Joe and I work out together all the time. He and his father have helped me more than anyone, and I'm really grateful to them," Jones explained in the local newspaper.

DAVID JONES FROM DUNCAN, OKLAHOMA, CLEARS THE BAR AT A MEET IN DUNCAN WHILE JOE PREPARES TO CATCH HIS POLE. JOE WAS NOT COMPETING DUE TO A PULLED MUSCLE IN HIS BACK. JONES WENT ON TO WIN THE COMPETITION WITH ADVICE AND HELP FROM JOE. THE TWO VAULTERS OFTEN PRACTICED TOGETHER.

"Last year as a junior was the first year I ever did much vaulting," Jones said. "I broke my arm as a freshman and broke my leg as a sophomore.

"In 1978, my best vault was 13-6 in the regionals, but that was my last meet. The 13-6 would have won any other regional by six inches. It got only fourth where I was, so I did not qualify for the state."

Jones also explained how Joe counseled him in his selection of equipment.

"I'm getting a new pole that is longer and heavier Wednesday. Joe says it will throw me up another six inches to a foot," Jones related.

Joe, who was recovering from a pulled muscle in his lower back, did not compete in the meet.

At the Southern Oklahoma Invitational Track and Field Meet held earlier at which Jones first cleared the 14 foot height, Joe exhibited another example of his sportsmanship by catching Jones' pole during the competition.

Joe recalls that the two vaulters would often practice together.

"He would often come up here (to Marlow) to practice or else I would go down there (to Duncan) to practice," Joe says.

Joe explained how much he loves to coach anyone involved in the sport of pole vaulting.

"It seems like I've been coaching my whole life. I always wanted to help somebody. Even if they were my competition, I wanted to help them. I would suggest, 'you should hold the pole here, or you should do this or do that.' I just wanted to help others," Dial said.

"I probably inherited that willingness to help others from my dad because he would help anybody. As a matter of fact, that's the way our whole family was. They would give you the shirt of their back. That's just something they always had done."

After high school, the two vaulters went their separate ways to continue competing in their chosen sport. Jones went on to pole vault for Arkansas State University while Joe went to Oklahoma State University.

Later, the two friends and former opponents became teammates.

"His last two years in college, he transferred to Oklahoma State so we got the opportunity to be teammates," Joe said.

Back injury

After being out of action for two weeks with a back injury in early April, Joe returned to competition with a vengeance. He had started the outdoor season in late March with vaults of 15-7 and 15-2 prior to the time-off due to the back injury.

Upon returning to competition, Joe had sub-par results (at least for him) at the Cowboy Relays, where he cleared only 14-3 and then a disappointing 14 feet even at the Arbuckle Conference Meet.

But then on a Saturday at the Chisholm Trail Invitational in Chickasha, Dial bounced back as he cleared 15 feet, 6 inches.

Two days later at the Stephens County Meet held at Joe's home track in Marlow, he soared over the bar set at 16 feet, edging ever so closer to the existing state record of 16-1.

As a matter of fact, on that Monday at Marlow, Dial had cleared the bar at 16-2 only to clip it off the standard on his way down. The state record certainly appeared to be within reach.

"All that is holding me back now is my bigger pole isn't in yet," Joe had explained on the previous Saturday at Chickasha.

Then on that following Monday in Marlow, Joe had his new pole and was ready to go.

The new pole was the same length (15 feet, 7 inches) but is rated to carry five more pounds (from 140 pounds to 145 pounds).

The difference was obvious as Joe missed only once on his way to attempting 16-2. He cleared 13-6, 14-0, 14-6, 15-0 and 16-0 all on his first attempts, while he needed only two attempts to clear 15-6.

Switching to a new pole in mid-season might provide some degree of apprehension to many vaulters, but not to Joe.

His theory on breaking in a new pole: "If you ain't scared of it, you can work with a pole one day and start using it in a meet the next day."

Which is exactly what he did.

Always seeking an edge, Joe was able to continue improvement even while he was out of action for those two weeks.

"While I was out, I studied pole vaulting a bunch. I watched a lot of film. It may have helped me," Joe added.

May 12, 1979 » Oklahoma Class 2A State Track Meet » Moore, Oklahoma

Joe claimed his second straight state championship with a vault of 14 feet, 6 inches, setting a new Oklahoma Class 2A record in the meantime. In the process, Joe broke the record of 14 feet set in 1971 by Travis Gartin of Tonkawa. Gartin tied his record the following year (1972). Jeff Dennis of Pauls Valley also tied the record in 1974.

Arkansas vaulting camp

In the summer of 1979, Joe attended the Track and Field Camp at Arkansas State University at Jonesboro, Arkansas, which was conducted under the guidance of Earl Bell. Bell, who would later capture the bronze medal at the 1984 Olympics at Los Angeles, had set a world record in the pole vault. Bell's presence was a major factor in Joe going to Arkansas to attend the camp.

"That's why I came here," Joe said. "I figured he could help me a lot."

Joe was able to improve his vaulting technique through the intense study of films. Films of himself taken primarily by his mother, Lena Dial, since his eighth grade year, and studying world-class vaulters like Bell, Billy Olson of Abilene Christian University and Jeff Buckingham of the University of Kansas, provided immeasurable assistance in his growth in the sport.

"Last year, we (Joe and his father, Dean) studied film just about every night," Joe recalled.

Dean Dial had plenty of time to coach and mentor his son since he was on disability retirement.

"I watched film of Buckingham because he's unusual — his size (5 foot, 6 inches) is similar to mine and also his style. I've watched films of Earl Bell and his style is unusual, too, in the long swing. I also watch Billy Olson. If anybody goes 19 feet, I think he will when he gets it all together," Joe predicted.

Small town pride

Like in many small towns across America, citizens would often identify with their local high school sports teams. Townspeople would eagerly share in their team's successes and lament in their team's defeats. Often, the businesses and citizens of these small towns would anxiously want to assist and support their local athletes in any manner possible.

The citizens in and around Marlow, Oklahoma, back in the late 70's and early 80's were no different. Joe Dial was their man. His growing fame and notoriety in the pole vaulting world was bringing national — and later worldwide — attention to the small southern Oklahoma town.

"That's one thing I really remember growing up. There were so many people in Marlow rooting for me to be successful. Early on, everybody kind of realized that I didn't go out and drink or smoke or run around and get into trouble. I had a lot of people would tell me this: 'If I ever see you do anything like that, I would stop you. You can't do that. You're going to be successful one day. You're going to be something.'"

Joe felt he was representing Marlow and its people, and he always took great pains to make the citizens back home proud, of not only his accomplishments on the athletic field, but also his actions as a human being.

But the sentiment went both ways.

Marlow was — and is — proud of Joe Dial.

Joe's mother, Lena Dial, recalls how the City of Marlow was always so supportive of Joe and all of his athletics accomplishments.

"The people of Marlow helped out in so many ways. They were always so proud of Joe. They put up signs on Highway 81 outside of town proclaiming Marlow "The Home of Joe Dial," she explained.

Joe reflects on the advantages and benefits of growing up in a small town.

"Marlow was a great town to grow up in. I wish my kids could enjoy the same experience," said Dial.

Another national age group record — 16-year-olds

In the summer of 1979 after Joe's sophomore year, he received several new vaulting poles. The new equipment evidently paid dividends because, along with coaching from his father, Joe cleared 16-6 in practice that summer. He then later cleared 16-2¼ in an Amateur Athletic Union (AAU) meet to establish a personal best as well as a new national age group record for 16 year- olds.

JUNIOR YEAR
MARLOW HIGH SCHOOL (1979–80)

Joe started his junior year of high school vaulting competition just as he finished his sophomore year — establishing more records and setting his — and others' — expectations to even higher levels.

January 18, 1980 » Oklahoma Track Coaches Indoor Winter Relays » Oklahoma City, Oklahoma

Joe broke in a brand new vaulting pole to a new national high school indoor record vault of 16 feet, 7¼ inches. Four of the nation's top young vaulters — Steve Stubblefield of Kansas City, Kansas; Gary Creed of Destrehan, Louisiana; Greg Duplantis of Lafayette, Louisiana, and Joe were invited to participate in a special competition of elite vaulters for the purpose of creating an atmosphere conducive to breaking records.

However, Stubblefield and Creed were no-shows and Duplantis suffered from a sub-par performance, clearing only the opening height. But it didn't matter as Joe was the star of the meet.

Joe warmed up for the record by winning the Class A high school pole vault at 16-3 in the morning session. He attempted the record in that session, but was unsuccessful on his three attempts.

Joe used a new blue SkyPole to set the mark. The previous national record was 16-7.

"I've done 16-8 in practice, but that's not on a regulation box," Joe explained. "Today was the first time on that pole. It's five pounds heavier than the other poles I use."

An additional five pounds is quite a lot to carry down the elevated board runway, especially for someone with such a small stature as the 5-8, 131 pound Dial, who lacks the muscular build of most elite pole vaulters. However, what Joe may lack in strength, he makes up for in speed and technique.

"I just stay at the bottom of the bending pole as long as I can," he said. "I started lifting weights last week, but I'm the same weight as last year."

"It was quite a deal for him," Marlow head track coach Darvis Cole said. "He's 16 and works harder than any man I've ever known. In practice this winter, he had already cleared 16-8, so this was really great that he got the record. He's an asset to Marlow, Stephens County and Oklahoma," Cole said.

However, Joe's record turned out to be rather short-lived.

Shortly after Joe set the record of 16-7¼ in Oklahoma City, another high school vaulter, Bill Lange of New Jersey, cleared 16-8 at a meet in Philadelphia, Pennsylvania, later that same night.

"If we had known about it, I think Joe could have handled 16-9 that night," Coach Cole said later.

"He (Joe) was really psyched up because of the competition at the meet," Cole added.

Joe recalled that he found out later that Lange was somewhat eccentric and a free spirit who actually competed barefoot. "He (Lange) was an unbelievable athlete. He had an impressive build and was super fast," Dial said in describing Lange.

In a later competition with Lange, Joe recalled how Lange's barefooted preference came into play.

"It started to rain and the runway began to get slick. As he started his approach and took off, his foot slipped and he fell on the runway. He then had to put on his spikes," Joe recalled.

January 19, 1980 » Sooner Indoor Relays » Oklahoma City, Oklahoma

Back-to-back meets were somewhat unusual, but this was one of those times. The Sooner Indoor Relays were held the night after the Oklahoma Track Coaches Association Indoor Games.

A national high school record was again set that night, but unfortunately, it wasn't by Joe. Greg Duplantis broke Joe's record just 24 hours after Joe set it, as he cleared 16-8¼.

Duplantis gave all the credit for his record to Joe and expressed the thought that Joe's jump from the previous night gave him the motivation and the emotional lift he needed to clear the new record height.

"Tonight, I didn't feel as good as I did last night," Duplantis said afterwards. "Joe Dial breaking the record last night was what did it."

Even Joe's vaulting poles had a prominent role in Duplantis setting the new record.

"The last three national records that Duplantis broke, he did using my poles. He went through his poles, so I offered him the use of my poles."

Joe's winning height at the Oklahoma Track Coaches Indoor Winter Relays forced him to re-assess the personal goals that he had previously set for himself.

"I set goals of 16-3 indoors and 17 feet outdoors for this year, but those are gone now," he said.

Joe was thinking in terms of 17-2 and higher. That would qualify him for the U.S. Olympic Trials.

"I'd like to get Jeff Buckingham's national mark (17 feet, ¾ inch for 17 year olds)," Joe explained.

Buckingham, a member of the University of Kansas track team, was at the time one of only three U.S. high school vaulters to ever clear 17 feet. Casey Carrigan, who was a member of the 1968 U.S. Olympic team, and Anthony Curran, who ended up going to UCLA, were the other two.

January 26, 1980 » Oklahoma Track Coaches Association Indoor Games » Oklahoma City, Oklahoma

This particular meet was a crucial turning point in Joe's pole vaulting career.

Joe burst on the national track and field scene as he became the first high school athlete in the nation to clear 17 feet indoors at this meet at the Myriad Convention Center in Oklahoma City. From this point on, Joe would be recognized as one of the elite pole vaulters — and not just on the high school level — in the entire country. The 17 foot jump set a national indoor high school mark, breaking the old record of 16-8½ by Steve Stubblefield which was set just three days earlier. Joe's 17-0 mark also established a new national age-group record for 17 year olds.

"I wasn't expecting it," Joe said after the meet.

"I want to start clearing 17-0 outdoors and then make 17-2¾ (the qualifying height for the Olympic Trials)," Joe added.

February 1, 1980 » Albuquerque Jaycees Invitational Indoor Meet » Albuquerque, New Mexico

Joe continued his streak of outstanding performances as he set another meet record by clearing 16-6, winning this meet for the second consecutive year.

First international meet

February 6-9, 1980 » Paris, France

Most high school track and field athletes may travel 100 miles or less to compete in a track meet. For Joe Dial, that distance is nothing.

While just a junior in high school, he traveled over 5,000 miles to compete in his first international track and field meet at Paris, France.

"This is my first trip outside the United States. I'm really excited about the opportunity," Joe said at the time.

With all of the expenses being covered by a French promoter, Joe was able to totally concentrate on the competition and his performance.

"It's going to get tough over there," Joe said as he contemplated his first international meet.

"I'm looking forward to it. No, I've never been anywhere like that, but, you know, I believe it will be easier to vault over there than it is here," he continued.

"There will be a bunch of folks around 17-8, 17-10 and if they're going to make it, then I'll have to make it, too. I hope to get closer to 18 feet there and I'm excited about going against the really good field competitors."

"I've got a chance to stay in France another week and jump against the Soviets," Joe said, "But it doesn't look like I'll be able to. I can't afford to miss that much school and I've already got several other meets lined up anyway. Hopefully, there will be other chances like that."

In the meet, Dial placed sixth with a leap of 17-¾.

"I'd thought I'd do a lot better than I did." Joe said.

"There were a lot of good jumpers here. I was really surprised at the quality of jumpers," Dial related after the meet. "The conditions were about the best I ever jumped in."

Brad Pursley from Abilene Christian University was the other American competitor to make the trip overseas. Pursley finished seventh, also at 17-¾, but since Joe had fewer misses than Pursley, Joe placed ahead of him in sixth place.

The 5 foot, 8 inch, 130 pound Dial was of the opinion that competing against older international athletes will definitely help him in the long run.

"I'm real little. I really don't know how I beat people so much bigger. I just trust in God," Dial said while attempting to explain his success.

But besides the action on the runway, Joe enjoyed several adventures which he had never previously encountered.

Oysters on the half-shell

Joe's first international trip to Paris included challenges off the track as well as those he faced on the pole vault runway.

"The pole manufacturing company who sponsored the meet expressed interest in having a couple of American pole vaulters to go to the meet. So Brad Pursley and I both went," Joe explained.

"The owner of Dema Sports, which is a major sporting goods company in France, took us out to eat after the meet.

"At the meal, he wanted Brad and I to try these raw oysters, but I was somewhat hesitant because they smelled really bad," Joe recalls.

"No, no. You must eat these," the sporting goods owner insisted.

But Joe was still not totally sold on the idea since the oysters smelled so rancid. But after several minutes of serious arm-twisting and going against his better judgment and not wishing to insult his host, Joe finally broke down and relented, eating just one oyster.

"I knew it smelled bad, but I went ahead and ate one," Joe explained.

Then waking up later in the middle of the night, Joe got deathly sick from food poisoning.

"I was throwing up and everything. I never felt so bad in my life."

With his bout with the food poisoning subsiding a little, in an attempt to get to feeling better, Joe decided to step outside the hotel in order to get some fresh air. As he strolled the sidewalks, he noticed some young men roaming the streets, all the while eyeballing him.

"They would see me and start moving my way. As I walked, they would start to approach me and I would retreat. This happened several times. It concerned me but fortunately, nothing happened."

"Here I was — a seventeen year-old kid from a small-town in Oklahoma roaming the streets in Paris at three o'clock in the morning. What was I thinking?"

French fries in France?

On that same trip, once when Joe was hungry, he went out in search of something to eat. Not being familiar with French food or the French language, he was seeking food with which he was a little more familiar.

Slipping into a little restaurant, he asked for a "hamburger."

The waiter did not understand what Joe wanted and apparently "hamburger" does not translate well into French.

Racking his brain to come up with some food that the French waiter would be able to better understand, suddenly the light bulb went off in Joe's head.

"I was thinking what would they understand. Then suddenly it came to me. French fries!" Joe exclaimed.

Thinking he had found some common ground, he attempted to explain to the waiter, "You have to know what french fries are — you're the ones who invented them!"

The waiter curtly replied, "No, no. Pommes frites. Pommes frites. Pommes frites."

Joe laughs today as he recalls the incident. "That's about the only foreign language I recall," Joe admits.

March 7, 1980 » Possum Kingdom Relays » Graham, Texas

Joe kicked off the 1980 outdoor season in fine fashion as he cleared 16-10 which resulted in a new Texas state record.

Joe entered this meet somewhat "under the radar." Being from Oklahoma, the Texas meet officials were not familiar with Joe and his pole vaulting talents. Joe kept "passing" on the heights while the other competitors were jumping. Joe informed the skeptical meet officials that he would pass until the bar reached 14-6. The meet officials didn't know what to think — they had never experienced any other vaulter with that degree of confidence.

Joe finally entered the competition when the bar reached 14-6 just as he had planned and then he didn't miss until it was raised to 16-6. Then he cleared that height on his second attempt. The 16-10 height set a new national record for high school juniors.

"The pits were so small I flew completely off the mat and landed on my back on the concrete. I just had a bad plant and the pits were so small," Joe recalled.

The previous junior class record was 16-9 set in 1979 by Dave Volz of Bloomington, Indiana. Joe and Dave would later go on to face each other many times in the future.

March 14, 1980 » Boomtown Relays » Burkburnett, Texas

Joe broke his existing junior class record by ¼ inch as he cleared 16-10¼.

"We had a unbelievable tailwind. I jumped on some new blue SkyPoles that the company had sent me and I was trying them out.

"It was probably at least 30 miles per hour wind at my back. The crossbar had been moved up to 17-2. I picked up my pole to make my approach on the runway and the wind picked the mat from the pit and totally blew it away. When that happened, the meet officials just stopped the meet. Imagine, if I had been in the air when the wind had blown the mat away?" Joe asked.

March 21, 1980 » Dickson Invitational Meet » Dickson, Oklahoma

Joe cleared 16 feet, 2¾ inches as he set a new meet and a new state outdoor record in the process.

In warm-ups, Joe discovered that the vaulting box had a hole in it so he took it upon himself to repair it by scooping cinders off the track and inserting and packing them into the hole. The repair effort must have worked since Joe went on to set a new state outdoor record.

Joe received an interesting request after the meet. A photographer from the local newspaper showed up late to the meet after Joe had already made his record-breaking jump. Wanting to document the record-breaking jump for inclusion into the newspaper, the local photographer asked Joe to place the crossbar back up on the record-breaking height and repeat the vault again so he could photograph the jump.

With disbelief at such a request, Joe replied that no, he couldn't do that! A person just couldn't simply clear a record-breaking height on demand.

But, in his always accommodating manner, Joe kindly told the photographer that perhaps he could make an 11 foot vault and the photographer would be welcome to shoot that photo. The photographer agreed, saying he could make the 11 foot vault appear to be the record-breaking height by using a different camera angle.

April 1, 1980 » Southern Oklahoma Invitational Meet » Duncan, Oklahoma

At the Southern Oklahoma Invitational Track Meet at Duncan, Joe set a new state outdoor record of 16 feet, 8¾ inches as he broke his own record of 16 feet, 2¾ inches, which he set just 10 days earlier in a meet at Dickson.

However, Joe had a close call on his way to the new state record.

Failing to clear the bar on his first two attempts at 16-7, he then cleared that height on his third and final attempt as he had perfect execution.

It then took Joe only one jump to clear the record height of 16-8¾.

Continuing on, Joe then had the bar set at 17 feet, ½ inch, but after three valiant attempts, and weary from prior jumps, he failed to clear the height.

The record was Dial's fifth consecutive vaulting record in as many meets.

"The funny thing was I made 17 feet in practice here Monday," Dial, who was 5-9 and just 135 pounds, explained following the meet.

"I had to go back to a smaller pole at the 16-7 height after I missed twice. I just wasn't ready for that bigger pole. I use different poles for different heights because their flexes are different."

Dial explained that he has about 20 different poles in his arsenal, but usually takes only five or six to a meet.

Joe's father explained Joe's passion for the sport and how he constantly strives for improvement.

"He talks to world class vaulters everywhere he goes," Dean Dial said. "Last summer he went to a pole vault camp at Arkansas State and got some pointers from Earl Bell and other top vaulters. And he works at it. He works out every day he possibly can," the elder Dial added.

"I'm trying to get 17-3 outdoors this year," Joe added.

Dial's first place finish in the pole vault led Marlow to a 1-2-3 sweep in the event as Mike Gatlin captured second place with Phil Cole taking third place.

Joe was very busy at this particular meet. In addition to setting a new state record, he was able to showcase his long jumping ability as he captured second place in the event with a leap of 19-10½. He was also given the opportunity to exhibit his speed as he claimed second place in the 440 yard dash in a fine time of 54.6 seconds.

How high can he go?

After the flurry of state records, and with 17-4½ being the then current national record, Joe was asked by Oklahoma City Sports Reporter John Martin how high he thinks he can ultimately go?

Joe had his answer ready.

"I really don't know. Some people think I may be limited because of my size (at only 5-9), but I try to overcome that with quickness. I felt confident I could go 17 feet, but I don't try to think about records. I'll just keep working on my technique and see what happens."

April 4, 1980 » Jets Invitational Meet at Western Heights High School » Oklahoma City, Oklahoma

Joe continued his streak of exceptional pole vaulting efforts as he cleared 16 feet, 6 inches.

That height would have easily been a state record except for the fact that Joe cleared 16-8¾ just days earlier during the Southern Oklahoma Invitational Meet at Duncan.

The unique aspect regarding Joe's performance was the fact that he did not miss until the bar was raised to 16-9. He successfully topped 14-6, 15-0, 15-6, 16-0 and 16-6 without any misses. Joe then had the bar raised to 16-9 in an attempt to break his recently-set state record, but missed on all three attempts.

Joe then took an unofficial fourth attempt at 16-9, and as luck would have it at, he cleared it.

April 5, 1980 » Konawa Relays » Konawa, Oklahoma

Joe established another state record as he soared 17 feet at the Konawa Relays and marked the first time he cleared 17 feet outdoors.

The mark erased his previous record of 16-8¾ set last week.

Joe was a record-setting terror — as the record at Konawa marked the third time Joe had set a new state record in the last 14 days. He has also set seven meet records so far during the 1980 season. It was just 24 hours after he set a meet record at Western Heights.

Joe was busy at this meet as he also finished fifth in the long jump with a jump of 20 feet, two inches and also ran legs on Marlow's 440 yard relay and mile relays teams, both of which finished in fifth place.

Marlow's pole vaulting threesome of Dial, Mike Gatlin and Phil Cole went 1-2-3 in the pole vault.

Joe's streak of records in the pole vault was attained despite the fact that the state of Oklahoma experienced a wet spring resulting in a number of meet cancellations and rescheduled meets. But the always positive Dial credited such weather for his recent surge of consistency, and the resulting push upward of the state record.

"Not only does bad weather cause cancellation of some track meets, but it really determines what a pole vaulter can do. I can still work on my endurance and sprint drills and even some on strength exercises, but weather has to be good to actually practice," Joe explains.

"Of course, I can always practice indoors and I do a lot, but it's a lot different because of the wind factor," he explained.

Respect

Even Joe's opponents often spoke highly of the talented up-and-coming pole vaulter.

"The sky is the limit for Joe," said Duncan High School coach Steve Cleveland. "He's got the talent. Height-wise, he's a world-class vaulter.

"What I like about him best is that Joe has remained a good country kid. All his success has not gone to his head. What's impressive about him is that he is not selfish or self-centered," Cleveland declared.

"He'll do everything the Marlow coaches ask him to. He'll run the quarter mile and the relays and compete in the long jump. He'll work to help the team."

Coach Cleveland even mentioned Joe's penchant for practice, noting that he often drives to Halliburton Stadium in Duncan to practice, depending upon the wind conditions.

April 11, 1980 » OSU Cowboys Relays » Stillwater, Oklahoma

Joe captured another meet title as be cleared 16-0.

Saturday, April 12, 1980 » Marlow Outlaw Invitational Meet » Marlow, Oklahoma

On an unseasonably cold and blustery day, Joe overcame the elements and equaled his state record of 17-0 he had just set a week earlier. The mark was good enough for another meet record. Again, Marlow's trio of pole vaulters — Dial, Mike Gatlin and Phil Cole — swept the event.

Those efforts helped the Marlow Outlaws to go on to record their first win of the year as they held off a late challenge to edge the defending Purcell Dragons 67-66.

With the temperature close to freezing, Joe took some unique steps in an attempt to stay warm.

"We had our family car at the back of the runway, off to the side. At Marlow, you could park there. I would hop in the car between jumps and warm my hands. It was so cold I kept my sweats on and didn't take my top of my sweats off until the bar got up to 17 feet," Joe said.

April 19, 1980 » Kansas Relays ; Memorial Stadium; University of Kansas » Lawrence, Kansas

Joe cleared 17-5¼, a national high school outdoor record and a world record for 17 year-olds. (See Part III — "Airborne In the Kansas (Relays) Skies" for additional details.)

Stephens County, Oklahoma: Pole Vaulting Capital

Anyone who follows track and field could not argue with the assertion that the Marlow Outlaws possessed the best trio of high school pole vaulters in the history of the state of Oklahoma. In fact, the three Marlow High School students, Joe Dial, Mike Gatlin and Phil Cole, may have been among the top trios of high school vaulters of any high school in America.

Joe, a junior, had set state, national and world records in the event almost too numerous to list, not to mention winning numerous prestigious awards along the way.

Mike, also a junior, has exhibited tremendous improvement as he has raised his personal best 21 inches to 14 feet, 9 inches since his 13-0 jump last season.

Phil, just a sophomore, has soared over the 13 foot barrier at several meets.

Anyone of these three athletes would likely be the best vaulter on many high school teams. But the combination of Dial, Gatlin and Cole proved to be great teammates all with the same objective: to sweep the Class 2A competition at the state track meet and led Marlow to a state championship.

May 3, 1980 » Class 2A Regional Meet » Clinton, Oklahoma

Marlow High School captured their first regional track and field championship in a number of years as Joe won two individual events as well as running on two winning relay teams.

Joe led a 1-2-3 finish for Marlow pole vaulters as he cleared 16 feet. Teammates Mike Gatlin took second (14-6) and Phil Cole was third (13 feet).

Despite limited practice time, Joe also claimed first place in the long jump as he soared 22 feet, ½ inch, setting a new Marlow school record. The jump was also the best in Class 2A.

"We started using Joe as a long jumper, but I wouldn't let him practice long jumping very much. During the week, he would practice his steps, but he wouldn't even jump. Long jumping is hard on your legs, and we didn't want to do anything that would mess him up for pole vaulting," Coach Cole said.

Danny Farmer, Scott Hall, Joe and Steve Patterson won the 440 yard relay in a time of 44.6 seconds, which was another new school record.

Hall, Dial, John Hazlitt and Patterson later combined to win the mile relay.

May 9-10, 1980 » Oklahoma Class 2A State Track Meet » Western Heights High School » Oklahoma City, Oklahoma

Joe set a new state record and Marlow again showcased its contingent of talented pole vaulters as the Outlaws placed 1-2-3 in the pole vault competition, which was exactly the team's goal. Joe captured first (17 feet, 1 inch), Mike Gatlin took second (15 feet) and Phil Cole, finished third (12 feet, 6 inches).

Joe and Mike were able to capture first and second place, respectively, fairly easily, but Phil Cole claiming third place turned into more of a battle.

"To sweep the state meet like that was very unusual. It was fun to just be a part of that feat," Coach Darvis Cole recalled.

"It was a really fun moment with the three of us going 1-2-3 at the state meet," Joe said.

In addition to his gold medal for the pole vault, Joe also captured the state title in the long jump.

"Joe Dial Day" in Marlow, Oklahoma; April 30, 1980

After Joe broke the state record and set a new national high school record at the Kansas Relays and qualified to compete at the U.S. Olympic Trials, the City of Marlow decided to honor their famous resident athlete with a day in his honor.

"I remember getting called out of class and being told they were going to have a "Joe Dial Day" in my honor. I had to go down to some local clubs, like the Lions' Club, and speak. It was all pretty neat," Joe recalled.

The official proclamation:

PROCLAMATION

WHEREAS, Joe Dial, having been a life-long resident of Marlow,

WHEREAS, Joe Dial has attended and received professional instruction in the Marlow Public School System,

WHEREAS, Joe Dial is an outstanding student and has excelled in athletic competition,

WHEREAS, Marlow is extremely proud of the record setting performance by this outstanding student and future community leader,

NOW, therefore, I, Harold "Dub" Watson, Mayor of the City of Marlow, do hereby proclaim, Wednesday, April 30, 1980 as JOE DIAL DAY for the City of Marlow.

Harold Watson
Mayor

ATTEST:

Marshall Long
City Clerk

State of Oklahoma Proclamation

After Joe set the national record at the Kansas Relays, he also received a Citation from The State of Oklahoma. On May 12, 1980, Joe received a commendation from the Oklahoma House of Representatives that was sponsored by State Representative Vernon Dunn of Stephens County, Joe's home county.

Meeting O.J. Simpson

Hertz Rent-a-Car sponsored the Hertz #1 Award to recognize the top high school athletic performer from each state. Of course, Joe was the Oklahoma representative due to his pole vaulting exploits.

O.J. Simpson, former National Football League star and later spokesman for Hertz-Rent A-Car, made the presentations of the "Number 1" trophy at the New York Athletic Club in New York City.

HERTZ SPOKESMAN O.J. SIMPSON
PRESENTS THE HERTZ NO. 1 AWARD
TO JOE FOR BEING HONORED AS
OKLAHOMA'S TOP HIGH SCHOOL
ATHLETE. JOE WAS A TWO-WINNER
OF THE AWARD WINNING IN BOTH
1980 AND 1981.

Joe was actually a two-time winner of the "Number 1" Award, winning it both his junior and senior years.

"I remember the first year, I was introduced to O.J. and he said, 'Joe Dial, it is good to meet you.'

"The next year after I won for the second time, I saw someone from the awards committee approach him when I was next in line and whisper something in his ear.

"When it was my turn to meet O.J., he beamed that big smile of his and said, 'Hey, Joe, it's good to see you again' like he remembered me from the previous year," Joe laughed.

"He no more remembered me than anything. He didn't know me from Adam. That person had simply whispered in his ear and told him that I was a repeat winner and he tried to come across as actually remembering me," Joe said.

Many years later, as he looked back on that meeting and reflected on the subsequent unfortunate events involving Simpson, Joe reminiscenced about meeting Simpson.

"Even back then he didn't tell the truth. He didn't remember me and then all this other stuff happens. But he seemed like a real nice guy, with lots of charisma," Joe related.

While Joe enjoyed his two days in New York City, he took in several interesting sights including Radio City Music Hall and the Rockefeller Center.

Joe mentioned an interesting sight that he came across during his visit.

"There was one place where all these guys were just laying in the streets. You couldn't even tell if they were alive or dead, but no one seemed to pay any attention to them," he explained.

LENA, JOE AND DEAN DIAL CELEBRATING JOE'S SECOND HERTZ #1 AWARD.

Joe later learned that they were some of the New York City homeless, sleeping in the streets and on the sidewalks in the city.

Dedication

Marlow High School Coach Cole fondly recalls how dedicated Joe was to his sport and the amount of time and effort Joe would tirelessly put forth in his constant efforts to improve.

"I would drive past the track field at different times, and it seemed like every time I drove by, I would see Joe and his dad out there practicing. For days and days, you would see Joe and his dad out there. I was worried that Dean (Joe's dad) might overdo it and burn him out, but Joe stayed with it and it certainly paid off," Coach Cole said.

"Joe's dad lived and breathed pole vaulting," Coach Cole said.

Plenty of shoes

Several major sport shoe companies were in their infancy stage and were actively promoting their products by giving away shoes and equipment to athletes who had a chance to qualify for the upcoming Olympic Trials. The companies realized that having an athlete wear their brand of shoe or equipment at the Trials, which would be televised in addition to receiving plenty of print coverage, would result in an enormous amount of free advertising.

After breaking the national high school pole vault record at the recent Kansas Relays, Joe's name quickly became known to the shoe companies and equipment manufacturers.

"Someone told me that all I had to do was to call the company up and they would send me free shoes and equipment," Joe recalled.

"I called Nike, Adidas, Puma, Brooks, ASICS, Pony and another company called, I think, Kangaroo. I just told them that I had just broken the high school pole vault record and was wondering if I could get some of your shoes to try," Joe said.

The shoe companies, always in search of the free advertising and national promotion, were more than eager to fulfill Joe's request.

However, their reaction far surpassed Joe's expectations.

"The boxes soon starting coming! Every company I contacted would send me boxes of stuff — two or three pairs of spikes, two or three pairs of flats, tee-shirts, warm-ups and hats. Just about anything they had. It was crazy! The stuff would just flood in!

"Everybody on my (Marlow High School) team was just about my size. So I started giving the equipment away to my teammates," Joe revealed.

Joe's teammates appreciated the opportunity for new — and even more importantly — free gear.

"It's amazing when someone had free stuff how it always fit better," quipped teammate Steve Patterson.

But Joe was sure to give all the companies who provided the free gear the exposure that each company desired.

"I would rotate what shoes I wore at the meets since I told them I would wear them. The ones I like the best I would wear at the Olympic Trials," Joe explained.

Dial named All-American

Joe was among a group of 13 Oklahoma high school athletes who were named to the first National High School Track All-American roster.

These 13 honored athletes were selected from more than 900,000 boys and girls competing in 28 different events at state track meets during the 1980 season.

In all, 365 All-Americans were selected for the 1980 season.

May 30, 1980 » Track & Field Association National Championship Meet » Cessna Stadium » Wichita, Kansas

Joe overcame some early misses to win the high school boys division of the Track and Field National Championships in Wichita, Kansas, as he soared 17 feet, 3¾ inches.

Joe beat out Steve Stubblefield of Kansas City and Greg Duplantis of Lafayette, Louisiana, who tied for second at 17-0. Both Stubblefield and Duplantis were frequent adversaries of Dial in competition.

History was made as it was the first time in any meet that three high school vaulters each cleared 17 feet.

Joe's vault was a new Track & Field Association meet record.

Joe later attempted a national record at 17-6¼ but failed to clear it.

"I was behind all day long. I was picking up silly misses. When we went to 17-3¾, I went to a new 17 foot pole and gripped at 16-1. I made it on my first attempt, but the other two guys (Stubblefield and Duplantis) missed their first attempt, so I took over first place," Joe recalled.

"I've been real close to 18 feet in practice. I want it real bad. But it's a long ways off, " Joe said after the meet.

It was at this particular meet that Joe also disclosed that he planned to clear 18 feet before he leaves the high school ranks.

Setting records was becoming second nature for the Marlow Outlaw. When pressed, the unassuming young vaulter told a local newspaper reporter that he had set records in nearly every one of the last 15 or so meets in which he competed.

Going to the U.S. Olympic Trials as just a high school junior

With such an impressive performance in the record books, Joe then set his sights on the United States Olympic team trials to be held in Eugene, Oregon, later in the summer.

Joe qualified for the Olympic Trials by virtue of his record of 17-5¼ vault earlier that spring at the Kansas Relays. The qualifying height for the Trials was 17-2¾.

Making the tryouts was actually Joe's goal this year, according to his father. Joe's high school coach, Darvis Cole, pointed out that Joe's determination and a rigid practice schedule have put him in a position to contend for national attention and a possible spot on the Olympic team. Coach Cole also noted Joe's positive attitude and outstanding skill set could potentially send him to international competition.

"In any track event, your mental attitude is real important, "Cole said. "He knows he can do it now."

But the thrill of attempting to qualify for the USA Olympic Track & Field team had to be tempered by the planned United States boycott of the 1980 Moscow Olympic Games in retaliation for the Soviet invasion of Afghanistan.

Joe expressed his displeasure with the potential boycott in no uncertain terms, but indicated he would still compete in an effort to make the USA team.

"I don't think they should do that (boycott the Olympics). You work all your life to do something then they won't let you do it," Joe opined.

The *Marlow Review* had a small story with Joe's thoughts and comments on competing in the upcoming Olympic Trials in Eugene, Oregon, scheduled for June 24, 1980.

From the *Marlow Review,* June 10, 1980:

"I'll just go up there and make the opening height," Joe told the Review. "They'll probably be starting at 17 feet or so. I'd be happy just to clear a bar up there. I sure don't expect to win it," Dial added.

"But I will go to the tryouts and see what I do up there," he said. "1984 — that would be about right for me," the young Dial explained.

Joe's father agreed.

He pointed out that in four years, his son would still be one of the youngest competitors. The tryouts in 1980 will pit his young son against "28 to 30 year olds."

"They will have 10 years of jumping on him," Dean Dial explained.

June 16-17, 1980 » National Junior Olympics Meet » Knoxville, Tennessee

"The Junior Olympics is the meet where Joe really wants to do well. If he places first or second, he will qualify for the 19-and-under U.S. team which will compete in meets against East Germany, the Soviet Union, and Canada, and in the Pan-American Junior Olympics," Dean Dial said prior to the National Junior Olympics meet at the University of Tennessee in Knoxville.

However, unfavorable weather conditions contributed to a seldom-seen sub-par performance by Joe as he managed to clear just 15-9. Two other vaulters beat Joe and three others tied him.

The loss was sufficient to knock the 17 year-old Dial out of international Junior Olympic competition.

The wind made a 180 degree turn after the competition started which resulted in the wind coming directly into the vaulters' faces.

"I have to have the wind at my back. They had kind of a head wind. It was raining and my steps just weren't on. I was clearing the bar by almost a foot, but I was falling on it because my steps were messed up and I wasn't getting enough acceleration.," he said.

Joe explained strong winds affected the rhythm of his starting run and then literally blew his thin, wiry frame off course.

"I was jumping outside my check point," he said. "One time I came down and almost landed off the mat. I guess you can't win them all."

June 24, 1980 » 1980 U.S. Olympic Trials » Hayward Field » University of Oregon » Eugene, Oregon

Going into the 1980 Olympic Trials, Joe had never "no-heighted" in a meet.

"I've never no-heighted in a meet and I'm just not going to no-height in this one," Dial declared, but unfortunately, that turned out not to be the case.

The *Marlow Review* featured an update on Joe competing at the U.S. Olympic Trails as related by his mother, Lena Dial. Joe had called his mother to update the family on how the competition at the Trials was unfolding.

"Joe said on his first attempt (at the opening height of 17-2¾) he was up and over it," his mother related from a phone call from Joe.

"Joe said, 'I almost had it' and said the wind wasn't too bad on that attempt."

Later in the meet, the wind became an issue for the high school junior.

"It was swirling around, blowing every which way," Joe had told his mother.

"He likes the wind behind him," Mrs. Dial said. "He doesn't like it from the side or blowing straight into him."

Another obstacle: the opening height at the Olympic Trials, 17 feet, 2¾ inches was the highest he had ever faced as an initial height in competition.

"He would rather start at about 16 feet," Mrs. Dial said. "He likes to work up to his larger pole. He doesn't like to get on the larger pole right off."

But getting on the larger pole right off is exactly what the situation dictated as Joe competed with 38 of the nation's best vaulters, with each one older, some as many as 12-13 years older, than Joe.

"He started at 17-0 at Wichita when he won that meet in 17-3. That's the highest starting point he ever had before," Mrs. Dial said.

The 17-3 effort at Wichita and the 17-5¼ mark at the Kansas Relays (a national high school record) had been Joe's only competitive efforts above 17-2¾.

As a testament to the degree of difficulty of the opening height, only 13 of the 38 vaulters were able to negotiate the opening height with an unbelievable 25 vaulters not clearing the opening height. For what it is worth, at least Joe was in good company among the "no-heighters." Earl Bell, who would later go to make two U.S. Olympic teams, Jeff Buckingham, Brad Pursley and Steve Stubblefield, all athletes against whom Joe had competed many times, were among the ones not advancing beyond the opening height.

Joe later explained his frame of mind as he competed on the big stage in the Trials.

"They called my name, and I heard the announcer say, 'Joe Dial on the runway.' I got up on the runway and heard all this noise. Clap! Clap! Clap! Everyone was clapping in Oregon. I couldn't figure out what was going on. I looked around and I was the only one competing. They were clapping for me! I put that little 16-5 pole down and I grabbed that 17 footer and put in there. I had a great time."

Joe, always wanting to learn as much as possible regarding his event, remained in Eugene after the preliminaries in order to watch the finals.

"Joe is staying over to watch," his mother said. "He'll learn something from watching. He's not bashful. If he sees someone doing something which might help, he'll go up to them and ask them questions."

The top three finishers in the trials who went on to make the United States Olympic Team were Tom Hintnaus (18-4¼); Dan Ripley (18-2½) and Mike Tully (18-2½).

Although most of the U.S. qualifiers came to the U.S. Olympic Track and Field Trials despite the U.S. decision to boycott the Games, many frankly admitted that with no Olympics, the trials just weren't the same.

Mike Roche, who made the 1976 team in the steeplechase, told the Eugene *Register-Guard* on one wet afternoon: "If these were the Olympic trials, it wouldn't be raining." Al Oerter, a four-time gold medalist in the discus said, "I knew it was not the Olympic Trials when I could sleep this week."

But the track-crazed city of Eugene saved the meet. Even as talk of a U.S. boycott persisted last winter and became a reality this spring, ticket sales remained brisk. The spirit of the crowds at Hayward Field is legend to the athletes and the support of the entire city is unrivaled in the U.S. Throughout the nine-day meet, the *Register-Guard* poured out six to nine pages of doting coverage each day. At one point, the newspaper sandwiched in a small sidebar on Pete Rose, calling him the "Al Oerter of baseball." That's the way it is in Eugene about track and field.

Joe was somewhat surprised and mildly shocked at the reception and the crowd's reaction at the Trials."All those people started clapping and chanting in rhythm when your name is announced and you make your run-up on the runway. It was very neat."

Time for rest

After such a whirlwind summer and the trip to the Olympic Trials, Joe returned home to Marlow to relax for a quick — and well deserved — respite from the rigors of competition and travel.

"All the travel was a lot of fun," Joe explained, "but right now I'm just running and lifting weights from about 10:30 p.m. to midnight. I can't jump in this summer heat because the pole just slips out of my hands."

Improving at the Arkansas vaulting camp

Under the watchful eyes of Earl Bell and several other world-class vaulters who served as instructors at the camp, Joe was able to discover a minor hitch in his form while vaulting.

"I was going off to the right side, sometimes even missing the mats. We watched my jumps on video tape and found out I was cocking my right leg which threw my direction off."

With this flaw corrected, Joe felt comfortable with his training plans and optimistic about his upcoming senior season.

"I'm just trying to get stronger in my upper body. I won't do anything with my legs except run. I never liked to lift weights with my legs, so I just let them take care of themselves," he declared.

As he was looking forward to his senior year, Joe had set some specific goals.

"I want to come out first in indoors in 1981. I'd like to do indoors what I did outdoors," he explained in reference to his 17-5¼ he cleared at the Kansas Relays. And outdoors, I'd like to go 18-0 in practice and if I can do it in a meet, that would be great," he added.

SENIOR YEAR
MARLOW HIGH SCHOOL (1980−81)

Joe entered his senior year at Marlow High School full of promise, facing high expectations and, perhaps most importantly of all, filled with anxious anticipation of new heights to conquer.

The question on everyone's mind was "How high can Joe go?"

Already the owner of the national indoor record of 17 feet and the outdoor record of 17 feet, 5¼ inches, Joe had consistently improved throughout his high school career, at least a foot and three inches each year since his freshman season

His record of improvement is remarkable and is likely unmatched in pole vault circles anywhere, anytime. As they often say of proven performers — "his reputation has preceded him."

That could be the case for Joe Dial, as now he was receiving invitations to premier meets and special competitions featuring the biggest and best-known names in the sport. Among the meets he accepted were the Millrose Games in New York City and the Star-Maple Leaf Games in Toronto, Canada.

To the question of how high can Joe go, his coach Darvis Cole weighed in with his opinion.

"The thing he wants, the thing we all want, is for him to become the first 18-foot high school vaulter."He pushed himself all fall last year and he felt he might have peaked out a little early. He didn't vault as much this fall and I think that will help him later on," Davis explained.

Cole noted that Joe has been clearing 17-2 fairly routinely in practice and even cleared 17-4 in what is affectionately known as "Pneumonia Downs," the old, damp and musty area at the University of Oklahoma that served for an indoor workout facility where Joe often worked out. Cole mentioned that Joe tried 18 feet and was over it but just knocked it off with his chest.

Cole also noted that compared to last year when Joe was a mere 5 feet, 8½ inches and 130 pounds, Joe looked a little heavier than last year and appeared to be a bit taller. "Joe seems to feel a bit more comfortable carrying the pole, although I'm not sure if that's due to increased speed or strength, or perhaps both," Cole explained.

New track coach

After having Darvis Cole serve as his high school track coach for his first three years at Marlow High School, Joe found himself with a new track coach as his senior year commenced.

Coach Cole had recognized that Joe and his track teammates were rapidly improving as a squad and would ultimately require more attention than he (Cole) was able to provide due to his other duties, so a new track coach was hired for Marlow High School.

Gary Boxley took over the reins of the Outlaws track and field squad.

Joe credits Coach Boxley with having the foresight and flexibility to allow him to develop and hone his pole vaulting skills.

"I had been running with all the other track guys — running sprints and intervals — before I would even practice my vaulting. The problem was after doing all that running, my legs were just too dead to do much in pole vaulting. I suggested to Coach Boxley if I could skip some of the running in practice so I could concentrate on my vaulting, it might be best. I assured him I would be willing to run any race in a meet and would always be prepared to compete. Coach Boxley could have simply insisted that I "do it his way" and practice with all the other track guys, like some coaches would. But instead, to his credit, he trusted me and let me practice as I saw fit. I really appreciated him for that," Joe said.

Joe was not the only Marlow High School track athlete to express a high opinion of Coach Boxley. Steve Patterson, Joe's teammate at both Marlow High School and at Oklahoma State University, credits Boxley with inspiring him to become a track coach.

"I actually first thought about coaching during my senior year in high school," Patterson said. "Our new coach, Gary Boxley, opened up a whole new world of track and field to me and instilled in me a complete love of the sport."

Obviously Coach Boxley influenced the two young men in a very positive way as he helped shape their lives. They both went on to outstanding active and coaching careers in the track and field world.

Joe, of course, would go on to his successful career in pole vaulting and then followed that with almost 30 years of coaching the sport, the majority of which were at the collegiate Division I level.

Patterson went on to parlay his "complete love of the sport" along with his coaching philosophy, competition experience, and his extensive level of track and field knowledge into a highly successful coaching career. For over twenty years, he racked up an impressive list of state championships as a track and cross country coach at three large Oklahoma high schools: Jenks, Edmond North and Lincoln Christian in Tulsa, before joining Coach Dial's staff at Oral Roberts University.

Coach Boxley's thoughts

"'Joe was such a great teammate to those guys. He went to a lot of places and did a lot of things, but he was so team-oriented his senior year. One of his big goals was to have Marlow be state champions that year."

Joe's dedication and lack of self-importance was evident in many ways. Putting his team first was of primary importance to Joe. As proof of this belief, Coach Boxley relates how Joe exerted himself when many athletes of his stature would settle to do less.

"He set the national record at Western Heights on a Friday and the next day at a meet at Konawa he ran the 4x100 relay, ran the preliminaries in the open 400 and qualified, then ran the finals in the open 400 and then ran the 4 x 400 relay. He did all that the day after he set the national record. To me, that shows you just how important it was to him to be a good teammate."

Boxley also explained that Joe followed a process to constantly improve that was a little different from other vaulters.

"Joe didn't do a lot of drills like athletes do today. He was a "jump guy." That is how he got better. He simply pole vaulted. There's a lot of guys who look good in the drills, but when it comes to jumping, they don't get it done. Joe got it done," Boxley said.

Another aspect of Joe's team-first attitude was how he would assist his fellow Marlow vaulters during a meet.

"He was always looking to how he could help our other vaulters. Counting steps, catching their poles, offering advice when needed, Joe was always interested in how he could help others improve and perform for the sake of the team," Coach Boxley divulged.

As previously mentioned, Joe opted not to play football his senior year in order to concentrate on his pole vaulting.

"I'm sure it was hard on Joe not playing football and competing with his friends. He would have no doubt made a great wide receiver with his speed. But by far, the best thing he could have done was to focus on his pole vaulting. That took him so far for all the accomplishments he was able to achieve," Coach Boxley said.

Fall off-season training

Joe's off-season training could be considered unusual at the time, and today perhaps "unorthodox" would be a more apt description.

"I think I got better athletically my senior year than I did my junior year. I really didn't lift weights much back then. All we did was practice once a week in the fall. Coaches (from the various colleges recruiting Joe) would come in and watch me vault. They would show up and I'd jump 17 feet right in front of them. They thought that was pretty amazing."

Joe went on to describe his unusual training routine.

"The only workouts we did was to vault once a week. My dad and I would hunt almost every afternoon. At one point while we were hunting, I would just hop out of our truck and run a mile. And that was it," he explained.

Weightlifting was somewhat looked down upon at that time.

"Back then, we heard that weight lifting would make you real bulky and tight. So we didn't do that much lifting," Joe said.

January 16, 1981 » Oklahoma Track Coaches Winter Games » Oklahoma City, Oklahoma

Despite a very late night of hunting the previous night that resulted in getting just a few hours of sleep, Joe started off his senior season in fine style as he cleared 17-4 at the Oklahoma Track Coaches Winter Games at the Myriad in Oklahoma City to set a new national indoor record. This accomplishment added four inches to his existing national record which he set in this same meet just a year ago.

Joe and his brother Jimmy went coon-hunting the night before and didn't arrive back home until the wee hour of 2 a.m. With Joe having to catch the bus to the meet at 6 a.m., there was not a whole lot of time for sleep or to enjoy any type of rest for that matter.

Joe's mom was waiting up and needless to say, she was not real pleased with Joe as he walked in, especially with such an important meet scheduled for later that day.

"You know you have a meet today, don't you?" Lena Dial asked Joe.

Despite being dead tired, Joe wasn't about to admit it. "I'll be ok," was Joe's simple reply. And later that day, he proved it.

Joe utilized a unique strategy in claiming the victory. He waited until everyone else had been eliminated before entering the competition. Once his Marlow Outlaw teammate, Mike Gatlin, went out at 13 feet, 6 inches, a personal best for him and good enough for second place, Joe went immediately to work on the runway in his usual business-like manner.

Joe requested that the bar be raised to 16-6, which he cleared easily on his first attempt. He then moved the bar up to 17-1 and cleared that height easily, breaking the old record.

Joe then had the bar moved up to 17-4, which he missed on his first attempt. But on his second attempt, he cleared the 17-4 height for yet another record.

Then with the bar set at 17-7, Dial missed on his three attempts to close out his night.

But, nevertheless, another record was set.

"I felt I could have made it at 17-7, but the standards were too far back. I watched a television replay and I cleared the bar, but I hit it on the way down. I couldn't get away from it," Dial related after the meet.

"But I'm satisfied. I guess I did all right for my first meet of the year and, hey, we won our class and that was important, too. We only had nine guys there while some of those other schools had busloads of people. So, yeah, it was a big day for us all."

In addition to his record-breaking performance in the pole vault, Dial also showed his versatility as he captured third place in the long jump and sixth place in the high jump.

Outlaws teammate Steve Patterson also enjoyed an outstanding meet as he won the 60 yard low hurdles, placed second in the 60 yard high hurdles and added a fourth place finish in the long jump.

Led by the performances of Dial and Patterson, the Outlaws went on to claim the team championship for Class 2A as Marlow edged out runner-up Madill, 67 points to 60½.

February 6, 1981 » Millrose Games, Madison Square Garden » New York City

The Millrose Games are historically noted as the pinnacle of the sport of indoor track and field. Enjoying the status of being the world's longest running and most prestigious indoor track and field competition, this high-profile meet annually attracted the very best vaulters in the world. The crowds are knowledgeable, rabid and loud. Back then, the sport of track and field was huge and Madison Square Garden was totally sold out.

Getting to the meet was almost more difficult than competing at the meet itself.

"It took me awhile to figure out the logistics. I carried my poles up this circular, winding ramp (in Madison Square Garden) to get to the level I needed to get to and it must have been about six stories up. By the time I got

COMPETING AT MADISON SQUARE GARDEN IN NEW YORK CITY WHILE STILL IN HIGH SCHOOL.

to the top, with carrying my poles and my other equipment, my legs were shot," Joe recalled.

"The experience of being in Madison Square Garden competing for the first time was amazing. The huge crowd seemed to be right on top of you," Joe recalls.

Usually vaulting in a high school track meet involved competing in front of a few hundred spectators in small southern Oklahoma towns as Dial often did. But then suddenly performing on one of the biggest and most relevant stages in the sport and before some 17,000 fans would be nerve-racking for most people.

But not Joe.

"I actually liked to get nervous before a meet. I liked that feeling of nervous excitement. You just can't get that feeling anywhere else. It took me awhile to get comfortable. They call your name and you're up. You're the only one up there. There's a little bit of a "scare factor" to it, but it always seemed to make me perform better. I'd run a little faster. I'd always try a little harder."

The meet attracted the best vaulters in the world. Several elite American vaulters including Earl Bell, Mike Tully and Billy Olson were there. Several of the top European vaulters were there as well.

The opening height was 16-6.

"That was pretty high for a high school kid to start at. I remember making it at 16-6, but I missed at 17 feet," Joe said.

"But all in all, the Millrose Games were a great experience!" Joe claimed.

Leaving New York City the next morning to return to Oklahoma City brought even more challenges. Something as simple as getting transportation from downtown Manhattan to the airport becomes a major ordeal when you are carrying five or six fiberglass poles and all are at least 16 feet long.

It's not your usual airline carry-on.

Joel described the reluctance that he often faced on the road with many cabbies refusing to load his poles for the cab ride.

"Since I would have to use towels or a length of rope to secure both ends of the poles to the taxi, many taxi drivers simply did not want to mess with the whole situation and would refuse to drive me and my poles.

"Once I was able to catch a willing cab driver and convince him to haul me and my poles, then I would have to negotiate getting the poles to the airport, through the terminal and make it to the airline ticket counter to check my poles," Joe said. "It was not always easy."

Feb. 14, 1981 » Toronto Star-Maple Leaf Indoor Games » Toronto, Canada

The next week found Joe in Toronto, Canada, competing in the Maple Leaf Games. The meet promoter also flew Joe's father to the meet. Joe cleared 16-6 there.

"I just remember there was a whole lot of snow everywhere and it was very cold. One specific thing I remember about that meet was that it seemed the lights in the arena were not very bright," Joe recalled.

JOE VAULTING FOR THE MARLOW HIGH
SCHOOL OUTLAWS.

February 28, 1981 » Oklahoma Coaches Indoor Meet » Myriad » Oklahoma City, Oklahoma

Joe improved his national high school record for the indoor pole vault as he soared 17-4½ to win the event at the Oklahoma Coaches Indoor Meet. That mark increased his indoor record set earlier this year also at the Myriad by one-half inch.

Joe, with a somewhat increased level of confidence, continued in an attempt to increase his record height to 17-8½. He came very close on all three attempts, but ultimately failed to clear the height.

"I was really jumping good. I just barely missed that 17-8½. Up to that point, that was the best I had jumped," Joe opined.

"Joe was well over the bar," Marlow head coach Gary Boxley said.

"I think he just needs to make a small adjustment in where he plants his pole. Joe is jumping super right now. He always seems to do extra well when he vaults in Oklahoma City," Boxley explained.

Joe earned ten team points with his victory in the pole vault. He also earned eight more team points with his second place finish in the long jump as he leaped 21 feet five and a half inches, his personal best for indoor competition.

Joe's teammate and close friend, Steve Patterson, added 23 team points by winning the 60 yard high hurdles in a time of 7.48 seconds and then claimed second place in the 60 yard low hurdles in a time of 7.40 seconds. Patterson also ran a leg on Marlow's winning eight lap relay team, which was good for 20 team points with Patterson getting credit for five points.

Behind Joe's 18 points and Patterson's 23 points, Marlow won the Class 2A team title with 80 points with Madill taking second with 62 points in the field of 28 high school teams.

Finally — rubberized runways at Marlow

At Marlow High School, like many high schools of that era, the pole vault runway consisted simply of a strip of asphalt, approximately three-feet in width, laid out adjacent to the football field sidelines.

With the hundreds, if not thousands, of jumps that Joe put in at practice and during meets on his home track, that particular runway received plenty of use.

In fact, Joe had run down that runway so many times that a person could actually see his footprints in the asphalt. With each step down the runway, Joe's spikes would scratch the asphalt just a little. And since Joe was so precise in his steps in his approach, and with his steps being so consistent from jump to jump, over time, those scratches slowly dug into the asphalt and actually became indentations in the asphalt surface.

"I had jumped so much you could sit there and see each one of my footsteps where I had dug it out over time," Joe explained.

About the same time, Oklahoma State University was installing a new track with a new rubberized surface.

"Coach Tate (OSU head track coach at the time) said we could have a couple of strips of the old rubber track. So we took the strips of rubber from the old track, cut it, loaded it into a horse trailer and hauled it to Marlow. We then put the rubber strips on the pole vault runway at Marlow. During my senior year, I actually got to practice on a rubber runway," Joe explained.

"It was a lot of work, but it made a real nice runway," Coach Cole added.

March 21, 1981 » Marlow Track Meet » Marlow, Oklahoma

Joe vaulted 16-6 at this meet on his home track to claim another victory.

March 28, 1981 » Southern Oklahoma Invitational Meet » Duncan, Oklahoma

"I remember this meet like it happened yesterday because a lot things happened at this meet," Joe recalled.

Joe cleared 17 feet to win the pole vault competition at the meet. But in landing, he twisted his foot, resulting in a bone in his foot being dislocated. He could only limp the rest of the day. Scheduled to run in the 4x400 relay, he had to scratch himself from that event. The extent of the injury did not bode well for the remainder of the season.

But things took an unexpected sudden turn — for the better.

"I woke up the next morning, and amazingly, I was 100% fine. I couldn't believe it. Right before that, with that injury, I thought it might be the end of my season," he remarked.

Sets National High School Record 17-9½

April 3, 1981 » Western Heights Meet » Oklahoma City, Oklahoma

Limited only by the lack of height of the standards, Joe nevertheless smashed the state and national high school pole vault records as he soared 17-9½ at Western Heights.

"I might have made 18 feet today, but they couldn't set the standards that high," Joe said, but adding that he was not necessarily disappointed about it.

Besides being forced to set the regular standards on boxes in order to achieve the record height, meet officials had to fasten two crossbars together.

"The crossbar was so heavy in the middle (because of two crossbars being fastened together), it sagged a lot. It was 17-9½ in the middle of the crossbar where I cleared, but it was actually 18-3 on the sides," Joe said.

"I'm satisfied in Oklahoma. That's high enough. Sure, I still want to get 18 (feet) or more, but if I don't, if I should break a leg or something, I'd be happy ending (his high school career) with the 17-9½."

A strong south wind estimated at 20 mph came around late in the meet. "The weather couldn't have been better for me," said Joe. "The wind was straight behind me."

Joe didn't even start competing until teammate Mike Gatlin was only other competitor remaining in the field. Gatlin had cleared 14-8, his best of the year and the second best in state (after Joe's). Gatlin fell out of the competition at 15-0, the height that Joe joined the event.

Joe went on to clear 16-6 on his first attempt, 17-0 on his second try, 17-6¾ on his first attempt and 17-9½ on his second.

When he cleared 17-6¾, he set new records in several categories: the state record of 17-1, which he had set at the 1980 state meet; his personal best of 17-5¼, set in last year's Kansas Relays, and the *Track & Field News* recognized national high school of 17-6, set by Steve Stubblefield of Kansas City, Kansas

Wyandotte High School, which he set two months after graduating from high school).

Dial's mark of 17-5¼ is the national high school mark recognized by the National Federation of High Schools.

"I knew Joe would get the record," said his father at the meet. "I'm tickled to death. Joe has worked hard for what he's done. He's earned the record. This is what he has worked for all along."

Joe said two adjustments helped him increase his lift. He changed the placement of his grip on his pole and changed the position of his left arm after he planted his pole and left the ground.

"I don't want to peak right now," he said. "I want to peak this summer."

The 17-9½ jump gave Joe the satisfaction of regaining the over-all mythical "Oklahoma Championship" and lacked only a half-inch from the American record for an 18-year old.

Joe also high jumped that day and cleared 6 feet and barely missed at 6-2.

April 10, 1981 » OSU Meet » Stillwater, Oklahoma

Joe has specific memories of his success at this meet and how close he came to clearing 18 feet.

"I had a great meet at OSU. I made 16 feet, then 16-6, 17 feet, and then I got on a bigger pole and made 17-6. Finally I tried 18 feet.

"I made it all the way over at 18 feet, but then I barely hit the bar with my arm as I went over. It was really, really close at 18 feet," he recalled.

April 11, 1981 » OU Meet » Norman, Oklahoma

The second meet in as many days didn't seem to bother Joe. In fact, he seemed to thrive on the competition as most great athletes do. The better the competition, the better he seemed to get.

He progressively increased the heights — first making 16 feet, then 16-6, 17-1, and then making 17-7 easily, clearing it with plenty of room to spare.

"I tried 18 feet again, but it wasn't as close," Joe said. "But this was still a real fun meet."

April 21, 1981 » Stephens County Meet » Marlow, Oklahoma

This particular meet provided the opportunity for an interesting "grudge match."

Joe and two of his long-time Marlow teammates, Steve Patterson and Scott Hall, were all entered in the 100 yard dash.

During all their years as teammates, the three speedsters had never raced head-on in the 100 yard dash.

"All the trash-talking for all these years finally came down to the one race," Joe recalls.

Scott Hall enjoyed an ultra-fast start to establish a quick lead on Joe and Steve.

"Once we got about halfway into the race, we both blew past Scott and then Steve pulled away from me at the end. Steve ran like a 9.7 and I ran a 10 flat," Joe explains.

"It was just a lot of fun to compete against friends of mine."

Joe also long jumped at this meet and uncorked a leap of 22 feet, 8 inches and then made 17 feet in the vault.

April 25, 1981 » Regional Track Meet » Chickasha, Oklahoma

Joe cleared 13-6 on first attempt and then turned the event over to teammate Mike Gatlin, who Joe was confident would win.

"Since I already knew my one jump at 13-6 would clinch second place (and qualify him for the state track meet), we knew Mike and I would get first and second place in the event. It didn't matter much to me as to who got first or second, as long as Marlow got all those points," Joe said.

Joe then proceeded to long jump for another victory and ran legs on both the 4x100 relay and the 4x400 relay.

Congratulations from the Oklahoma Governor

Joe received a handwritten note from the Governor of Oklahoma, George Nigh, praising him for his accomplishments.

April 30, 1981

Joe,

I continue to be proud of your athletic accomplishments. More than that, I am proud of the fine personal reputation that you have.

18 feet – look out!

Congratulations!!

George Nigh

May 1-2, 1981 » Oklahoma Class 2A State Track Meet » Western Heights High School » Oklahoma City, Oklahoma

A major controversy arose during the Class 2A state meet in the pole vault competition regarding some tape Joe had applied to his fingers in an attempt to prevent blisters. One of his opponents filed an official protest resulting in a delay of over an hour in the competition.

"They tried to disqualify Joe because of the tape on his fingers. It was a very chaotic situation. The officials weren't even sure if Joe had the tape on his fingers on each of his jumps," Coach Boxley recalls.

By the time the protest was settled and the competition resumed, Joe had lost any desire and reason to continue. Joe was ready to concede the state title to his teammate, Mike Gatlin. It was only after being convinced by his coaches of the unique distinction of being a four-time state champion, did Joe continue in the competition and ultimately succeed in winning his fourth state title. Joe cleared 15 feet, 6 inches while Gatlin captured second place as he recorded a 15 feet, 1 inch vault

Joe also captured the state title in the long jump with a leap of 23-5½, which was a new meet record as well as a new state record. He also ran legs on Marlow's 4x100 meter relay team and 4x400 meter relay team as Marlow was runner-up for the team title in Class 2A at the state outdoor meet.

Kent Hall, Scott Hall, Joe and Steve Patterson made up both relay teams. Marlow's 4x100 meter relay team had the fastest qualifying time going into the meet and had an excellent shot at winning the state title. But unfortunately, Marlow's lead-off runner "flinched" at the starting gun that resulted in a false start and the team's disqualification.

Marlow's 4 x 400 relay team went on to finish second in a time of 3:20. For any high school foursome to record 3:20 in the 4x400 relay is an impressive feat, but for a smaller school like Marlow to record that time is remarkable. Joe recalls that he ran about a 50.6 split on his third leg followed by Steve Patterson, who ran a very impressive 48 second anchor leg.

Ultimate team player

There has always been a lot of discussion about being a "team player" and what exactly that phrase means and how does one qualify to be referred to as a "team player?"

There are many definitions of what constitutes being a "team player."

"Being unselfish," "putting the team first," and "doing whatever it takes to win" are all clichés that quickly come to mind.

The sport of track and field is especially difficult to illustrate this characteristic due to the sport's individualized nature of events. But Joe exhibited not only his "team first" attitude but also his compassion and caring for his teammates.

A key example was the 1981 state track meet.

"I remember that I made 13-6 and my teammate Mike Gatlin made 15-1 at the state meet, which put him in first place and me in second and we were the last two vaulters left. Even though I could go much higher and get first place, it really didn't matter to me. Our team was going to get the same number of points whether we finished first and second or second and first. It didn't really matter to me. So I decided to just accept second place with Mike winning the state title."

But then Joe's coaches approached him to explain the situation.

"Nobody's ever won the state meet in all four years, so if you would win this year, it is a big deal," they explained.

Joe had not realized how important it was to be the first person to win the state championship all four years, an achievement that could never be topped.

So, only after some prodding and with a little reluctance, Joe continued in the pole vault competition and ultimately won his fourth state championship in four years as he cleared 15-6 with Mike Gatlin taking second place.

Joe was also very cognizant of the importance of his teammates getting the recognition they deserved, even though most everyone's attention was focused on Dial and his exploits.

"I certainly don't mean to sound egotistical about this, but every year, I would try to let him (Mike Gatlin) win regionals. I would take just one jump at regionals in order to qualify for the state meet and then go off to long jump and run the relays where we could pick up more points. Mike was always the second best vaulter in the state. It was just that we came along at the same time. I wanted him to get some of the recognition that he deserved," Joe declared.

Tacos and transmissions

Many successful and famous athletes often end up in commercials pitching some of their favorite products or services. Joe was no exception.

Although his commercial pitches were not on a national level, they were nonetheless interesting, not to mention unique.

Joe had a first cousin who owned a chain of Taco Bells in Oklahoma. The cousin encouraged Joe to perform in one of the local commercials being produced.

"Just say whatever you want to say," the cousin urged Joe on the set during filming of the local commercial.

Joe's personal favorite Taco Bell menu item happened to be the bean burrito.

Told just to be natural, Joe's spontaneous line, after a number of outtakes, was, "Yea, try the bean burrito; it just gives you that little 'pffftttt.''

"It was so hilarious it would make you cry. He ran with that version on local tv in the Ardmore, Oklahoma, area and the commercial ran for a long time locally," Joe said.

Joe's other endeavor into the world of television advertising involved AAMCO, the automotive transmission repair company.

The basic premise of the commercial, which ran state-wide, was: "Congratulations to Joe Dial for setting all the records in the pole vault. Here at AAMCO — honk! honk! we support champions!!"

May 23, 1981 » Golden South Track Classic » Winter Park, Florida

The Golden South Track Classic certainly lived up to its name as Joe Dial and Greg Duplantis, two of America's top high school pole vaulters, faced-off in a duel for the ages at one of the most prestigious high school track meets in the country.

Besides their similar highly-respected status in the pole vaulting world, the two young men possessed several other similar traits.

One was physical size. Joe is 5 feet 8 and 132 pounds, while Duplantis is 5 feet 7 and 135 pounds.

But perhaps the most important common element of the two athletes was how they each were introduced to the sport for which they were striving for the pinnacle of success.

Each caught the pole vaulting bug via a close family member.

Duplantis' older brother, Robert, was a successful high school vaulter and got Greg started in the sport. Joe picked up his first pole at age five at the behest of his father, Dean Dial, who was one of the top vaulters in the state of Oklahoma and was also encouraged in the sport by older brother, Rex, also very successful as a former state champion.

Duplantis' vaulting credentials were almost as impressive as Joe's.

He had won the Louisiana prep title as a freshman, became the No. 1 high school vaulter in the nation as a sophomore with a 16-6 leap and as he entered the Classic, he owned a 17-7 vault to rank only behind Joe.

Joe's resume was well-known to track and field fans. A four-time high school state champion, a world record holder for 17 year olds, and with a 17-9½ vault to his credit, a match made in heaven was sure to transpire.

With that background set and with the high expectations in place, Dial and Duplantis did not disappoint.

Two local Florida vaulters, Mike Woodruff and John Linge, battled in the "preview" event as both cleared 15-0 but each missed at 15-6.

Then the two world-class jumpers, Dial and Duplantis, took to the runaway for the "'main event," raised the bar six inches and commenced their duel.

The *Orlando Sentinel Star* reported that the duo kept "a majority of the 3,000-plus fans 'oohing and aahing' with every vault."

The battle finally ended with both athletes clearing 17-4, but with Joe being declared the winner with fewer misses, having cleared both 17-0 and 17-4 on his first attempts.

Both Dial and Duplantis went on to attempt 17-10½, which would have been a new national high school record, and both gave great effort before the excited crowd of spectators. Joe came the closest to clearing the height as he actually cleared it only to jar the bar loose with his hand on the way down.

"If my dad had been here, I would have made it," Joe said after the meet. "He would have made sure I concentrated on technique.

"Sometimes I tend to get away from my technique. I get too involved in the crowd. When I finally got it together for last jump, I got a good one, but I couldn't get my hand out of the way," Joe explained.

June 13, 1981 » Abilene Christian University Meet » Abilene, Texas

Joe cleared 17-6, but Greg Duplantis, while using one of Joe's poles, cleared 17-10½. Dale Jenkins also cleared 17-10½ as both broke Joe's existing national record of 17-9½.

June 27, 1981 » OU Summer Track Meet » University of Oklahoma » Norman, Oklahoma

Joe regained the national high school record as he cleared 17-11 at an All-Comers summer track meet at the University of Oklahoma.

July 11, 1981 » Olympic Training Center » Colorado Springs, Colorado

Greg Duplantis and Joe were invited to train at the Olympic Training Center at Colorado Springs, Colorado. While at the training center, Greg and Joe were scheduled to vault against the the Soviet Union junior team. But with the politically charged atmosphere between the U.S. and the Soviet Union at that time, the Soviet junior team did not show up. With the opposition's failure to show, the Americans simply ended up competing in what basically could be referred to as an intrasquad meet, competing among themselves.

Joe and Greg both cleared 17-6 and then it was announced that the bar would be raised to 18 feet.

It was always Joe's dream and lifelong ambition to be the first high school vaulter to clear 18 feet. However, Duplantis was the first vaulter up with a shot at 18 feet.

"Greg decided his pole was too small, so I loaned him my pole again," Joe recalled.

Sure enough, as Duplantis was soaring over the bar, he hit the bar, but somehow it stayed up on the standards.

Joe's dream of becoming the first 18 foot high school vaulter was apparently wiped out, and to rub salt into the wound, Duplantis did it using Joe's vaulting pole!

But wait.

Since it appeared to be a record-breaking jump, the meet officials had to measure the height in order to ensure that it was indeed the record-breaking height.

"When they re-measured, it turned out the official height was announced at 17-11¾," Joe recalled.

"As soon as he made it, I knew it wasn't 18 feet," Joe said. "When they measured it, sure enough, it wasn't. I knew I could make it then. I knew I should be the first one over 18 feet."

With Duplantis's vault now officially just under the magical 18 feet barrier, Joe possessed renewed hope of becoming the first over 18 feet.

With Duplantis enjoying incredible success using Joe's poles, Joe decided on a unique course of action. He simply gave Greg his pole.

"After that meet, I just gave Greg one of my poles. I told him, here, take it. You've broken three of my national records. You can just have it," Joe told Greg.

The fact is, Greg and Joe had been tremendous friends all through high school as they often competed against each other at elite meets around the country and even overseas. They still remain good friends today.

August 11, 1981 » OSU All Comers' Meet » Oklahoma State University » Stillwater, Oklahoma

Joe finally attained an important and highly desired milestone — being the first high school athlete to clear 18 feet as he cleared 18 feet, ¼ inch. The height was also a new senior class record. Since Joe had not yet entered college, he was still considered a high school athlete. Therefore, he had the opportunity to set a new senior class record.

August 25, 1981 » OSU All Comers' Meet » Oklahoma State University » Stillwater, Oklahoma

In another OSU All Comer's meet, Joe upped his national high school record to 18-1¼. He attempted 18-4 and almost made it, but hit the bar with his hand as he went over.

Besides, the 18-1¼ for the senior class record, here are the class records also set by Joe:

Junior class best (1980) 17-5¼

Sophomore class best (1979) 16-2¼

In total, Joe had a total of 15 jumps that exceeded the existing high school record of 17-6½.

The Jim Thorpe Award

The Jim Thorpe Award is awarded annually to Oklahoma's most outstanding athlete. Joe was named a recipient of the Jim Thorpe Certificate of Excellence in 1981 signifying him as one of Oklahoma's most outstanding high school athletes.

Flying to meets: 16 foot poles are not carry-ons

As one might expect, transporting 16 foot vaulting poles represented some interesting challenges.

Even before the increased security concerns and precautions that 9/11 later brought, traveling to meets with the poles could present obstacles that most people never faced.

"Most of the time, my dad would drop me off at the airport in Oklahoma City and I would be able to get my poles on without much trouble. It usually went fairly smooth," Joe recalled.

"I was flying so often — pretty much every week — that after awhile they kind of expected me. I remember flying American Airlines a whole bunch. After awhile, the guy at the ticket counter at the Oklahoma City airport got to know me and if there was ever any opening, he would try to bump me up to first class."

Joe and fellow vaulting competitor and friend, Greg Duplantis, shared in telling of issues and incidents and even confrontations — not on the runway — but at airline ticket counters, while traveling with the pole vaulting poles.

"I haven't been at an airport yet where the ticket agent has failed to tell me I couldn't take the pole on the airplane," Duplantis offered with a sigh. "I used to get mad. Now I just tell them what page to check in their manual."

Joe has his own "strange but true" pole story.

He recounted the time he was to compete in Paris and a French airline official told him he would have "to saw the pole in half" in order to get it on the plane.

Perhaps the most unusual situation involving poles and an airliner was in 1984 when an airline loaded Joe's poles by opening a window in the pilots' cockpit, sliding the poles through and then permitting the poles to be simply stored on the floor in the aisle where they remained for the duration of the flight.

But once the poles are safely tucked away on the plane, the battle is only half over. In addition to their interesting experiences of transporting their poles, each competitor also has their unique way of securing their poles on the road.

Joe always tried to pack two lengths of rope with which to tether his poles to the front and rear bumpers of the car.

On the other hand, Duplantis prefers the "towel technique."

This method involved clamping the ends of two towels under the sides of the hood and trunk, which form loops into which the poles can be inserted for the ride.

Getting from the airport to the arena or stadium for the actual competition, often became a competition in itself.

"Once I landed, the airlines people would usually bring my poles out and then someone from the meet would pick me up or I would just take a taxi. I would have the address written down which I would show the driver and ask them to take me to that place," Joe explained.

"But often, once the taxi driver saw that I was carrying the long poles with me, they wanted no part of the ordeal of loading, transporting and unloading the poles and they would simply refuse service to me. I would then have to wait for another cab with the hope that the next cab driver would be willing to haul my poles," Joe claimed.

Traveling in Europe could be especially challenging, especially when traveling with five or six poles.

Getting from city to city for his various meets, Joe frequently traveled by several modes of transportation — bus, train, airplane — and each had its unique set of challenges.

"Sometimes in the larger cities, especially in Europe later in my career, I would take a subway to the arena where the meet was scheduled to be held," Joe explained.

With the rapid opening and closing of the subway doors, one can imagine the potential problems a person would encounter when he is trying to manhandle five or six long poles.

"I would often have to jockey for position to the door when my destination stop was coming up. Even then, I would have to bump people and knock into some with my poles. I received a lot of dirty looks and I'm sure, a lot of choice words under their breath," Joe explained with a grin.

"I would say, 'I'm getting off at the next stop' but of course, most people on the subway didn't speak English and didn't understand anyway.

"I got into several blow-ups with people just for that very reason."

HIGH SCHOOL TRACK 1982
$3.50

JOE DIAL
Men's Prep Athlete Of 1981

JOE WAS NAMED THE NATIONAL PREP ATHLETE OF THE YEAR IN 1981.

Named Prep Athlete of the Year

Joe and sprinter Denean Howard of Granada Hills, California were honored as they were named the 1981 High School Athletes of the Year by *Track & Field News*.

A press release outlined the accomplishments of each athlete:

Howard, a junior, succeeded her sister, Sherri, as the leading scholastic woman track and field athlete. Denean won The Athletics Congress Senior 400-meter race and the TAC Junior 200. She also ran a personal best of 51.65 seconds in the 400 meter dash as she finished second in the United States' dual meet against the Soviet Union.

Joe's resume including breaking the national scholastic pole vault record five times and becoming the first high schooler to clear 18 feet with leaps of 18¼ and 18-1¼.

Dueling record keepers

Confused about the maze that record keeping seems to be trapped in?

There are indoor/outdoor records. Age group records. Class records. High school records.

Don't feel bad. The record-keeping authorities operate under different criteria, often resulting in confusion, even among the athletes and coaches.

The National Federation of High School Associations ("NFHSA") and the highly respected publication *Track & Field News* have different opinions and criteria in regard to recognizing high school records.

Records set while an athlete is still enrolled in high school will be recognized by NFHSA as the official high school record.

However, *Track & Field News* takes a more liberal view in recognizing high school records made through summer competition until the athlete has actually started college.

Thus the difference results in some confusion involving Dial's numerous records.

Record mania

The old adage, "records are made to be broken," could have definitely been attributed to Joe Dial.

As proof, Joe broke the outdoor record five times during his senior year at Marlow High School. as he made 17-6¾, 17-9½, 17-11, 18¼ and 18-1¼.

But Joe was not without stiff competition.

Dale Jenkins from Abilene, Texas cleared 17-10½ on June 5 to break Dial's 17-9½. Greg Duplantis made 17-11¾ on July 24 to better Dial's vault of 17-11.

But Joe returned the favor and grabbed the record back on August 11 as he soared over 18-¼ while competing at an All-Comers meet at OSU.

Then for good measure, Joe came back two weeks later and he upped his record mark another inch to 18-1¼ during another OSU All-Comers meet.

"All I was worried about was getting over 18 feet," Joe explained. "I wanted to be the first one to do it. It was kind of a mental barrier for me. That's awful high. But I just felt I should be the first one."

"I was more consistent at the higher heights (than Jenkins or Duplantis). I had 15 vaults over 17-6 and Duplantis had only two or three," Joe added.

Joe was constantly looking for every advantage to improve and strengthen his hold on the record book.

"When I cleared 18-1¼ (on August 25, 1981 for the National High School record) I needed to bend the pole more. At the time, I didn't know that. I sent off to get a movie showing how the world-class vaulters did it. I was on the film, too, and I looked at the other jumpers. I could see the difference," Dial explained.

Joe was in great company on the video. Besides Joe, the other top vaulters on the video included Thierry Vigneron of France.

PART III

"AIRBORNE IN THE KANSAS (RELAYS) SKIES"

April 19, 1980

Never in the long and storied history of the Kansas Relays, one of the most respected and prestigious track meets in the country, has a high school athlete been named the meet's Outstanding Performer.

That is until Joe Dial came long at the 1980 meet, the 55th annual edition of the Kansas Relays held in Memorial Stadium on the University of Kansas campus in Lawrence, Kansas.

Dial entered the meet with no knowledge that the world age-group record for 17 year-olds was 17 feet, ½ inch until he had broken it three times.

He soared over the bar at 17-1¼ and then 17-3, which qualified him for that year's Olympic Track and Field Trials.

Then he hit the "big one."

Joe set a world age group record for 17-year-olds as he cleared 17 feet, 5¼ inch on his third — and final — attempt. It was also a national high school high school record as well. To add icing on the cake, it was also the first time that two high school vaulters cleared 17 feet in a meet.

"I don't even remember the first two (attempts)," Joe said at the time. "I don't remember running down the runway or anything. The only thing I remember is that one vault. It was like slow motion for me. When I planted, I felt a little under and then stiffened my arm into it. When I stiffened, it gave me the penetration to make it. The pole bent into it," Joe explained.

"Everything before that is a blank, but the last one felt really good. I had an easy wind blowing at my back and that gave me confidence."

Once the realization sank in of his accomplishment, Joe was somewhat in a state of disbelief.

"I jumped off the mat and ran back down the runway. All the cameras started shooting and everybody wanted to talk to me. The crowd went wild. It (the crowd) was roaring. That was the biggest outdoor meet I've ever been to."

With the adrenaline level running at an all-time high, Joe asked that the bar be set even higher — at 17-8¼ — in an attempt to even better the record. Unfortunately, he failed to clear the height on three attempts.

Joe later said he decided to enter the Kansas Relays when he learned that Steve Stubblefield, from Kansas City, Kansas, had jumped 17-0½ last week at a meet in Wichita.

"I thought I'd better get up there and beat that," said Dial. "I tried not to let him bother me, but when he cleared 16-0 by a mile-and-a- half, it scared me."

Near perfect jumping conditions — a gentle tailwind from an open end of the stadium and 74-degree temperature — factored greatly in his performance, Dial said. He also cited the springy Tartan surface of Kansas' Memorial Stadium runway as a major factor.

"I've never vaulted under conditions like these. I'm more used to asphalt runways and stuff."

And the weather?

"Heck, where I come from, I did 17-0 in 42 degree weather in my warm-ups. That's like a 17-5 jump here. I think I can do it again, given the right facilities."

In setting world age-group, national prep and Kansas Relays records, Dial cleared 15-6 on his first try, 16-0½ on his second, and then cleared 17-1 and 17-3 on his first attempts. In all, he had six misses in jumps.

One strange and unusual result from the meet: the record mark (recorded in the high school division) was actually 1¼ inches higher than the winning height in the open pole vault division.

Joe's record-breaking performance earned him the title of the Meet's Outstanding Performer over hundreds of athletes competing on the high school, junior college, college, university and open division levels.

"I feel pretty good," Joe said of his record breaking performance. "I really didn't expect to do it (break the record), but I got a really big pole."

Joe's mother, whose duty it was to film Joe while vaulting, admitted to having a minor case of the butterflies as she watched her son establish a national record.

"I got a little bit nervous. That's the reason the film kind of jumps around. I got more nervous than Joe did," she explained.

Joe's coach from Marlow High School, Darvis Cole, admitted the performance was not particular surprising.

"Of course, we were thrilled to death that it happened," Cole said. "But we felt like all along he had the potential to do it. Being there with top-notch vaulters helped him decide he could get over the high one," Cole added.

Cole also remembers Joe's record-breaking feat bringing some degree of notoriety to Marlow as Joe and the town received national attention.

"Joe almost needed his own press secretary, he was getting so much publicity. I remember I got a phone call one Saturday morning. It was Sports Illustrated. I was shocked when they called. They wanted to talk to me about Joe's national high school record."

The Kansas Relays weekend had been a long weekend for Joe.

It had started on the previous Thursday afternoon with Dial competing in a high school meet in his hometown of Marlow. He ran the 440 yard dash and long jumped. That was followed by the seven-hour drive to Lawrence, arriving at 5 a.m. The long drive exhausted Joe.

"I came in here dead tired," said Joe.

He spent the day Friday watching the meet action from the grandstands.

"I slept some in the car, but I got a good night's sleep (Friday) night," Joe said.

The rest apparently paid handsome dividends with the new record.

Afterwards, Joe reflected on his remarkable feat and outlined his near future plans. "I do think I can go higher," he said.

"My goal is to do it at the (U.S. Track Federation) championships in Wichita next month or the Olympic Trials in June. I didn't expect to do it (break the record) so soon because I've practiced at 17-5 but never made it. The most I ever did was 17-2," he said.

What makes his achievement even more remarkable is that it was accomplished under less than ideal conditions in the horseshoe-shaped Memorial Stadium.

"I got lucky and got a tailwind. But you can't tell what the wind will do there. It's always swirling. At Wichita (Cessna Stadium), the stadium is open on both ends and the wind blows right down the runway. That'll get you to flying. That's where Earl Bell (of Arkansas State) broke the world record (at 18-7¼)," Joe pointed out.

His performance also bettered some of his vaulting friends and colleagues, including Jeff Buckingham of the University of Kansas, who had claimed the Open Division title with a vault of 17-4.

The personable Dial had somewhat mixed feelings.

"I wasn't expecting to do that (defeat his colleagues). It kind of made me feel bad beating them. but I can't wait for them. Dan Ripley and Terry Porter were there and both are 18-footers. They said they were impressed with me."

Joe noted that he thinks he could soon join the 18-foot vault club with using another pole. He pointed out that a pole manufacturer was at the Kansas meet and expressed tentative plans to build poles more specifically catered to him.

"I have a 16-5, 160 (pound) pole and held at 15-6 on it. That's the highest grip I've ever used. They're going to send me a 16-5, 160 pole where I can hold it at 16 feet," he added.

Fan mail from opposing fans

Shortly after Joe's record-breaking performance at the Kansas Relays, he received a letter from a gentleman who lived in Lawrence, Kansas. His name was Odd Williams and he identified himself as a graduate of the University of Kansas.

In his letter, Mr. Williams spoke highly of the University of Kansas and called the University one of the finest universities in the country. He also stated the success of the track program at KU is well known throughout the country.

Mr. Williams also noted that KU track coach Bob Timmons is "one of the finest and most consistent men I have ever known" and is hopeful that Joe will give "serious consideration to attending the University of Kansas."

Williams closed his letter with saying that regardless of Dial's decision concerning his higher education, "we wish you continued success."

Mr. Williams also enclosed some press clippings from local newspapers of coverage of Dial's record-breaking performance at the Kansas Relays.

ODD WILLIAMS
BOX 530
LAWRENCE, KANSAS 66044

April 21, 1980

Mr. Joe Dial
Marlow High School
Marlow, OK 73055

Dear Joe:

Congratulations on setting a world's record in the pole
vault at the Kansas Relays this past week-end. I imagine
you have copies of these three sports pages but thought
maybe you could use some extra ones. The picture in the
Topeka Capital-Journal is especially good.

I live in Lawrence and am a graduate of the University of
Kansas and am naturally biased but do sincerely believe it
is one of the finest universities in the country. In addition, the success of the track program here at KU is known
throughout the country, and there are few schools which
can rival the number of championships won through the years.

I have known Coach Bob Timmons for 30 years, and he is one
of the finest and most consistent men I have ever known.
He is respected by his peers and is a very popular member of
this community. I think you could also say that people
here take track and field most seriously, and of course
people here are hopeful that you will give serious consideration to attending the University of Kansas.

It was a great thrill to see you clear 17-5¼ inches and
set a world record in the process. Regardless of the decision you make concerning your higher education, we wish
you continued success.

Again, congratulations!

Sincerely,

Odd Williams

Odd Williams

OW:ds
Enc

PART IV

HIGH FLYING COWBOY

Top recruit

With Joe's impressive resume of high school pole vaulting titles, national records and international experience, he was a prime target of almost every major university who sought him for the potential points he could produce in track and field meets in the ultimate hope of yielding a national championship.

Due to NCAA regulations, a prospective student-athlete is limited in the number of campus visits he could make. Joe waded through the hundreds of letters that he had received through the years from the numerous universities recruiting him. After serious and careful consideration, Joe narrowed his list of schools to visit down to the following: Oklahoma State, Oklahoma, Alabama, Tennessee, Florida and Texas-El Paso.

At several of them, and those shall remain nameless, there was some type of inducement offered in an attempt to entice Joe to commit to their school.

"It was almost like a story book. One school showed me a brand new Z-28 Trans-Am T-top. Black. Glass packs. It was a really sharp car," Joe recalled.

"They said, 'hop in here.' So I did."

Joe turned over the ignition to start the car and gleefully listened to the roar of the powerful engine.

"WOW! That's great," was Joe's response.

"They said to me: 'You sign with us, it's yours.'"

But that school lost in the race for Joe's services.

One of the more practical inducements that one school offered was a video camera, which the offering school emphasized could be utilized to help video tape Joe's vaults in order to assist him in improving his vaulting skills. Another school didn't beat around the bush and simply told Joe to bring them "his best offer" he had received and that they would beat it.

Since Joe's recruitment took place in the fall semester of his senior year at Marlow High School, he did receive the unique opportunity to take in many of the top collegiate football games in the country. Most schools Joe visited would schedule him to visit their particular campus on a weekend in which their football team played host to a key game. All the more to impress upon the young and impressionable Dial of just another reason to bring his attendance, along with his world-class vaulting skills, to their institution of higher learning.

And since the vast majority of schools on Joe's list were collegiate football powerhouses, Joe experienced a season of college football that few, if any, football fans had ever had the pleasure of witnessing in person.

As Joe reflects back on the experience of his visits, a sly grin comes over as he chuckles at the thought entering his head.

"I do remember that of all of those big games I was invited to while on my visit to their campus, with the exception of one game, the home team always lost. I must have been bad luck," Joe laughed.

The one exception was the University of Oklahoma. Joe recalls when he visited the Norman campus on his official visit, the Sooner football team was taking on their long-time rival, the Nebraska Cornhuskers. Joe distinctly recalls watching an OU running back pointing toward the north end zone just prior to a play. The next play, sure enough, OU went the 70-some yards to the north end zone to score, the same direction that the OU player had just motioned prior to the play.

After weighing all his options and considering all his offers, Joe selected Oklahoma State University. As an added bonus, his father, Dean, agreed to coach the OSU vaulters on a volunteer basis.

"Yeah, I picked OSU because I could stay close to home and my dad could help me," said Joe. "Besides, OSU has a good atmosphere and I like the guys on the team and the coach, Ralph Tate. I visited Tennessee, Alabama, Texas-El Paso, Florida and Oklahoma before the indoor season started. I made my mind up during the outdoor season. I really don't remember when."

Joe's mother remembers the decision being a very difficult one for Joe.

"Joe really liked Coach J.D. Martin at OU. He liked him extremely well. The coach would let Joe practice there indoors when it was cold. But Joe kept saying that he thought he was more fitted for Oklahoma State than he would be at OU. J.D. was always super nice to Joe. But Joe thought his background was better for OSU. We weren't rich people. Dean and I didn't tell him where to go. We told him to go where he wanted and where he would feel the best about school. That was our concern — where he would be happy," Mrs. Dial explained.

One of the Joe's primary concerns regarding competing in his home state was the apparent lack of adequate pole vaulting facilities. Joe commented at the time that the OSU Cowboys have responded to those concerns by purchasing a new vaulting pit and seemed to have adopted a new and fuller appreciation for the pole vault event than they previously held.

"I feel a lot of pressure on me to win the Big Eight championship," Joe said at the time. "I should win the Big Eight if something doesn't go wrong. As far as the nationals go, I don't know. I could be anywhere from first to sixth. Dave Volz of Indiana has gone 18-3¼ and he should be improved. I know I'm going to be improved.

"I didn't win vaulting against those 18-footers. I didn't feel too bad. Now that I'm in college, I'll have to start jumping. Nineteen feet depends on how strong and fast I am."

Compared to his senior year in high school, Joe had grown a little bigger and a little taller, now 5 foot 9 and 140 pounds. He had also added more speed, now down to 10 flat for 100 yards.

As previously mentioned, Joe wanted to stay relatively close to home and Oklahoma State located in Stillwater, Oklahoma, just 2½ hours away from Marlow, definitely fit that criteria.

"I wanted to be close to home. I get back every chance I get," Joe explained. "The people here in Marlow are happy that I'm doing good. They know what I've done, but I'm just another person. I don't let it go to my head or anything. I can't stand people who think they're big shots."

Joe recalls that the most impressive campus he visited was at the University of Tennessee with its massive football stadium and trademark orange and white checkerboard-painted end zones.

"Before the game, they even let me walk out onto the field while the players were warming up," Joe said.

During Joe's junior year at Marlow High School, he was named the *Track & Field News* Athlete of the Year, a very prestigious honor in the track and field world. So Joe was one of the top recruiting targets his senior year. That honor was one of the main reasons he received all the attention during the recruiting process.

"Everybody assumed I would go to OU. Once I decided to attend OSU, out of all the phone calls I ever had to make, the call to J.D. Martin was by far the toughest.

"Mom and Dad insisted that I call J.D. and tell him personally about my choice. He had been so nice to me and my family during the recruiting process and even before that time when I was vaulting in high school. J.D. was a super guy and later gave me my first job out of college as an assistant track coach," Joe said.

"What made my decision even more difficult was that I had visited OU since I was in the eighth grade for track meets, summer meets, and practice sessions. Another item we had in common was that J.D. was also an excellent pole vaulter back in his day. When I would see him at my high school meets, I would always go up and talk to him. He was a super nice guy," Joe explained.

Teammates for years

Steve Patterson and Joe were teammates at Marlow High School and later at Oklahoma State University. Besides being football and track teammates in high school and track teammates at OSU, there were also roommates during their college years.

STEVE PATTERSON (#11) AND JOE (#83) WERE ALSO FOOTBALL TEAMMATES AT MARLOW HIGH SCHOOL.

"We spent lots of time at each other's house. He would spend several days at my house, then we would spend several days at his house. We were very close," Joe recalls.

In high school, Patterson and Dial could almost form their own two-man track team and give most teams a run for their money. Dial would inevitably win the pole vault and most likely the long jump, while Patterson would dominate both the high and low hurdles as well as the sprint events. The two then often combined with two other teammates to compete, and often win, the sprint relays.

"Joe and Steve were the backbone of our track team," Coach Cole recalls.

Joe recalls how he and Patterson ended up at Oklahoma State University.

"Coach Tate of Oklahoma State was so smart. Nobody recruited Steve for track but Coach Tate apparently saw something in Steve's track potential that others obviously missed," Joe said.

Joe recalls his conversation with Coach Tate.

"I'll give you and Steve a full ride scholarship if you will both come to Oklahoma State," Joe recalls being Coach Tate's offer.

It didn't take Joe long to decide and to pose the question to his teammate.

"The next time I saw Steve, I put a simple question to him: 'Steve, do you want to go to college?" Patterson quickly replied in the affirmative. Patterson went on to an outstanding track and field career along with Joe at Oklahoma State where he ran sprints, hurdles and relays.

"We both fit in so well at OSU. Besides teammates, we were roommates in college. We're still great friends,'" Joe explained.

As a matter of fact, when Joe was inducted into the Oklahoma Sports Hall of Fame, he asked Patterson to be his presenter. (See Part XI.)

Patterson went on to be a highly successful high school coach in Oklahoma in both track and field as well as cross country — for both boys and girls.

He served as head coach of track and cross country at Edmond North, Lincoln Christian and Jenks. While leading each of those programs to championships, he enjoyed his greatest degree of success at Jenks High School.

He coached the Jenks Trojans to a host of state titles — five boys cross country titles (including four consecutive crowns (2012–2015); two girls cross country titles; three boys track championships and one girls track championship. All of these titles were captured while competing in Class 6A, the state's largest class. He also spent one year at the University of Tulsa serving as the strength and conditioning coach for the Golden Hurricane football team.

Dial's and Patterson's paths were never far apart in high school and college and their relationship continued in a number of ways.

Patterson coached Joe's middle son, Tommy, at Jenks High School during Tommy's four years of high school competition. Of course, like father-like son, Tommy competed in the pole vault, where he won two Class 6A state titles and nearly broke his father's high school record at the Kansas Relays.

The most recent major intersection of Joe's and Steve's careers occurred in the summer of 2016 as Joe hired Steve as an assistant coach on the coaching staff at Oral Roberts University. Steve served there one year before accepting the position of head track and field coach at Union High School in Tulsa.

STEVE PATTERSON AND JOE WERE STANDOUTS FOR THE MARLOW OUTLAWS TRACK TEAM.

More than just teammates — best friends

While Joe and Steve were school-mates and then teammates for a number of years, their relationship went much deeper. One could even say they were more than best friends. They even think a lot alike.

To wit, Patterson's comment on spending time with Joe as a youth almost mirrors exactly Joe's comment.

"I would say that I spent more time with Joe than I spent with my family. During the summers, I would spend a week at his house and then he spend a week at my house. We spent a lot of time together," Patterson recalled.

"We did a lot of hunting, a lot of fishing. a lot of frog-gigging. That's what we did and we did it almost every day during the summers."

When asked about what he remembered best about Joe, Patterson had a ready answer.

"His work ethic. No one could outwork Joe. It just wasn't possible. Joe and his dad would go out and vault eight to ten hours a day in the summer. Sometimes they would turn the headlights on their car so Joe could still jump after dusk. They weren't going to lose any opportunity to practice. It was almost that Joe willed himself to be good. He simply outworked everyone."

Patterson also noted that Joe and his father did more than just put in practice time on the pole vault runway. The Dials looked and worked for every possible advantage that Joe could muster that could potentially make him a better vaulter.

"The times that they weren't out actually practicing, they spent time watching film of other vaulters. They would look at what made other vaulters successful and constantly look for ways for Joe to improve," Patterson explained.

Joe's dedication to practice and his quest for constant improvement were almost legendary. Patterson recalls that Joe would often vault some 100 to 120 times a day in the summer. Patterson notes that is an unbelievable number considering the amount of effort and strength required and the degree of stress and tension placed on one's body — not to mention the impact and potential of injury brought on by one's body landing from some 16 to 18 feet heights.

What about the chances of suffering from burn-out resulting from so much practice and constant attention to pole vaulting that it almost became an obsession?

"Joe wanted to be great and Joe's dad wanted him to be great. They wanted to him (Joe) to succeed and were going to do whatever it took to make that happen. They left it all on the runway," Patterson articulated.

That particular passion and complete dedication to the sport that Joe exhibited in high school continued on as Joe competed in college.

"He still practiced in college more than anybody I've ever seen. There were probably some people who may have had as much or more athletic ability than Joe, but they didn't have the same passion, the same work ethic, the same desire to be great as Joe," explained Patterson.

"He structured his life to be great in the pole vault. His whole life was built around pole vaulting. That's what did it for him," Patterson explained.

Respect from one vaulter to another

Despite the disappointment and heartache of losing Joe to Oklahoma State University, OU Coach J.D. Martin held great respect for Joe and the Dial family at that time and still maintains a friendship to this day.

"It was his decision. I hated it (Joe going to OSU) for obviously selfish reasons because I wanted him for my team. But he had to do what he thought was best for him. I respected him for that and wished him well," Martin recalled.

Perhaps some of that respect resulted from a deep-seeded bond that existed between the two men resulting from a common interest and shared talent.

You see, Coach Martin was a world-class pole vaulter in his own right. Being a three-time All-American and the 1960 NCAA Outdoor Champion in the event provided him a unique insight and instant credence that not many other recruiters could offer.

In an somewhat ironic twist of fate, back in 1960 Martin vaulted 15 feet, 9¾ inches — higher than the existing world pole vault record. However, due to the lack of certification of that particular meet, that record-breaking effort unfortunately could not be officially recognized.

As noted previously, Coach Martin was always helpful to Joe.

"He and his dad used to come to OU and use our facility. We had an indoor facility called "Pneumonia Downs" located underneath the east side of Memorial Stadium. It was jokingly called "Pneumonia Downs" due to it being cold and dark with the occupants being somewhat susceptible to catching pneumonia. Joe and his dad would come up and when we (the OU track team) finished practice, we would leave and they would go in and practice," Martin explained.

Martin recognized early on that Joe possessed qualities and a work ethic that would translate into becoming a great athlete and a world-class pole vaulter.

"When he was in high school, Joe had certain qualities that no one else had. He was tenacious — almost ferocious. You have to have speed to be good pole vault and he was quick!"

"What amazed me was that he was fearless. In those days, those fiberglass poles would often break. And when a vaulter would break a pole during competition, typically that would be the end of the day for that vaulter because of the mental aspect. Mentally, they were destroyed for the rest of the day. They would have to build up their courage to vault again," Martin said.

It was similar to getting bucked off a horse, in which the most difficult course of action is to get right back on the horse, no matter how hesitant or intimidated the rider might be.

Snapping a pole vault pole and falling on an unpadded surface from 15 to 18 feet high is no doubt scary. But the remedy is much the same. The vaulter needs to get right back up and try it again. But that is easier said than done.

Except for Joe.

"Snapping a pole could happen to Joe, but he would get right back up and get on with his next attempt like nothing happened. Nothing seemed to bother him," Martin said.

"Joe could break a pole, but that wouldn't stop him. I was always amazed at how he could perform and his aggressiveness in being a competitor. He had great technique and form and speed. He was just a great athlete.

"I have known Joe since he was a kid, and he's always been a first-class guy as far as I was concerned. To me he is more than just an athlete. He is a great citizen," Martin concluded.

FRESHMAN YEAR, OKLAHOMA STATE; 1981–1982

Jumping with cows, pigs and other animals

Joe's indoor practice facility at Oklahoma State University was rather unique to say the least.

"When I signed with OSU, I mentioned to Coach Tate that we would need someplace to practice indoors," Joe recalled.

Coach Tate wholeheartedly agreed and after some thought and discussion, came up with a solution. Tate contacted several officials from the Animal Husbandry Department on campus and a mutual decision was made to install the pole vault practice facility in the Animal Husbandry Building.

"We built the runway in the building. It was really great, other than the smell that is. Cows, pigs and other farm animals were there. It was like a rodeo arena on the inside with a pole vault runway. If we were going to jump at 4 o'clock in the afternoon, we would come in and turn the heaters on about one o'clock, and it would be pretty nice by the time we came to practice.

"It was a great place at the time, but really not by today's standards. We made a wooden runway about 140 feet, the regular length," Joe remarked.

"It could smell a little bit now and then, and I would go through a lot of shoes. You've got to watch your step," Joe laughed at the time. "We would get on one of our vaulters if they happened to be having an off-day. 'You are pole vaulting so bad, we can't figure out if that's the cows or your pole vaulting that smells so bad.'"

Joe's high school coach, Gary Boxley, attests to the strong smell emanating from the facility.

"You could go in there for two hours and then walk out and you would smell just like cow shit. The smell would be imbedded in your clothes. It wasn't the best place in which to jump, but it got the job done," Coach Boxley added.

"I jumped in there from my freshman year (1981–82) until the year I broke the world record (1986). All those years and I never even noticed there was a light over the pit. The world record at the time was 19-2. I made 19-1 and then we put the bar on 19-8, six inches over the world record. I went in there and "caught one." I went over 19-8 and all of a sudden I heard an explosion! I had no clue what had happened, but all this glass landed around me in the pit," Joe said.

JOE'S FATHER, DEAN DIAL; JOE
AND JOE'S MOTHER, LENA DIAL.

"As I cleared the bar, I was so high that my feet went into this big light — a huge light bulb — right above the pit. That was the very last time I practiced in there," Joe declared.

Joe did admit at the time that it will be nice to get into the outdoor season. "If you jump in too nice a place, then when you go anywhere else, you're disappointed. Anyplace I go now — it's nice."

Early setback at college

Early in Joe's college career, he suffered what in retrospect could have easily been a career-ending injury during a practice session.

"Everything was going good. I was having a good practice. I tried to vault and went over the bar and landed right square on the mat. There was cement under the mat, but the mat was so bad and so thin, I went through and hit my back, breaking my back in two places," Joe explained.

The injury occurred just some six weeks after Joe arrived at OSU and left him unable to practice for two months.

"I couldn't do anything — no running, no lifting, no anything, all during that time" Joe lamented.

Once his back healed, Joe was anxious to get back into action. His first day back on the runway, he remembered that there were quite a few anxious people present to watch his return to action.

"I just remember getting back on the runway getting ready for my regular run just like I did in high school a thousand times, with my regular pole, just like I had always done. I brought the pole down and planted, and it threw me in the dirt."

Joe's pole "catapulted" him clear of the vaulting pit onto the dirt floor of the Animal Husbandry Building.

"I forced myself to get up off the dirt floor and go try it a second time," Joe said.

This time, the pole catapulted him even farther away from the pit, onto a metal bar that served as a fence as part of the rodeo arena that was in the building," Joe said.

It was obviously not an auspicious return to the sport.

Years later, Joe was talking with one of the coaches who was present that day watching Joe's attempted comeback.

Paul Parrot, who was coaching at an area college at the time, related to Joe his thoughts after witnessing Joe's early failed attempts in which he kept getting tossed away and missing the landing pit.

"I just had to leave after watching that. I asked myself, is this kid an absolute lunatic? He's going to kill himself. I have to leave. I can't watch this stuff, " Parrot later told Joe.

January 16, 1982 » Eastman Invitational Indoor Relays » East Tennessee State University » Johnson City, Tennessee

Fully recovered, Joe's first-ever collegiate meet at East Tennessee State was a success as he won with a vault of 16-6. Joe's vaulting friend, Greg Duplantis made only 15-9. Both athletes were severely disappointed.

"I was just awful," Joe openly admitted.

January 29, 1982 » Missouri Triangular Meet » University of Missouri » Columbia, Missouri

In a triangular meet involving the University of Kansas, Oklahoma State University and the host team, the University of Missouri, Joe recalls this as one of the most exciting meets from a strictly personal perspective.

Joe was facing off with KU's Jeff Buckingham, who was one of Joe's long-time fiercest competitors.

Joe explains the scenario: "Buckingham and I were battling it out. It came down to the last event as to which team would win the meet. The whole meet was already over with the exception of the pole vault and Jeff and I were the only vaulters still left. It so happened that the team scores were so tight, that whoever won the pole vault, that vaulter's team would win the meet," Joe said.

As the bar continued to rise, Buckingham and Joe kept clearing and advancing the height. Then with the bar set at 17 feet, 2 inches, Buckingham missed on all three of his attempts. Joe missed on his first two, but cleared the bar on his third, and final, attempt.

"As soon as I cleared it on my last try, all my teammates ran over and mobbed me in the pit. Since I had won the pole vault, OSU had won the meet. They all piled on top of me. It was one of the most fun times I had in all the time I was pole vaulting," Joe reflected.

February 6, 1982 » Oklahoma Track Classic » The Myriad » Oklahoma City, Oklahoma

Now fully recovered from his back injury he suffered in the fall, Joe proved he was back to full strength as he cleared 18-0 to win the event. The 18-0 is his best indoor effort to date and just an inch and a quarter shy of his high school record he set outdoors last year as a senior at Marlow High School.

"I finally got my run-up back to my regular high school distance. I was just so happy to make that," Joe said.

After clearing the 18-0 height, Joe had the bar set at 18-9¼ in an attempt for a world record indoors, a mark that Billy Olson had cleared earlier at the Mason-Dixon Games in Louisville, Kentucky.

"I just wanted to see what it looked like. I wanted to be able to say that I tried," said Joe. "I felt like tonight I could have gone 18-4."

Unfortunately, Joe did not come close in any of his three attempts at the world mark. Yet, new ground had been broken, and it was certainly no disappointment to miss getting a new world record at 18-9¼. To illustrate just how important Joe's success at this meet truly was, only two American vaulters cleared 18 feet in the previous 1981 indoor season.

February 13, 1982 » Millrose Games » Madison Square Garden, New York City

Joe finished fifth in the pole vault as he cleared 17-4½. Earl Bell won the event at 18-6½.

February 26-27, 1982 » Big Eight Conference Indoor Meet » Lincoln, Nebraska

At the University of Nebraska, Joe broke the Big Eight indoor pole vault record with an 18 feet,½ inch leap as he smashed Kansas' Jeff Buckingham's conference mark of 17-4. In addition, it was a personal best for Joe.

"I knew it would take an 18-foot vault to win the competition," Joe said. "I wasn't as worried about setting records today as I was about just winning the meet."

Joe cleared the record-breaking vault on his second attempt, but failed to clear the bar when it was raised to 18-3. "I believe I could have gone higher if I had brought a bigger pole," Joe explained. "The facilities were the best I've ever jumped on by far."

Joe's victory was even sweeter after a minor run-in with vaulter Doug Lytle of Kansas State University during the competition.

Joe had a habit of setting his can of spray stick-em on the runway in order to help mark his steps on his run-up. The can was off to the side of the runway, completely out of the way of all the competitors and not bothering anyone.

"I'm sitting there and all of a sudden Lytle walks over and kicks my can. What the heck was he doing?" Joe asked.

Retrieving the can and placing it back in its original spot, Joe was more determined than ever to not only defeat Lytle, but to win the Big Eight title, and he ultimately did both.

Joe's teammate, David Swezey, placed fourth in the vault with a 17-¼ leap and in the process qualified for the NCAA Indoor Championship. Three years earlier, Swezey from Mannford, Oklahoma, had walked on at OSU with a personal best of just 12-6.

As a team, OSU was edged out of second place by Iowa State, 80-79. The Kansas Jayhawks captured the conference crown with 94 points.

In an interesting, yet unusual, side note, Tyke Peacock of the University of Kansas established a Big Eight record in the high jump as he cleared 7-3¾ inches.

What was so unusual? Peacock had played and scored six points for the Jayhawks basketball team in their game against Iowa State in Lawrence earlier that afternoon. Peacock took a charter flight from Lawrence and didn't arrive at the arena in Lincoln until after the high jump competition had already started. With little time to prepare and hardly any time to warm up, Peacock managed to not only win the competition, but set the Big Eight record in the process.

March 6, 1982 » Frank Potts Invitational » Boulder, Colorado

Joe set an NCAA Freshman pole vault record by clearing 18-3, a personal best for him at an invitational indoor meet at the Frank Potts Invitational at the Balch Fieldhouse on the University of Colorado campus.

Joe remembers the field house to be dark and dingy and where the vaulters would start their run-up in the dark and then come in running into the light. The stands were very close to the back of the pit with the fans seemingly right on top of the pit.

"I figured out then that I really liked the altitude and that place really worked for me," Joe said. "Everything seemed to come so much easier."

After clearing 18-3 on his first attempt, Joe had the bar moved up to 18-6¾ and came close to clearing that height which would have been good enough for an American indoor record currently held by Earl Bell.

Joe did not miss often at the meet. In fact, he did not have a miss until he reached 18-6¾. Up to that point, he cleared 16-6, 17-0, 17-6, 18-1½ and 18-3 — all on his first attempts.

"I thought I might hit 18 (feet) today because I've been jumping pretty well lately," Joe said. "But I didn't think I could go this high indoors. I really didn't think I could do it."

The vault was Joe's best to date, either indoors or outdoors. He cleared 18-1¼ outdoors to set a new national high school record last summer. At last week's Big Eight indoor meet, he soared 18 -½ to win the conference title.

"I think I can hit 18-6 outdoors, he said. "In fact, I might have made it today with a bigger pole. But I wasn't planning on making that type of a jump."

With that jump, Joe became only the tenth American in history to clear 18 feet indoors and has performed that feat in three different meets.

March 12-13, 1982 » NCAA Indoor Championship Meet » Pontiac Silver Dome » Detroit, Michigan

Joe recalls that there were a number of great vaulters at this meet and the competition was fierce. Mark Strataman ended up winning the title with a vault of 17-9. Joe placed fourth with a vault of 17-5¾.

The Cowboys mile relay team placed third in a time of 3:11.63. Texas-El Paso won the team championship as OSU tied for 14th place overall in the team standings with 10 points.

March 26, 1982 » Letter from David Boren, United States Senator

The letter from Senator Boren congratulated Joe for being named to the National High School Track All-American team for the 1981 season.

DAVID BOREN
OKLAHOMA

WASHINGTON OFFICE:
440 RUSSELL BUILDING
WASHINGTON, D.C. 20510

STATE OFFICES:
621 NORTH ROBINSON, SUITE 350
OKLAHOMA CITY, OKLAHOMA 73102

ROBERT S. KERR BUILDING
440 SOUTH HOUSTON
TULSA, OKLAHOMA 74127

MUNICIPAL BUILDING, ROOM 115
400 NORTH MAIN
SAYRE, OKLAHOMA 74858

United States Senate

WASHINGTON, D.C. 20510

MEMBER:
COMMITTEE ON FINANCE
RANKING MEMBER:
SUBCOMMITTEE ON ESTATE AND
GIFT TAXATION
MEMBER:
SUBCOMMITTEE ON INTERNATIONAL
TRADE
SUBCOMMITTEE ON SOCIAL SECURITY
AND INCOME MAINTENANCE PROGRAMS
MEMBER:
COMMITTEE ON AGRICULTURE,
NUTRITION AND FORESTRY
RANKING MEMBER:
SUBCOMMITTEE ON AGRICULTURAL
RESEARCH AND GENERAL
LEGISLATION
MEMBER:
SUBCOMMITTEE ON AGRICULTURAL
CREDIT AND RURAL ELECTRIFICATION
SUBCOMMITTEE ON FOREIGN
AGRICULTURAL POLICY

March 26, 1982

Mr. Joe Dial
703 South 7th
Marlow, OK   73055

Dear Joe:

I have just learned that you have been named to the National High School Track All-America roster.

Congratulations! I am extremely proud of you as I know your family and your Marlow area fans are. For you to have been selected from more than 900,000 boys and girls competing in state track meets across the country during the 1981 season is a tremendous honor.

Under separate cover, I am sending you a calendar which was published by the United States Capitol Historical Society. You will note an important event is listed for each day in the year. Since this is the 250th anniversary of the birth of the father of our country, George Washington, this year's items are all about him.

I hope this calendar will serve as a reminder of your senior Senator's pride in your achievements and his best wishes for your continuing sucess in whatever you undertake.

Sincerely,

David L. Boren
United States Senator

DLB/wrc

March 27-28, 1982 » Texas Relays » University of Texas » Austin, Texas

Fighting 30 mile per hour cross winds, Joe uncharacteristically no-heighted in the regular collegiate competition held on Friday. The next day was the Open competition in which Coach Tate was able to get Joe entered. To combat the strong cross winds, the Open competition was held on the track.

Joe was able to clear 17-8 while Billy Olson of Abilene Christian University won the event with a jump of 18-2.

April 17, 1982 » Kansas Relays » University of Kansas » Lawrence, Kansas

Joe captured his first collegiate Kansas Relays pole vault title as he cleared 17-0 in the 57th running of the Kansas Relays. Joe outdueled his Big 8 rivals Doug Lytle of Kansas State and Jeff Buckingham of Kansas to capture the crown.

JOE COMPETING AT THE RALPH HIGGINS INVITATIONAL AT OKLAHOMA STATE UNIVERSITY AT STILLWATER, OKLAHOMA.

May 1, 1982 » Ralph Higgins Invitational » Stillwater, Oklahoma

Despite the 38 degree frigid conditions, rain and cold, the familiarity of vaulting on his home track apparently set well with Joe as he cleared a career-best 18-4½ to capture first place. That effort increased the previous NCAA freshman, all-time Big Eight and school record best of 18-3. It was also the third best vault in the world in the year so far, behind Billy Olson's 18-8¾ and Dan Ripley's 18-5.

Joe attempted 18-6¾ three times, but after a near miss on his first attempt, he didn't come as close on his subsequent attempts.

"I was surprised that I vaulted that high," Joe said. " I warmed up terrible."

OSU Head Coach Ralph Tate was pleased with his team's effort and performance."Dial and Butler (James, who won both the 100 and 200) keep proving themselves as world-class athletes. There is no telling how good they can be because they keep improving with every meet. In fact, our entire team keeps improving with every meet. They ran extremely well Saturday and it shows as they set 13 season best marks."

In an interesting side note, OSU sophomore Garth Brooks finished fourth in the javelin with a toss of 188-10¾. You may have heard that Garth later went on to a "successful" career in a "different" field.

Dr. W.D. McCollum, OSU benefactor and long-time fan, attended the meet. That night, there was a banquet for the track and field program. At the banquet, Dr. McCollum spoke to the group and announced that he was so impressed with Joe's success that he had decided to donate $100,000 to the OSU track and field program.

New technique

Prior to the Eastman Relays at the East Tennessee State University campus in Johnson City, Tennessee, Joe saw Dave Volz of Indiana University utilize a somewhat controversial new technique. Volz would grab the crossbar as he soared over it to prevent it from falling off the standards. Volz initiated the technique and Joe used it in a meet during the season.

"I saw Volz do it at a meet and I started trying it in practice," Joe said. 'Then I read an article written by Volz where he explained the technique and I have had a lot of success with it.

"What actually happens is that you push down on the crossbar and sort of pin it against the support and the upright. When you think about it, the technique makes a lot of sense," Joe explained.

Critics of the technique claims it is inconsistent and is not always successful. Joe disagreed.

"I've had a lot of success with it in practice, and I'm one for one in meets so I will stay with it," Joe said. "It seems like the worse you miss the jump the better chance you have of pinning the bar. That time I put it back up there. I must have missed the bar by five or six inches.

"If you just barely nick the bar it seems like it is a lot harder to pin it. When I did that in the meet I was laughing when I landed in the pit. It was unbelievable."

Even though the technique is actually legal, Dial and Volz have had their critics.

"After I did that first time, a lot of the other guys said it was a bogus jump," Joe explained. "That kind of talk doesn't bother me one bit. The Europeans have been doing it for years and it is just now catching on over here. I think you will be seeing a lot more of it this year and the years to come. The other jumpers have the same opportunity that I do to try it, so that doesn't really bother me at all," Joe revealed.

When Joe employed the new technique in a meet at Hanover, New Hampshire, he was the subject of criticism from Dan Ripley, who finished second to Joe.

"I already had the meet won by then, and it didn't really enter into the final outcome," Joe related. "It was just something that happened. It was not something that I really planned to happen. It just happened naturally."

May 14-15, 1982 » Big Eight Conference Outdoor Championships » University of Oklahoma » Norman, Oklahoma

Going into the meet, Dial expected his stiffest competition would be from Doug Lytle of Kansas State University who defeated Joe in the NCAA Indoor Championships in March and who had cleared 18 feet outdoors (18-0¼) a week before Joe did. However, Joe defeated Lytle at the Big Eight Indoor Championships earlier in February.

"He (Lytle) was really mad at me when I beat him at the Big Eight Meet," Joe said. "He really cussed me out. He's kind of cocky."

However, Joe's concerns turned out to be unfounded as he cleared 18-0½ on his final attempt to claim the Big Eight title at the conference meet held at Norman.

The leap established a new meet record. It was also a "double" for Dial as he had won the Big Eight Indoor pole vaulting crown back in February.

But the title didn't come without a battle with a stiff cross-wind.

"That's sure the highest I've ever vaulted in a cross-wind," said Joe. "I'm a terrible jumper in a cross wind."

The event came down to three contestants — Dial, Lytle and David Swezey of OSU — who had all cleared 17-7. At that point, Swezey had one miss but

Dial and Lytle were both perfect. If neither had cleared the next height (18-0½), the event would have ended in a tie.

"Making 18 feet on my last attempt was a big win for me," Joe claimed.

"I thought Lytle was going to beat me after I missed those first two times at 18-0½," Joe said. "I felt like I was going to hit the bar going up on that third attempt. I was really scared."

Swezey, a fifth-year senior from Mannford, Oklahoma, who had never vaulted higher than 15-9 before this season, had a great effort and almost cleared 18-0½.

Swezey was quick to attribute his rapid success to coaching. "The reason I've improved so much is because of Mr. Dial and Joe," he said.

"I remember being so happy after the meet for me and Swezey," Joe added.

June 3-5, 1982 » NCAA Outdoor Championship Meet » Brigham Young University » Provo, Utah

The extreme windy conditions in central Utah greatly hampered Joe at this meet.

"I had a good warm-up and felt great. Just then, a huge tailwind came in," Joe said.

The sudden change in wind pushed Joe totally out of synch with his steps, and he missed all three of his attempts.

"I ended up no-heighting. I was so upset. I made a butt out of myself. I threw my spikes up against the fence in a fit of frustration," Joe recalled.

"After the no-height, I told myself I would never show my failure in that way again. So I learned a good life lesson from that NCAA meet. I never did that again."

Joe completed his outstanding freshman year by clearing 18 feet at five different meets, indoor and outdoor together.

SOPHOMORE YEAR, OKLAHOMA STATE; 1982–1983

After an outstanding freshman season, Joe had high expectations — along with just about everyone else — in the track and field world.

As a testament to his increasing skills, during his sophomore year at OSU he cleared the 18 feet height a total of 23 times. He attributed his performance to his efforts in getting into top physical condition and improving his technique.

"I improved so much during my sophomore year. I worked out quite a bit with the sprinters at OSU. I was probably in the best shape of my life at that time," Joe claimed.

"I would run all the jumps from my freshman year over and over in my mind, playing them over and over. I watched my videos and noticed my hands were a little too far apart on the pole. Sometimes, I couldn't swing up all the way. Then it hit me like a brick in the head. I just brought my hands in a little closer.

"As soon as I moved my hands in, my swing got so long, that 18 foot jump got to be pretty easy after that," Joe explained.

Joe even went as far back to study video tapes of himself in action during his sophomore year in high school in order to determine the optimum placement of his hands.

"I found out that the best distance from the bottom of my top hand to the top of my bottom hand is 22 and a half inches," Joe explained. "Once I figured that out, I was able to go to the next level," Joe declared.

January 8, 1983 » Dartmouth Relays » Hanover, New Hampshire

For Joe's first indoor meet of the season, he traveled solo to New Hampshire. Joe's travel expenses for meets like this were often covered by a benefactor of the OSU track and field program through the athletic department.

Joe's keen eye for all details regarding the pole vault event caught an anomaly that other athletes may not have noticed. Joe noticed the vault box was only six inches deep rather than the standard eight inches.

"Even with just a two-inch difference, that could have a big impact on your vaulting," Joe explained.

Joe went on to capture the meet title with a vault of 18-2. After the meet, one of the meet officials informed Joe that his vault had established a state record for the state of New Hampshire, and it was the first time any vaulter had cleared 18 feet in the state. In fact, Joe was the first vaulter to clear 18 feet in the entire New England region that included the states of Maine, Vermont, New Hampshire, Connecticut and Massachusetts.

January 15, 1983 » Eastman Invitational Indoor Meet » East Tennessee State University » Johnson City, Tennessee

"Coach Tate always liked to go this meet because they (East Tennessee State University) had a large indoor track almost 300 meters in length," Joe recalled. "For runners, this was a great place to run. And it was a great place to pole vault as well."

Joe was absolutely correct on all counts. The Dave Walker Track at East Tennessee State is 280 meters in length. And, yes, it was a great place to pole vault, especially for Joe.

Joe proceeded to set a new meet record here as he vaulted 18-0, breaking the old record of 17-6.

There is a side story to this meet. Joe readily admitted his weakness at that time to playing a certain video game that was popular in that era, Donkey Kong.

"I just loved that game," he admitted.

As the OSU track team was preparing to leave the team hotel to visit some local site, Joe opted to stay back at the hotel after discovering a Donkey Kong video game in the lobby of the hotel.

"I could put a quarter in and end up playing for over an hour," Joe says with a sly smile. "The machine lists the all-time record and I ended up breaking the all-time scoring record that time," Joe said.

"What's funny is I don't even play video games now, but man, was I hooked on Donkey Kong back at that time."

January 29, 1983 » Sooner Indoor Relays » The Myriad » Oklahoma City, Oklahoma

In one of his favorite venues, Joe cleared 18-4¾, the highest indoor vault of his career at that time at the Sooner Indoor Relays before deciding just after midnight that he was too exhausted to attempt the next height of 18-6¾.

"I was just too tired. I started warming up at five o'clock. That's seven hours," Joe said. "I'm in shape, but nobody can do that."

Besides the fatigue factor, Joe had other demons he was fighting. He was battling the blaring music of a Mexican Mariachi band which was performing next door in a convention banquet hall at the Myriad. The music seemingly grew louder — and more distracting — as the night wore on.

"I was having to fight that, too," Joe said. "I was so tired my mind was starting to play tricks on me. I just couldn't concentrate anymore."

Some confusion reigned as well regarding the height of Joe's successful jump. The marker indicated the bar was set at 18-6¾, which would have established a new NCAA indoor best. But after Joe cleared the bar on his third attempt, it was re-measured and determined to actually be 18-4¾.

"That really depressed me," he said.

Joe had started the competition at 17-3, the highest at which he has ever opened any competition. He proceeded to clear 17-3, 17-8, 18-0, and 18-3½ with no misses. He then made 18-4¾ on his third try.

February 25-26, 1983 » Big Eight Conference Indoor Meet » Lincoln, Nebraska

Joe captured the Big Eight indoor title as he cleared 18 feet. Jeff Buckingham from the University of Kansas was enjoying a phenomenal year and had showed tremendous improvement during the year, but Joe was able to edge him out for the indoor crown.

March 11-12, 1983 » NCAA Indoor Championship Meet » Pontiac SilverDome » Pontiac, Michigan

In one the most competitive fields in the pole vault event ever at a national meet, Joe was among a bevy of the best vaulters in the country. Jeff Buckingham, Doug Lytle, Brad Pursley and Dave Volz were just a few of the better-known elite contenders. The competition was so tight and intense that Joe remarked, "The pole vault was so stacked. It took jumping 18 feet just to get eighth place."

A somewhat lesser-known vaulter, Felix Bohni from Switzerland and attending San Jose State University, captured the national title as he cleared 18 feet, 5½ inches. Joe's friend, Brad Pursley from Abilene Christian University finished second while Joe, Dave Kenworthy of the University of Southern California and Jeff Buckingham from the University of Kansas all cleared 18-3. Based on the number of misses, Kenworthy was awarded third place, Buckingham fourth and Joe fifth.

April 9, 1983 » OSU Invitational » Oklahoma State University » Stillwater, Oklahoma

Due to the rainy conditions and the wet runway, the pole vault competition was moved indoors to the OSU Animal Husbandry Building, where Joe had practiced many times in the past.

Perhaps it was that familiarity with the environment that enabled Joe to vault 18-5¼, his best jump of the year at that time.

May 21, 1983 » Big Eight Conference Outdoor Meet » Oklahoma State University » Stillwater, Oklahoma

Jeff Buckingham of the University of Kansas exacted a degree of revenge on Joe as he defeated Joe in a controversial finish for the Big Eight outdoor pole vault title. Joe had earlier defeated Buckingham in the Big Eight indoor meet and now Buckingham returned the favor with his win at the conference outdoor meet.

However, the result was not without a tinge of controversy.

Joe recalls the windy conditions in Stillwater on his home track the day of the pole vault finals.

"The wind was really, really, bad. We would have to wait a long time for it to calm down. I would start and then stop and then start up again on my run-up. Buckingham would do the same thing. We were just trying to wait in order to get a calm wind."

When it was Buckingham's turn to vault, he was standing on the runway, pole in hand, waiting for the wind to calm down.

Once a vaulter's name is called, they have a two-minute window in which to initiate their vault or else a miss is declared and charged to the vaulter.

Buckingham was standing on the pole vault runway as his two-minute window ran out. As the event judge was pulling the red flag out to signify expiration of time and the resulting charged miss, Buckingham took off running down the runway. And then he cleared the bar.

Despite an argument from Cowboy coach Tate that time had expired and therefore Buckingham should have been charged with a miss, Buckingham's successful jump was nevertheless allowed to stand. The official ruling was that Buckingham was "in the process of going" at the time the red flag was pulled.

That disputed jump actually won the event for Buckingham as Joe finished second.

Afterwards, Joe took the high road in the face of his controversial defeat.

"I didn't actually mind the ruling. Jeff was a great guy and a good friend. I wasn't going to fight the ruling. He and his whole family were nice people. I didn't want to be a sore loser," Joe graciously explained.

June 5-6, 1983 » NCAA Outdoor Championship Meet » Robertson Stadium » Houston, Texas

Felix Bohni of San Jose State University swept the NCAA pole vault titles for 1983 as he followed his indoor title by claiming the outdoor title at the NCAA outdoor championship meet at Robertson Stadium on the University of Houston campus. Joe captured second place as he cleared 18-3.

"It was the only time that I put my hand on the bar that it cost me. The bar was at 18-6. I went over all the way and barely touched it with my hand and knocked it off. If I had made that, I would have won it," Joe explained.

Joe's close second place finish and being edged out of the championship was to serve as a challenge in what was to come in the next two years at the NCAA championship meets, both indoor and outdoor.

European travels

In the summer of 1983, Joe traveled to Europe for a series of track meets with a group of track and field athletes that comprised the "Athletes in Action" team. Most of the athletes making the trip did so through the generosity of sponsors. Joe's sponsor was Dr. W.T McCollum from OSU who was a frequent OSU track and field benefactor.

The team started the ten-city tour with two meets in Hungary, and Joe won both by jumping 5.50 meters, or 18 feet, one-half inch. The next meet was in Sweden where he again won at the identical height of 5.50 meters.

While in Sweden, Joe stayed with a host family that would put athletes up during the competition and provide them a place to stay. His stay with that particular family made a couple of deep impressions on Joe in two areas that he fondly recalls today — food and sleeping.

"The people I stayed with fixed me this reindeer stew. Oh my gosh, was it good. It was kind of like my wife's bear stew. It had that flavor — just really had a nice punch to it. I really loved it," Joe said.

The other impression was in regard to the amount of sun a northern country like Sweden would receive in the summer.

Much like Alaska, aka "The Land of the Midnight Sun," Sweden likewise enjoyed extremely long days of sunshine in the summer months.

"The bedroom they had me use had these special blinds on the windows. You roll down these blinds and they would totally block out all the sunlight, making the room completely dark. Otherwise, you would have sunlight coming into the room, even late into the night, and have difficulty falling asleep," explained Joe.

Another meet was in Prague, Czeckosvolokia, where Joe remembers the city "as needing a good scrubbing. Everything was just dirty looking."

Despite the appearance of the city, Joe remembers the track facility in Prague as being an extremely good place to pole vault.

"The track was so old that it was hard and really fast. The pole vault runway was not perfectly level, and you would first start running uphill a little and then run downhill a little as you approached the pit. I made 18 feet there and probably could have gone higher," Joe recalls.

When Joe was preparing to depart to return home, his host family presented him a sheep rug, similar to a bear rug.

"It was solid white and it was beautiful," Joe fondly recalls.

But alas, upon entering the United States at New York City, customs officials would not allow Joe to bring the rug into the country and he was forced to leave it behind.

"They took it out of my bag and wouldn't even let me bring it in. Man, was it beautiful!" Joe said.

Despite some up and downs, the hassles of travel, and the challenges of eating strange food and living in new and unknown environments, Joe was pleased with what he had accomplished during the six week European trip. But as usual, Joe was driven to improve and was already thinking of what he needed to do in order to make that happen.

"It was definitely a good summer. I was really consistent in my jumping. I was already looking forward to next year. But the trip helped to open my eyes. I saw a lot of really great vaulters in Europe that were better than me. I realized that I really needed to get better if I wanted to compete on their level."

On these trips, the members of the track team would often visit churches in the area. Some of the churches that the group visited would have been considered "underground" churches, ones that the powers that be in that particular nation may not approve of or were aware of. The visiting American athletes would visit the local residents, sing songs and sometimes give testimony, which would be translated into the local language.

Joe often took Bibles with him to pass out to some of the people who attended the services. Several times when entering a foreign country he would carry the Bibles in his pole bag, just to lessen the possibility of the Bibles being confiscated.

"That's how we snuck the Bibles into some of the countries," Joe explained.

Often, these Bibles had far-reaching effects — beyond what most people could imagine. Joe related one such example.

"I had given a Bible to a Soviet pole vaulter, Igor Trandenkov, whom I had gotten to know. He later won silver medals in both the 1992 Olympics (Barcelona) and the 1996 Olympics (Atlanta) as well as placing third in the 1993 World Championships.

"He was very gracious and thanked me for the Bible. A number of years later, when I was in Europe in 1995, we were able to meet again and I remember what he said to me in his somewhat stilted English.

"Joe, you remember you give (sic) me Bible long time ago? I still have Bible and I read it all the time. I am Christian now."

Train ride in Hell

Back to the European trip during the summer of 1983.

Kory Tarpenning, a pole vaulter who would later go on to finish second at the 1984 NCAA championship meet behind Joe and who also went on to finish in fourth place at the 1992 Barcelona Olympics, was on the trip.

"We were in Budapest and I had won the meet. The local officials asked us if we would be willing to stay a few more days and compete in the next meet. If we would be willing to stay the few extra days, the officials said they would pay for our flights to the next stop where we could catch up with the rest of our team, so we agreed to stay and compete. Then after that next meet when we were to fly to the site of the upcoming meet, they backed out of their promise of flying us."

Joe and Kory called the Athletes in Action team administrator and asked for advice as to what to do next, "We're struck in Hungary and don't know how to get out. What should we do?" they quizzed the administrator.

The AIA administrator informed them that the next track meet was scheduled for Switzerland. His specific instructions were: "Get to Zurich, Switzerland, and then get a train to the hotel in the mountains, where we'll be staying."

It turns out it is a 18-hour long train ride across Europe from Hungary to

Switzerland. To get to the train station to start their trip, Joe and Kory loaded their poles on the bus which would take them to the train station.

Once settled on the bus, Joe suddenly realized that sitting directly under the poles which had been stashed on the overhead rack was probably not the safest or wisest place in which to sit.

"Kory, let's not sit here. If those poles fall, it's liable to kill us. Let's sit behind them, " Joe suggested.

Then noticing a large pot hole in the road off in the distance ahead of the bus, Joe suddenly had a premonition of something similar to an automobile accident.

"It was like a car wreck. You may see it coming, but there's nothing you can do about it. It's just going to happen," Joe thought to himself.

Sure enough, the bus driver hit the pot hole directly. The two sets of pole carriers, with each carrier holding about eight vaulting poles, came crashing down on an unsuspecting local citizen who had been sitting in the seats previously vacated by Joe and Kory.

"This guy was tall and long-necked and got hit squarely in the head with the poles which knocked him out cold. Suddenly, the natives on the bus became restless. We quickly had a bus full of upset people yelling at us in a language we didn't even understand. Finally, we asked one of the passengers who was somewhat conversant in English what they wanted, and he said they are demanding money for this guy's hospital bills," Joe related.

After a few minutes, the injured passenger regained consciousness, but the uproar from the other passengers continued throughout the trip to the train station.

After arriving at their destination, as Joe and Kory unloaded their poles to prepare to depart from the bus and make their way to the train station, they found themselves being followed by the mob of still-angry passengers demanding some form of restitution for their fellow injured passenger.

After being followed by the intimidating group for a short distance, Joe's patience finally grew thin.

"I dropped my poles and threw my bag down, turned around to the group and told them 'to come on, let's go right now!'" as Joe invited them to get physical.

Suddenly caught off-guard, the group's edginess level was turned down a few notches and they retreated somewhat.

About that time, a good Samaritan bystander came up to Joe and explained, "You don't owe that guy anything. The health care here is free. Whatever care he needs won't cost him a dime."

The once angry group slowly then began to disburse, permitting Joe and Kory to continue their trip without further interference.

As Joe and Kory purchased their train tickets, all they could afford were tickets to stand, similar to purchasing "Standing Room Only" tickets at a baseball game. The train was completely full, mostly with women and children. So for most of the 18 hour train ride, Joe and Kory were forced to stand with only occasional respites when they would grab a vacated seat for a few minutes when a passenger departed the train and before the next passenger claimed that particular seat.

"I remember standing up during the night, trying to fall asleep. There were wall-to-wall people most of the time. It was hot and stuffy. There was no air conditioning. It was truly the train ride from hell," Joe laughs.

Once they arrived at the Zurich train station, the two guys were to make a connection to the next train which would take them to their appointed hotel located in the mountains. After a near snafu where the pair almost boarded the wrong train, they finally arrived at their destination.

A driver from the hotel was on hand to accompany them from the train station to the hotel. As they made small talk, the driver soon realized that Joe and Kory are Americans. He asks each of them where are they from. Kory replies Oregon and Joe tells him Oklahoma.

"Where about in Oklahoma?" the hotel driver asks.

"Marlow," Joe tells him.

"Marlow? Are you kiddin' me? Do you remember the restaurant right outside town? My parents owned that," the driver claims.

Joe and the driver went on to share bits of information from their little slice of the world. The driver also disclosed that his sister knew Rex Dial, Joe's older brother.

Half way around the world and you run into another person from your small Oklahoma hometown. What a small world we live in.

JUNIOR YEAR, OKLAHOMA STATE; 1983–1984

Goal: to make the 1984 U.S. Olympic Team

With the 1984 Summer Olympic Games set for Los Angeles, it signaled a return to the United States for the first time in 52 years and Joe relished the idea of making the U.S. Olympic team. The last time the Summer Olympic Games were held on American soil was in 1932 when they were also held in Los Angeles.

"I can't tell you how badly I want to make the team," Joe said at the time. "It can do so much for a person. I'm young enough that there is still '88 and '92, but a person never knows what might happen in that time," he reasoned.

According to the January, 1984 edition of *Track & Field News*, Dial was ranked eighth among all U.S. vaulters in 1983. Jeff Buckingham of the University of Kansas was the top-ranked vaulter in the U.S. and ranked ninth best in the world. Pole vaulting seemed to be an event dominated by the Europeans. A teenager from the Soviet Union, Sergey Bubka, who won the World Championships at Helsinki, Finland, last year by clearing 18-8¼, was ranked number one in the world.

But Joe was confident in his ability and felt he was coming on as he cleared 18-8 in practice.

"I've been taking some fair shots at 19-0," he said. "I really think I can clear that this year."

Like many American vaulters, Joe seemed to compete better indoors, but he believed last summer's European tour, which provided him immeasurable experience with vaulting in less than ideal weather and in dealing with unfavorable wind conditions, had really benefited him.

"That gave me so much confidence," Joe said. "I am mentally tougher."

During his European tour last summer, Joe competed in a total of 13 meets and was very successful. He won eight of the meets and cleared 18 feet in nine meets. His best performance in clearing 18-4¼ actually came in a meet that he did not actually win.

Upon returning home after the tour, Joe enjoyed a brief respite from training to allow his sore back to fully heal. During the fall when Joe undertook a weight lifting program, he gained 11 pounds, going from 137 to 148 pounds. Preparing for the 1984 outdoor season, Joe revealed his weight has leveled off at 144 pounds.

"I really worked hard in the weight room. I worked on my upper body and core. Working out really helped my confidence."

With many years of top-flight vaulting experience behind, Joe realized the importance of pacing himself over the long season, especially in an Olympic year.

"I don't want to get burned out indoors," he said. "I want to do good in the indoor meets, but I want to be careful."

Joe considered maintaining a low profile during the outdoor season, with an emphasis on training and conditioning rather than competition.

January 6, 1984 » Sunkist Invitational Meet » Los Angeles, California

At this particular meet, Joe got his first impression of Sergey Bubka, the young Soviet pole vaulter who had taken the sport by storm and who would literally dominate the event for years.

Despite suffering some bad luck and misfortune at the Olympic Games, at which Bubka won only one medal (a gold medal at Seoul in 1988), he managed to win gold at six consecutive World Championships from 1983 to 1997 (1983, 1987, 1991, 1995 and 1997).

But perhaps the most impressive aspect of the Soviet vaulter was his accumulation of world records.

Bubka broke the world record for the men's pole vault some 35 times during a ten-year period of his career. He broke the outdoor world record 17 times and the world indoor record 18 times. Even more impressive was the fact that Bubka lost his outdoor world record only once in his impressive career. Thierry Vigneron of France broke Bubka's record on August 31, 1984 at the Golden Gala International track meet in Rome.

However, Vigneron's hold on the record was extremely short-lived as Bubka subsequently reclaimed the record just minutes later on his next run.

But at the Sunkist Meet, Joe jumped 18-4½ on his first jump as did Billy Olson. At 18-6½, Joe passed and went for 18-8. Bubka and Vokof both made it.

"I tried for 18-8 but missed it and Billy made it, so I had to settle for fourth place," Joe said.

When Joe finished competing, he went into the stands to sit and to watch the remainder of the competition. Fellow vaulter Jeff Buckingham was sitting next to Joe, and they both exchanged glances as they watched Bubka. Both vaulters were impressed and totally entranced by Bubka's obvious level of superiority.

"Bubka is using a 17 foot pole and gripping right at the end of it. Before this, everyone was gripping at 16 feet at the highest," Joe noted.

The bar was then raised to 18-10 but Bubka missed his first attempt.

Then it happened.

On his second attempt at 18-10, Bubka cleared the bar by at least a foot, resulting in a simultaneous joint epiphany for Joe and Jeff.

"Jeff and I immediately looked at each other incredulously as our jaws dropped and said, 'It's over.' We didn't mean so much this particular competition being over, but the actual sport of pole vaulting itself. The entire pole vault scene changed at that particular moment. This is not even the same event," Joe recalled thinking.

"Everything changed from that moment. It was so surreal. The pole vault event as we knew it was over. With Sergey Bubka, this is a whole new ball game," Joe commented at the time.

Bubka continued on to set a new indoor record that night as he soared over the bar at 19-1½. It was early in the young Soviet's career, and it was Bubka's third world record on his way to the aforementioned 35 world records.

Through their competition and common time spent on the runway, Bubka and Joe became good friends.

"I felt very comfortable going up to him and talking. When he first came to America, he had a different mindset of America. One of the funnier things about him was he assumed everyone in America was a millionaire," Joe recalled.

Bubka was universally acknowledged as the premier vaulter in the world. He was head and shoulders above everyone else. Bubka's dominance and influence in the sport would soon become apparent as most vaulters followed his example and raised their grips on the pole.

January 7, 1984 » Sooner Invitational Meet » The Myriad » Oklahoma City, Oklahoma

The next morning, a Saturday, Joe flew back to Oklahoma City for a meet that night at the Myriad in Oklahoma City. Joe made the return flight back from Los Angeles just fine, but unfortunately, his vaulting poles did not. However, always being prepared for the worst case scenario, Joe's dad had a second set of poles for Joe that he brought from home to the Myriad just in case.

Joe jumped 18-4½ for the second consecutive night.

"I was really locked in that night," Joe recalled.

January 14, 1984 » Albuquerque, New Mexico

Joe recalls this particular meet specifically as he decided to make a minor modification in his approach on the runway.

"I changed my run-up that day. I did a couple of walking steps, then took off on my run," Joe explained. "That's why I can recall this specific meet since I changed something in my jump."

Whatever Joe changed, it obviously must have worked as he went on to capture the meet title by soaring over 18 feet, 6 inches.

"It seemed like I always jumped good in Albuquerque," Joe noted.

January 21, 1984 » Sooner Indoor Relays » The Myriad » Oklahoma City, Oklahoma.

Joe set a record of 18-6 on his "home track" at the Myriad Convention Center during the 10th Annual Sooner Indoor Relays, breaking the previous record of 18-4¾.

The pole vault competition lasted so long into the night that arena workers were disassembling the wooden board track when Joe was still trying to finish his event.

"I just remember I really had to focus on my jumps with all the noise and distraction going on. I had to keep telling myself: stay focused, stay focused."

February 25, 1984 » Big Eight Indoor Championships » University of Nebraska » Lincoln, Nebraska

Joe won his second Big Eight Indoor title as he cleared 18 feet.

March 10, 1984 » NCAA Indoor Championship Meet » Carrier Dome » Syracuse University » Syracuse, New York

Joe captured his first of four NCAA titles as he cleared 18 feet in the cool environment of the Carrier Dome on the Syracuse University campus.

Joe actually preferred vaulting in the smaller arenas because vaulting in a large cavernous domed stadium, such as the Carrier Dome, especially in the winter, often presented some unique challenges; namely that it was freezing cold inside, much like it was outside in the elements in early March in Syracuse, New York.

"It was so cold in there that I had to wear a coat all the time. I would take it off just as I was about ready to get on the runway," Joe explained.

"When the heaters would kick on in that dome, there would be a breeze, a slight head wind, coming at us. It seemed strange to be indoors and have a head wind at us."

Jammin' on the road

GARTH BROOKS AND JOE WERE
TEAMMATES ON THE OSU TRACK
TEAM. GARTH THREW THE JAVELIN
FOR THE COWBOYS TRACK TEAM.

While at Oklahoma State University, Joe was a teammate of another athlete who would ultimately go on to bigger and better things.

When Joe and Steve Patterson roomed together, one of their next door neighbors was a javelin thrower for the Cowboys by the name of Garth Brooks.

"On lots of road trips to meets, we would take three vans: one for sprinters, one for the distance guys and one for the field event guys. Sometimes, I would ride with the field event guys just so I could listen to Garth and the guys play their music on the way to the track meet. We had another discus thrower named Dale Pierce who played the banjo and guitar. That was pretty cool," Patterson recalled.

"I remember several times on bus trips, Garth would ask us what we wanted to hear. I would just say someone like Merle Haggard. Not only would he sing Merle Haggard songs, he would even sing better. I remember thinking to myself, 'Man this guy is really good.' He was pretty impressive," Joe added.

Garth and Joe, both very competitive individuals, also found themselves face-to-face in some good-natured wrestling.

"I don't know what it is about college, but you get in those dorms and everybody wants to wrestle each other," laughed Joe.

Garth, the javelin thrower, turned singer

Joe clearly recalls Garth as a good javelin thrower in his college days.

"I saw him throw 218 feet his senior year in practice a few days before the Big Eight Championship Meet. I was out there vaulting when he threw it so we stopped to measure it.

"I got excited and told Garth, 'Oh my gosh, that's going to place big time at the Big Eight meet coming up,' " Joe said.

GARTH AND JOE REMAIN GOOD FRIENDS TODAY. LEFT TO RIGHT: GARTH BROOKS, LENA DIAL (JOE'S MOTHER); JOE DIAL, TRISHA YEARWOOD AND SHAWNA DIAL MEET BACKSTAGE PRIOR TO GARTH'S AND TRISHA'S CONCERT AT THE CHESAPEAKE ENERGY ARENA IN OKLAHOMA CITY ON JULY 15, 2017.

"Don't tell coach," Garth pleaded to Joe.

"Why?" asked Joe.

"Well, then coach will expect me to do it at the meet. I don't do real well when there's lots of pressure on me," was Garth's explanation as recalled by Joe.

Joe remembers that conversation for its irony.

"Garth is in the most pressure-filled situations ever at his concerts and he always comes through like a champ. It's just amazing what he would conceive as pressure at a track meet, I consider it fun. And what I conceive as pressure, like playing before an audience of several thousand people and singing, that would be intense pressure to me."

Joe recalls the day that Garth finished school and was moving on in order to prepare for his life's work.

Joe walked down the hall where he saw Garth packing his things in preparation for moving out.

"What's going on here?" Joe asked.

"Movin' out. I'm done here," responded Garth.

"Wow. What's your plans?" Joe asked.

"Well, I'm going to Nashville. My mom knows some people there and I'm going to try to get into singing," replied Garth.

"Hey, great. I'm all for you. Good luck out there," Joe said.

Within five short years, Garth found his niche and as they say, the rest is history.

May 14, 1984 » Big Eight Outdoor Championship Meet » University of Nebraska » Lincoln, Nebraska

Joe claimed his second Big Eight outdoor title as cleared 18 feet.

June 2, 1984 » NCAA Outdoor Championship Meet » University of Oregon » Hayward Field » Eugene, Oregon

Joe captured his first NCAA outdoor title while Oklahoma State teammate Eric Forney took third at the NCAA Outdoor Championships at venerable Hayward Field on the University of Oregon campus in Eugene, Oregon.

Joe cleared 18-2½ to bring home the gold and set a new NCAA meet record.

The two Cowboy vaulters helped the OSU Cowboys team score 46 points and capture ninth place in the men's team championship race. Host Oregon won the men's division with 113 points.

Both Dial and Forney easily qualified for the finals as the field was cut down from 25 to 14 with 17-2¼ being the cut-off for the finals.

Joe just had to make one vault in the preliminaries as he passed on the opening height of 16-10¼ and then needed just one attempt to clear 17-2¼.

"It was a perfect day for vaulting," said Joe. "I'm just hoping it's the same kind of day for the finals. They have a fast runway here, and the tailwind today was great," Joe told a reporter after the meet.

In the finals, Joe defeated the defending NCAA Felix Bohni of San Jose State University, as well as long-time rival Steve Stubblefield of Arkansas State and Dale Jenkins of Abilene Christian, the NCAA Division II champion.

With the win under his belt, Joe then set his sights on the Olympic Trials scheduled for Los Angeles later in June.

"I know I can jump well enough to qualify for the Olympics, but it is just a matter of jumping well on the right day," Joel explained.

"There are about ten vaulters in the United States that have a shot at qualifying for the Olympics, and it's just a matter of who jumps the best on the qualifying days," Joe added.

All-American

Joe's outstanding performances during the 1984 season were recognized as he was named to the 1984 All-American Track and Field Team by the All-American Board of the NCAA Division I Track and Field Coaches Association.

Narrowly misses making the 1984 U.S. Olympic team

June 17, 1984 » 1984 U.S. Olympic Trials » Los Angeles Memorial Coliseum » Los Angeles, California

The 1984 U.S. Olympic Trials were held in the Los Angeles Memorial Coliseum, the same venue that would host the 1984 Olympic Games just a month later.

After the first round in the pole vault competition, the finals were delayed by some 40 minutes as the run-up direction was reversed to take advantage of the tail wind. Five of the twelve finalists fell out of the competition by the time bar reached 18-4¾.

Earl Bell, Dave Kenworthy, Brad Pursley and Joe all cleared 18-4¾. Joe cleared 18-4¾ on his second attempt, while Earl Bell cleared it on his first try. Based on the number of misses, Bell took third place and the last spot on the U.S. Olympic team. Joe, by virtue of his fourth place finish, was designated as the first alternate.

Doug Lytle enjoyed one of the best vaulting days. Although he hadn't done much that year, he had the meet of his life that one day as he jumped 18-8¾.

Mike Tully won the Trials at 19-½, setting a new American record in the process. Lytle was second with his 18-8¾ while Bell took third place.

The Coliseum was one of the more interesting venues where Joe competed.

"I thought the whole place was neat. They had the 1932 Olympics there and the impressive pillars on the one end of the stadium were awesome. It was really a nice place," Joe observed.

At the Olympic Games, the Americans enjoyed an impressive showing in the pole vault as Tully captured the silver medal clearing 18-6½, and Bell captured the bronze medal as he and Thierry Vigernon of France each cleared 18-4½.

August 31, 1984 » Rome, Italy

Joe again traveled to Europe during the summer to compete and soon found himself going head-to-head against some of the best in the world, including Thierry Vigneron from France and Sergey Bubka from the Soviet Union.

At a major meet in Rome, Bubka and Vigneron went 1-2, as both men broke the world record. Joe placed an impressive third at 18-4½.

"I was real consistent at 18-4½ that year," Joe said.

The battle of Bubka and Vigneron had several interesting and unique twists.

Vigneron cleared 19-4½ to break Bubka's record that was set just a month and half earlier in London.

"I can remember Vigneron smoking a cigarette while he was waiting for his turn to vault," Joe recalled.

Then it was Bubka's turn on the runway. For some reason, Bubka didn't get started on his approach within the allotted time limit and was charged with a miss. With that being his third miss at that height, Bubka was then declared out of the competition.

"He was done, finished for the day," Joe explained.

Joe and Larry Jessee, who was Joe's friend and a fellow vaulter, then went to Bubka's aid in an effort to get his assessed miss forgiven so Bubka could remain in the competition.

"Larry and I approached the meet officials and tried to get Bubka reinstated. We wanted to intervene on his behalf. We told the officials, 'Hey all these people came here to watch this great pole vault competition and to watch Bubka.' We tried to make any kind of excuse in order to give Bubka another chance in stay in the competition. And then sure enough, they reversed course and did allow Bubka to remain in the competition," Joe explained.

Bubka, obviously motivated by Vigneron taking the world record away, cleared 19-5¾ just a few moments later to regain the world record.

Bubka later went on to set the world record another 13 times over the next ten years. He held the record of 20 feet, 1½ inch, set on July 31, 1994 and that would last for an amazing 20 years until Renaud Lavillenie of France broke it in 2014 by clearing 20-2½ on February 15, 2014.

This meet also had another strange twist.

"What's crazy about this meet is that everyone who was at the Olympics, held a month earlier in Los Angeles, was here, with the exception of Bubka, who was not because of the Soviet boycott of the '84 Olympics. And I got third at this meet," Joe explained.

Who knows what the results at the Olympics would have been if Joe had qualified for the Games? Through their competition, Bubka and Joe held mutual respect and admiration for each other. Their relationship evolved into a good friendship.

In later years, Joe would often assist Bubka in communicating with meet officials since Bubka's mastery of the English language was somewhat limited.

"I was probably Bubka's first American friend and we still stay in touch. He calls me 'my buddy Joe,'" Joe explained.

"I got along with all the Soviet vaulters. I seemed to have a good friendship with all of them. And I even became friends with the French vaulters," Joe declared.

1984 was also a milestone in Joe's vaulting career. It was the first year that he was ranked in the top ten pole vaulters in the world as he cracked the list at number 10.

SENIOR YEAR, OKLAHOMA STATE; 1984–1985

JOE VISITING THE EIFFEL TOWER WHILE COMPETING
IN A MEET IN PARIS, FRANCE IN 1985.

January 12, 1985 » World Indoor Games; Paris, France

During Joe's senior year at Oklahoma State, he was hitting his stride as the new year, and a new season of competition, was coming on.

"I had just made 18-10 in practice and was really training well. It seemed that I had gone to a whole new level. I was coming off a great '84 season and everything was rolling well," Joe explained.

Unexpectedly, Joe received an invitation to compete at the World Games to be held in Paris.

Never one to turn down an opportunity to compete, Joe gratefully accepted. As an added bonus, Joe was even able to take his father on the trip.

"This was the first time that I had ever vaulted into a pit where the front pads came way out in front. When I ran down the runway, it felt like I was running into a tunnel. The optics were just strange. I was just really off. I was never very comfortable. I had never jumped on a pit like that before. It really messed me up on my pole plant," Joe explained.

Even with the unfamiliar surroundings of the pit, Joe ultimately cleared 17-4, which was substantially below his normal height. "It was really bad," he added.

Soon, that style of pads became the norm in the sport. After much practice and more exposure to the new style of pads, Joe soon grew more comfortable and regained his confidence and resumed his elite level of vaulting.

January 26, 1985 » Kansas Invitational » Anschutz Pavilion » University of Kansas » Lawrence, Kansas

Joe cleared 18-2½ inside Anschutz Pavilion on the University of Kansas campus. Joe was pleased with his performance as he had always considered the Jayhawks' home indoor track a difficult place in which to vault.

February 9, 1985 » Arkansas Invitational » University of Arkansas » Fayetteville, Arkansas

Joe continued his string of outstanding performances as he broke the NCAA indoor record with a vault of 18-7⅝.

February 23, 1985 » Big Eight Conference Indoor Championship Meet » University of Nebraska » Lincoln, Nebraska

Joe captured his third Big Eight Conference indoor pole vault title as he cleared 18 feet.

March 2, 1985 » University of Colorado » Boulder, Colorado

In a final tune-up prior to the NCAA Indoor Championships, Joe again broke the NCAA indoor record again as he edged up the record by clearing 18-7¾.

March 9, 1985 » NCAA Indoor Championship Meet; Carrier Dome » Syracuse University » Syracuse, New York

Talk about déjà vu. Almost every aspect at this national championship meet was a repeat of the previous year's NCAA indoor championship meet. It was the same meet location (Carrier Dome at Syracuse University); same finish place for Joe (1st place); and the same uncomfortable elements in the Carrier Dome (cold air and a slight head wind from the vents).

However, the one important difference was Joe's winning height of 18-6 that proved to be an amazing half-foot better than his winning height last year.

"I then moved the bar up to 18-10 to try to get the collegiate record that Billy Olson had set when he was at Abilene Christian," Joe recalled.

But, unfortunately, Joe was unable to clear 18-10 and the collegiate record would have to wait for another day.

**April 19-20, 1985 » Kansas Relays; Memorial Stadium » University of Kansas »
Lawrence, Kansas**

Joe traveled to familiar territory to Lawrence, Kansas, and the Kansas
Relays where it seems he always performed well going all the way back to his
junior year in high school when he set a national high school record.

At this edition of the Kansas Relays, Joe claimed a couple of impressive
victories as he cleared 18-8 in the Open Division on Saturday to win that
crown and was named the meet's Outstanding Performer. That mark was a
new Kansas Relays record as well as a new personal record for Joe.

In the Collegiate division competition held the previous day on Friday, Joe
also won that event with a vault of 18-5.

May 3, 1985 » OU Invitational Meet » University of Oklahoma » Norman, Oklahoma

With his intense level of training and preparation, his recent record performances combined with his physical condition and mental determination,
Joe's confidence level was approaching an all-time high.

His hard work and dedication obviously paid off as Joe soared over the
crossbar at 18-9.

"I really smoked it. I had a really big jump. I knew then I was ready for the
next step," he said.

Joe sets new American Record

**May 12, 1985 » Big Eight Conference Outdoor Meet » Kansas State University »
Manhattan, Kansas**

After a dismal rainy and cold start to the Big Eight Conference outdoor
meet, the sun suddenly fought through the clouds to reappear much to Joe's
delight. Once the weather broke and the rain ceased, vaulting conditions
turned ideal.

"It was perfect conditions to vault — a nice ten-mile per hour tail wind
made it ideal to jump," Joe said.

Joe captured the Big Eight pole vault championship as he cleared 19-1½.
In the process, he also broke the American record held by Mike Tully of the
New York Athletic Club in 1984 by a half-inch.

Joe set the record on his first attempt at that height as he barely brushed
the bar. The jump was the fourth highest in pole vault history at the time.

In addition to being the fourth highest vault in history, that vault was significant for a number of other factors:

- It was a track facility record beating Kansas State's Doug Lytle's mark of 17-5.
- It was Big Eight Conference meet record beating the record of 18-5 held by Jeff Buckingham of the University of Kansas.
- It was a national collegiate record previously held by Buckingham of 18-10¾.
- It was a new American record bettering Tully's 19-1.
- And just for good measure, it closed the gap on the World Record of 19-5¾ set by Sergey Bubka of the Soviet Union.

JOE CELEBRATING SETTING A NEW AMERICAN RECORD AS HE CLEARED 19-1½ TO WIN THE BIG EIGHT OUTDOOR CONFERENCE CHAMPIONSHIP AT MANHATTAN, KANSAS ON MAY 12, 1985.

To add to his impressive performance, Joe did not miss an attempt during the competition. He first cleared 17-7, then 17-11; 18-2; 18-5½; 19-0; and 19-1½ — all without any misses.

Joe could have elected to go even higher, but he respectfully declined. The world record was within reach, but he waited for that achievement for another day for a unique reason.

"It's not very often you can end a pole vault competition feeling good. You usually leave after three misses. This way, I left on a great note," Joe reasoned at the time.

"Right now I'm so fired up it's unbelievable. Plus. I had already PRd (set personal records) twice and the odds of doing it again were pretty slim.

"Dad expected me to do it (clear 19-1½) more than I did. It didn't surprise him at all. Of course, one of the reasons for that is Dad and I had been talking about how to jump 20 feet."

Joe proceeded to address those who may have doubted him in the past.

"People say I can't do it, but they've been saying that forever. They said I couldn't go any higher when I jumped 12-7 in the eighth grade and again when I set the national high school record at 17-9½. What they don't know is that Dad and I know more about pole vault than anyone else."

As the old saying goes — it's not bragging if it's true.

JOE RAISED THE AMERICAN RECORD TO 19-2½ AT THE OU INVITATIONAL MEET IN NORMAN, OKLAHOMA ON MAY 19, 1985. AT THE TIME, IT WAS THE THIRD HIGHEST VAULT IN THE HISTORY OF TRACK AND FIELD.

May 19, 1985 » OU Invitational » University of Oklahoma » Norman, Oklahoma

Joe put his "doubters" to rest for good as he raised his American record height in the pole vault to 19 feet, 2½ inches on a sunny Sunday afternoon at an NCAA Qualifying Meet at the University of Oklahoma.

After Joe had set the American record (19-1½) the previous week at the Big Eight Conference Meet at Manhattan, some competitors in the sport still appeared to be somewhat apprehensive of Joe's American record status.

Not that anyone doubted the authenticity of Joe's ability or of his actually attaining the record, but it seems the accepted culture in track and field circles is something to the effect that when a competitor accomplishes a recording-breaking performance, then everyone wants the athlete to repeat the feat.

Joe said he hopes the other U.S. vaulters, Mike Tully and Billy Olson in particular, will now show him a little respect. It was Tully's record of 19-1 that Joe broke a week ago.

"They said I don't have the height, that I'm too short; that I'm too small; that I'm too weak, " said Joe. "Well, what do they have? The Tully's, the Olson's? If I'm not that good, what does that make them?"

With his new American record of 19-2½, at the time, it was the third best in the history of track and field. The only two better jumps were by world record holder Sergey Bubka of the Soviet Union at 19-5¾ and Thierry Vigneron of France who had vaulted 19-4¾.

Joe was believed to be the only vaulter in the world to have cleared 19 feet so far in the year 1985. Asked if he now considers himself to be the world's best vaulter, Joe replied, "I don't know, but I'm jumping over 19 feet. I guess right now at the moment I am, but next week I might not be."

After he cleared 19-2½ on his third attempt, he attempted 19-4⅜ but just came up short under the bar both times. Seeing he had lost his strength, he retired for the day.

"I was zapped, mentally and physically," he said.

No wonder he was tired. Joe made eight vault attempts on the day and made four of them. He entered the competition at 18-2 and at that point, only one other vaulter, Steve Stubblefield, was still alive in the competition.

Joe cleared 18-2, 18-5 and 18-10, all on his first attempts. Stubblefield passed at 18-2, cleared 18-5 on his third try, then bowed out of competition at 18-10.

Joe then opted to go up to 19-2, but encountered an unforeseen issue.

The meet officials needed 15 to 20 minutes to arrange the standards to accommodate that height and to get the crossbar to stay on the standards without blowing off.

Undeterred, Joe spent the idle time pacing up and down the runway, running sprints on the infield or sitting on the grass with his back to the vaulting pit.

Carrying the same pole he used to break the American record two weeks earlier, Joe's first attempt was not successful. On his second attempt, Joe raced down the runway, planted his pole, attained the necessary height, only to catch the crossbar with his upper body on his way down.

But there was no contact on his third try. Joe sailed clearly over the bar, although it did bounce around a little as he came down, perhaps from the southerly wind which provided a nice tailwind most of the afternoon.

But the bar settled back in its place and after meet officials measured and then remeasured, it was finally determined that Joe had cleared 19-2½ instead of 19-2.

Joe then attempted two jumps at 19-4⅜, but without success and then called it a day.

"From now on, I'm going for the world record, not the American record anymore," he said.

At age 22, Joe still qualified as a youngster in the pole vault, an event which traditionally has been dominated by athletes in their late twenties and even into their early thirties.

The future in the sport of pole vaulting for Joe looks to be bright and full of promise.

May 25, 1985 » SMU Invitational » Southern Methodist University » Dallas, Texas

In a final tune-up meet before the NCAA championships, Joe traveled the short distance to Dallas and the campus of Southern Methodist University. Two of Joe's chief rivals at the time, Mike Tully and Billy Olson, were also present.

"That's where Billy started talking some smack and trying to get me riled up. Probably because I had broken the record twice. I was apparently stepping on his territory (Texas) and I had jumped higher than he ever had," Joe explained.

"Are you going to jump today, Joe?" Billy whined. "Are you scared today, Joe?"

After several minutes of constant whining, Joe's patience soon drew thin.

"You better hush, Billy, or I'll hush you up," threatened Joe.

Despite Joe's warning, Billy's taunting continued relentlessly as Joe grew weary and decided that he could not tolerate any more.

Joe flew towards Billy on the runway, ready to take him down. Billy suddenly changed his tone and demeanor.

"What's the matter, Joe? Can't you take a little kidding?" Billy jokingly answered.

Getting back to the competition and with the NCAA championships coming up in just four days, Joe took it relatively easy, making 18-7 after just a short run.

"You are really jumping good," Tully remarked to Joe after Joe's last vault.

May 29-30, 1985 » NCAA Outdoor Championship Meet » University of Texas » Austin, Texas

Joe won his fourth straight NCAA pole vaulting title (two indoor and two outdoor) as he battled intense heat and cleared 18 feet, 6 inches at the NCAA Outdoor Track and Field Championships.

Joe attempted 19 feet three times. He failed to clear the height but he came close. On his first two attempts at 19 feet, each time he barely nudged the bar knocking it off the standards. On his third and final attempt, he didn't quite have the needed height and came down squarely on the bar.

"There's no way anybody can jump 19 feet every time out. You have to miss sometime," Joe rationalized.

Joe's toughest opponent at this meet was not another athlete. No, rather it was the unbelievable heat he had to endure at Memorial Stadium on the University of Texas campus.

The pole vault finals commenced at 1 p.m. — about the same time that the high heat was beginning to take effect. By 3 p.m. when the vaulting competition was only about half-way through completion, Joe noticed that a thermometer on the floor of the stadium registered 120 degrees. It possibly could have been even hotter since 120 degrees was the highest measurement possible on that particular thermometer.

"It was so hot on the turf down on the field," said Joe, "that when I ran down the runway, it burned the soles of my feet."

But that was not the worst of his worries. What bothered him most was how hot his pole vaulting pole would become each time he laid it down on the turf. In fact, his pole would get so hot that he would literally burn his hand each time he picked it up.

"The heat was about to melt my pole," Joe said, "So I stated putting ice packs on it to try to keep it cool."

The intense heat had another adverse effect on Joe as well — sweaty palms.

"Every time I would grab the pole, my hand would get so sweaty that I could barely hang onto the pole. I was afraid my hand was going to slip off when I went to plant the pole.

"I think I could have jumped 19 feet if it hadn't been so hot. I felt good running down the runway, but I didn't have any confidence when I went to plant the pole. I was afraid my hand would slip."

Joe was perfect on his first three heights. He made 18-0½, 18-3 and 18-6 on his first attempt at each height. He didn't record a miss until attempting 19-0.

"All three jumps at 19 feet were close," Joe said.

June 1985 » L. A. Invitational » Los Angeles Memorial Coliseum » Los Angeles, California

Joe cleared 18-8¼ at the venerable Los Angeles Memorial Coliseum to win the pole vault event at the last track meet held in the world-renown facility before it was renovated. The historic Coliseum had played host to both the 1932 and 1984 Olympic Games.

"I made 5.70 meters (18-8¼) and then had the bar raised to 19 feet," Joe said. "I came close, but wasn't able to clear it."

But Joe remembers the meet for something that all vaulters fear.

"Brad Pursley came up short on his vault and landed right back in the box. He hit his head and it knocked him out. They had to get a stretcher to take him off."

Joe recalled that the vaulters in the competition that day became pretty apprehensive after the accident. "I remember Mike Tully saying, 'Ok, that's it. I'm not jumping any more today.'"

July 13, 1985 » U.S. Track and Field Championships » Indiana University-Purdue University at Indianapolis Track and Soccer Stadium » Indianapolis, Indiana

In the finals, Joe recalled a stiff head wind which the last four competitors had to deal with. With Joe being the smallest and lightest competitor, any head wind would have the most significant impact on him.

"I cleared 18-5 and 18-9 on my first attempts. It turned into a big showdown between Mike Tully, Billy Olson and me," said Joe.

Joe went on to clear 18-9¼ to claim the title. "It was probably the most intensive meet I've been in. It was tough mentally. I was bound and determined not to lose that day. It was a big turning point for me," Joe said.

Besides the top-notch and challenging competition, there was another significant factor in Joe's desire to perform well at this meet.

"This was the first time that I was competing for Nike. I had just signed my contract with Nike between the NCAA meet and the U.S. championships. The team was Nike Athletics West. I was determined to show them (Nike) that they had made a good decision in selecting me for their team. The Nike Athletics West team was the elite team for Nike," Joe explained.

Size doesn't matter

While most elite pole vaulters at that time ranged in height from around 6 feet, 1 inch to 6 feet, 6 inches or so, with a strong, muscular build, Joe (at only 5 feet, 8½ inches and a slight 148 pounds) was usually the smallest vaulter in any meet in which he competed.

While his less than somewhat imposing stature may have been often overlooked or taken for granted by his opponents, Joe nevertheless refused to back down from anyone on the runway or track. In fact, he often used his size to his advantage in the event.

Soon, his competitors learned to respect the ultra competitive nature of the wiry Dial as the young Oklahoman began dominating the national and international pole vaulting scene.

FIVE CONTINENTS

From his humble beginnings in tiny Marlow, Oklahoma, the sport of pole vaulting enabled Joe to travel to all corners of the world to witness many sights and experience numerous events that most people would never have the opportunity to do.

Among his travels, he visited and competed on five separate continents. Of course, North America, including the United States as well as Canada, was the site of many of his competitions. Previous sections of the book detailed Joe's competitions in South America (Sao Paulo, Brazil) and Australia (Perth). He competed in numerous Asian meets, including several events in Japan. His most traveled continent after North America was Europe. He competed in Europe many times, commencing as far back as his junior year in high school and also during several summers while attending Oklahoma State and later. He traveled extensively all over the continent, visiting many countries in the process and experiencing the lifestyle of the native Europeans, with whom he would often stay while competing.

Below is a summary of several of Joe's international meets along with some of his other significant post-collegiate competitions as well as several important life milestones.

1983 » Athletes in Action Meet » Stockholm, Sweden.
Joe won the meet as he cleared 18-½.

1984 "The World Victory Tour"

In late summer and early fall 1984, Joe competed in a number of meets throughout Europe as part of what was referred to as "The World Victory Tour."

"It was one of the greatest times I had in track," Joe said in looking back at the experience. "Traveling all over Europe was an incredible experience."

The athletes participating on the tour represented some of the biggest names in the sport at the time. They included Steve Williams, former sprinter who equaled the world records in both the 100 meters and 200 meters and was also a member of a world record-setting 4x100 meter relay team; Larry Jessee, who held the American record in the pole vault and winner of some 100 international meets; Ray Flynn, an Irish miler with some 89 sub-four minute miles and two Olympic Games appearances to his credit; Brian Theriot, a 800 and 1500 meter runner from UCLA; Benn Fields, silver medalist in the high jump at the 1979 Pan-American Games; Darrin Clark, a sprinter from Australia who finished fourth in the 400 meters at both the 1984 and 1988 Olympic Games; and Thomas Jefferson, American sprinter who took the bronze in the 200 meters at the 1984 Olympics and Joe.

"With the exception of Thomas Jefferson and me, most of the guys were going out on their careers and Thomas and I were just coming in. So it was really good for us," Joe explained.

Since it was last major competition for many of the athletes, they referred to the tour as the "World Victory Tour — 1984."

"I went to so many track meets in Europe in 1984, it was great. It was the summer after my junior year at OSU," Joe explained.

How Joe got involved in the tour was almost by happenstance.

"I had seen in *Track & Field News* about a meet in Oslo, Norway. So I flew to Oslo, but it turned out they didn't have the pole vault event at the meet. But then I heard of a meet to be held in Sweden in a couple of days, so I decided to go there," Joe explained.

Arriving at the meet in Sweden, Joe faced an ultra impressive field including two previous Olympic champions from Poland — Wladyslaw Kozakiewicz (1980 Olympic gold medalist) and Tadeusz Slusarski (1976 Olympic gold medalist and the 1980 Olympic silver medalist).

Joe recalls the meet as having somewhat the appearance of a dream.

"There were cottonwood trees all over the place with millions of the white seed pods floating through the air so that it looked like it was snowing," he recalled.

One could almost say that Joe's dream continued as he ended up defeating both of the defending Olympic gold medalists as he cleared 18-4½.

"When I won that meet, Andy Norman, who was the biggest meet promoter in Europe, invited me to come on their tour. We were based in London. Larry Jessee and I had our own personal private room at the Auckland Hotel in London. It was an older hotel but at the very top of the hotel was our private room. We would fly out of London to a meet and then fly back. We would hit the road again and then fly back."

The Victory Tour covered many locales stretching all over the European continent. From Sweden in the north to Italy in the south; from London's Crystal Palace in the west to Budapest in the east, the tour consisted of about 15 meets.

Rome; Budapest; Crystal Palace twice; Stuttgart; Brussels; Rovereto, Italy; and Stockholm were just some of the meet locations. Joe remembers there were even pole vault events held in the street.

With the sport of track and field enjoying huge popularity in Europe, most of the meets played to capacity crowds of enthusiastic and knowledgeable track and field fans.

Joe has specific memories of just about every meet from the tour.

"I got second place jumping 17-10½ at Stockholm, but it was one of the coldest track meets I was ever in. It was 32 degrees with mist and rain and snow. I barely had any feeling because it was so cold."

At one meet in Italy, the perseverance and dedication of European track fans were on full display. With the vaulters encountering difficulty in getting their poles shipped in, the pole vault competitors were delayed in arriving. As a matter of fact, the rest of the meet had been completed with the exception of the pole vault. But approximately 5,000 loyal fans remained in the stadium for the sole purpose of watching the pole vault competition.

"They just waited for us. There were two French guys, and Larry Jessee, Eric Forney and I were all there. We got a police escort — complete with sirens — from about an hour out of town all the way into the stadium. They drove us onto the track, and we exited the vehicle on the track in front of everyone. It was so cool," Joe explained.

Travel methods between these meets often varied among trains, planes and automobiles. On one occasion, Joe's group was traveling by private automobile in Germany on the Autobahn.

"We were driving this small car with all of our poles on top of the car. Larry (Jessee) was driving and he had that little car maxed out on the Autobahn (portions of which carried no speed limits or on some portions only advisory speed limits). We were flying through the area. But there were Mazeratis and Ferraris passing us like we were standing still," Joe described in wonderment.

Getting close to their destination, Joe noticed the car's engine beginning to sputter. Then white smoke began to spit out from the car's exhaust, a sure sign of engine burn-out possibly caused by lack of oil in the engine.

Within view of the group's destination and with the engine seemingly disintegrating, the group managed to coast in to their appointed location just as the engine totally gave out with the occupants bailing out and the keys being handed over to a meet organizer.

Despite such hijinks, Joe enjoyed the camaraderie and friendliness the group offered, especially to a younger guy such as himself. Finding himself surrounded by veterans, not only in the sport of track and field, but who had years of international experience and extensive travel knowledge, was reassuring to Joe.

"So many of the guys on the tour were very talented in ways other than track and field. Ray Flynn who was often called "Father Flynn," could play the piano and often played in the lobbies of the hotels where the athletes stayed.

"It was just cool to travel with guys who were really veterans and who had competed internationally for a number of years," Joe added.

July 13, 1985 » USA vs. Germany Dual Track Meet

Joe's favorite memory of this meet did not take place on the pole vault runway or even at the stadium. It was actually at a rather unusual location — the local airport.

"I remember getting off the plane in Germany and all the U.S. athletes were walking from the airplane to the terminal dressed in our official USA gear. Along the entire way where we walked, German soldiers were lined up with each one holding machine guns. We walked between the rows of soldiers.

"With their complete German uniforms, including the high black boots and the machine guns, it reminded me of an old German movie," Joe stated.

For the record, Joe did win the pole vault competition as he cleared 17-4.

"The weather conditions were pretty nasty, cold and rainy. Not great conditions in which to vault," Joe recalled.

From Germany, Joe traveled on to Zurich, Switzerland, for another meet.

"I just remember I didn't do very good and I was really tired. It had been a long season and I had accomplished pretty much all my goals that I had set for myself — broke the collegiate record; became the first vaulter over 19 feet; set the American record; won the NCAA national title; won the United States Track & Field championship."

Joe decided to go home to rest and work out about a month and a half.

Being recharged after his period of rest, Joe returned to Europe for the completion of their outdoor season.

His first stop was back at Zurich, but Joe freely admits, "I didn't do too well there."

Next was Brussels, Belgium, where he won the meet with a jump of 18-8.

"I then wanted to go for the American record, but the meet officials would not let me raise the bar to the height I needed.

"No, we must stay with progressions," meet officials informed Joe.

"I won the meet and I'm the only one left. I should be able to put the bar at any height that I want," Joe insisted.

Even fellow vaulter Earl Bell argued on Joe's behalf and informed meet officials that Joe should be permitted to set the bar at any height he choose. But their arguments were to no avail.

So the bar was set at the next progressive height — 19 feet.

"I came pretty close, but didn't make it," Joe said disappointingly.

Often, the pole vaulting competition would last hours and would be the last event to finish at a meet. That was the case at Brussels.

"When we left the stadium, it was like we had rock star status. Thierry Vigneron (French vaulter who was a world record holder), Larry Jessee (Joe's friend and fellow vaulter) and I got into a limousine provided by meet officials to take us back to our hotel. We had to fight our way through the people and duck our heads to get through the crowd to get into the limo. They had to have security to keep the people back. You have to realize that track and field is really popular in Europe with many serious and ardent fans. It was just crazy!" Joe recalls.

February 1,1986 » Hearnes Center » University of Missouri » Columbia, Missouri.

Joe set the indoor World Record at 19-4¾. See the Prologue for a complete description.

PART VI

RECORD-BREAKING STREAK

Three American records set in less than two weeks

Joe competed in three meets in April 1986 and amazingly each time broke his American record.

Joe started his amazing record-breaking run as he was already in possession of the American record of 19-2¼ from the previous May (1985).

On April 12, 1986, Joe cleared 19-2¾ at the John Jacobs Invitational Meet at the University of Oklahoma. Eight days later, he cleared 19-3½ at El Paso, Texas. Then just five days after that, he upped his American record to 19-4¼ at Norman, Oklahoma. Such a feat of establishing three American records in the pole vault in just a 13-day period had never been accomplished previously or since.

These impressive performances by Joe were the subject of a full-page feature in the June 1986 issue of *Track & Field News*.

Following are additional details on each meet as Joe totally dominated the American pole vaulting scene and inflicted a direct assault on the American track and field record book.

April 12, 1986 » John Jacobs Invitational Meet » University of Oklahoma » Norman, Oklahoma

Looking for any way to improve, Joe was willing to make some drastic changes in his basic approach to pole vaulting.

Shortening his runway approach from 132 feet to 117 feet, he also lowered his grip on the pole, moving down to 16 feet, 3 inches from 16 feet, 6 inches.

With those changes, the last thing Joe thought he was capable of was setting any new records.

Joe's vault of 19-2¾ broke his American record of 19-2¼ set last May at the same John Jacobs Field on the University of Oklahoma campus. However, this record was not set in the same spot as the 1985 record. The Jacobs Field pole vault runway has two vaulting boxes — one at the south end and one at the north end.

Last year Joe had set the American record at the north end of the runway. The new record was set at the south end as meet officials attempted to position the vaulting area to take advantage of a slight head wind from the north.

However, by the time he entered the competition, the wind had shifted to the south, resulting in a slight head wind.

"I think the wind came from every direction today," Joe commented after the meet. "When I cleared 18-10, the wind was in my face all the way down the runway."

Once he cleared 18-10, Joe had the bar moved up to 19-2¾. He missed on his first attempt at the record height as he hit the bar on his way down.

But on his second attempt at the record, he had sufficient height and just barely brushed the bar on his way down. The bar shook for what seemed like an eternity before ultimately coming to a stop while still perched on the standards.

"The wind never stayed the same, so I wasn't sure which pole to use. On my 18-10 jump, it blew right into my face, but I went down there and just smoked it. I didn't see how I could miss the American record after that.

"I missed my first jump because my pole was a little soft. So I went up to a stiffer pole and I must have cleared by at least five inches. I brushed the bar coming down, but it had no trouble staying up."

Joe then moved the bar up to 19-6½, but missed on all three attempts.

On his third and final try, he appeared to have the height but grazed the bar again coming down. After rattling around, then appearing to remain on the standards, it finally fell.

"My third try at 19-6½ was the first time I had a tailwind. I cleared by at least three inches and I was on the mat in the pit before the bar fell. But I was just really happy to be jumping that high."

"It doesn't make any sense that I would jump high today," Joe said after the meet. "I shortened my approach, so I wasn't running as fast. And I didn't hold as high on the pole because I haven't been practicing vaulting much lately. All I've been doing is running and lifting weights. I haven't vaulted in a week."

On subsequent analysis, had Joe cleared 19-6½, it would have been the second highest vault of all time, ranking only behind the then world record of 19-8¼, held by Sergey Bubka of the Soviet Union.

"That's the best I've vaulted this year," said Joe. "I think I could have cleared 19-8 or 19-10 on that last jump (at 19-6½), but I had them move the standards back two inches. If I hadn't done that, I don't think I would have hit the bar on the way down."

April 20, 1986 » Safeway Olympian Invitational Meet » El Paso, Texas

Joe was able to raise his American record by less than an inch to 19-3½ at the Safeway Olympian Invitational Meet at El Paso, but he was able to do it seemingly with great ease.

"I was able to clear everything up through the American record on my first jump. On a day when I have the feel on my poles right away, I usually clear everything on my first try. Jumping just isn't hard at all.

"I made 19-3½ so easy. I just floated over. Nineteen (feet) really seems like 17 feet now. Nineteen (feet) is nothing as a mental barrier for me anymore.

"I tried 19-6½ again and got over on my last try but knocked it loose with my chest. But I am excited about being able to jump at home the next week," Joe excitedly said.

April 25, 1986 » Sooner Invitational, University of Oklahoma » Norman, Oklahoma

For the third time in less than two weeks, Joe set a new American record as he cleared 19-4¼ at the Sooner Invitational Meet at the University of Oklahoma.

"It was the most perfect day for pole vaulting with a strong south wind," Joe remarked. "It was a perfect tailwind. There was no doubt in my mind that I was going to break the record that day."

Prior to his record vault, on Joe's first two attempts at 19-¼, he missed badly — sailing under the bar. Then on his next vault, he seemed to get an additional source of energy and lift as he easily cleared the bar with about six inches to spare.

"That was the best comeback vault I have ever seen," said Larry Jessee, the former American record- holder in the pole vault who had been training in Norman with Joe for the past week.

"It was like an eight-hour work day out there. I warmed up at 11:30 and took my try at 19-7¼ at 7 o'clock. There were more than 20 vaulters to begin the competition and they started at 15 feet," Joe commented regarding the long day.

"I made 18-1 and 18-7 on my first tries, but when I went to 19-¼, the tailwind had died way down. I missed twice and then decided to use that bigger pole but slow my run a little. I thought somebody lowered the bar on me. I made it and I swear it felt like seventeen feet. I must have had eight inches clearance everywhere," Joe said.

The 19-4¼ vault put Joe on his way to breaking the American record for the third time so far this season.

"I just smoked that. I must have had six inches everywhere on that one. What happened was that when I tried to run faster in my approach, the timing of the pole's recoil and my run weren't together. But when I slowed down, everything worked together and away I went.," Joe said.

After clearing the 19-4¼ height, the third best vault ever outdoors, Joe had the bar moved up to 19-7, an inch and a half below the world record of 19-8½ held by Soviet vaulter Bubka.

"If I clear 19-7," he said making his first attempt, "It's over for the other boys. No other American can touch me."

Joe missed on his first attempt at 19-7, but then was making his approach for his second try when a small child standing along the runway suddenly screamed. With his concentration broken, Joe quickly pulled up and stopped.

"I kind of jammed something. I rolled my tendon on the outside of my left leg," Joe explained. After consulting with a trainer, Joe reluctantly decided that would be it for the day.

"There's no need to jump while I'm hurt. I don't want to hurt it any worse than it already is," Joe reasoned.

"Besides jumping higher again, I was happy to be able to hold my concentration over such a long competition and still do the job.

"I think I jumped better today than I've ever jumped in my life," said Joe, "I think those last two jumps were the best of my life. They were both so easy."

The next day, Joe's leg was still extremely sore and tender and he encountered difficulty just walking. He initially used crutches then gradually was able to walk, then jog. However, the injured tendons in his left leg took longer to heal than first thought. It would be almost two full months before Joe returned to the runway to compete at the United States Track and Field Championships at the University of Oregon in June.

But no one could deny that the previous two weeks were perhaps the greatest streak of outstanding pole vault performances, not only by an American but by any athlete ever, in the history of track and field.

Stoking the competitive fires

Joe's athletic successes at this time along with his string on American records seemed to have stoked his fire for vaulting and heightened his enthusiasm to even new levels for facing Sergey Bubka and continuing his desire to be the first vaulter to clear 20 feet.

Joe shared his thoughts at the time.

"Right now, I feel I'm jumping as well as Bubka ever has. I've seen all his record jumps and my 19-1/4 and 19-41/4 jumps compare equally to his.

"Since I shortened my approach run and slowed it down, I'm able to control the pole better. I weight 155 and I'm using poles designed for vaulters who weigh 200 pounds or more. Plus I want to raise my grip from 16-4 to 16-7.

"Now I'm going to train for a month before The Athletics Congress (TAC) meet. Last year, I peaked early because of the college season. But my plan for this year was to have a few meets early in the season, then train for TAC.

"I want to break the World Record at TAC and jump 20 feet. I don't see 20 (feet) as a barrier either. The first place you conquer anything is in your mind, and I've always been a big dreamer. You've got to dream things before you can actually do them, and I definitely can see myself jumping 20 feet.

"I know some people think I should jump in every big meet in the U.S. But, hey, I'm getting ready here at home to meet Bubka. I want to go to the Soviet Union for the Goodwill Games and put it on him.

"What I like most about all this is that it's still early in the year. I know I can jump 20 feet. I just can't wait. When it's all said and done, I'm going to be on top," Joe proclaimed.

But the leg injury Joe suffered at the Sooner Invitational in late April turned out to be more serious than initially anticipated and shelved his momentum that he built up.

June 18, 1986 » United States Track and Field Championships » University of Oregon » Hayward Field » Eugene, Oregon

Joe finally returned to competition after being out for almost two months. Despite the lingering effects from the injury and his limited practice time, Joe cleared 18-8 and claimed third place.

JOE, HIS MOTHER LENA DIAL AND WIFE SHAWNA STAND IN FRONT OF THE "HOME OF JOE DIAL" SIGN OUTSIDE MARLOW, OKLAHOMA. THE MARLOW CHAMBER OF COMMERCE ERECTED THREE SIMILAR SIGNS ON HIGHWAYS LEADING INTO MARLOW TO RECOGNIZE JOE SETTING A NEW AMERICAN RECORD IN THE POLE VAULT.

Marlow, Oklahoma: Proud Home of Joe Dial

The City of Marlow honored their hometown hero in 1986 by erecting three signs on the outskirts of town proclaiming Marlow as the hometown of Joe Dial. Two signs inform approaching motorists on Highway 81 — from Rush Springs to the north and from Duncan to the south. A third sign was installed on Highway 29 for motorists coming from Bray to the east of Marlow.

The signs read, "Joe Dial, American record holder and NCAA Champion pole vault champion at 19-2½."

Even though Joe later raised his all-time best vault, the signs indicated his highest effort at the time the signs were installed. The signs remain there yet today to welcome visitors to Marlow.

"It was really fun to get the signs put up in my honor. I remember right after they put the signs up, we noticed someone had shot a bullet through the sign on the north side of town," laughed Joe.

Taking mom and dad to Holland

In 1986, a meet promoter from Hengalo, Holland, contacted Joe to inquire about Joe coming to Holland and competing in a meet and wanted to see what Joe thought. At this point in his career, Joe often held the upper hand in negotiating his appearances at meets. Having possessed the world record earlier that year, Joe's market value to European meet promoters had never been higher. Joe's appearances at European track meets would substantially increase the already strong demand for tickets by the rabid European track and field fan base. The result was often a much larger volume of ticket sales and additional revenue for the meet promoters. So naturally they were anxious to get Joe to agree to terms.

"I'll come to your meet if you'll fly my mom and dad on a round-trip ticket, and fly me over along with payment for my appearance," was Joe's proposal.

The promoter readily agreed to Joe's offer. Joe's parents were able to see him compete for the first time in Europe. After the meet in Hengalo, Joe continued to compete in other meets while his parents enjoyed traveling across Europe, including Germany and Switzerland via train while they enjoyed taking in the sights. Joe's father was somewhat a history buff and enjoyed seeing the Rhine River and the adjoining countryside. After some seven days, the Dials returned to Oklahoma and their home in Marlow.

Meeting his future wife

Shawna Bailey lived in Oklahoma City and as a youngster enjoyed playing softball, basketball and running track. She attended Western Heights High School in Oklahoma City.

In the ninth grade, during a pep assembly for the football team, the wooden bleachers on which the students, including Shawna, were sitting and stomping their feet — had collapsed sending Shawna flying some 10-12 feet to the gym floor.

Faculty members and the school's coaches immediately came to her aid, but everything seemed fine with no sign of obvious injuries. However, just to be safe, Shawna's mother later took her to the hospital for x-rays, which proved negative at the time. But years later, Shawna was diagnosed with a ruptured disk that ultimately required surgery.

"I couldn't participate in athletics after that injury, but I wanted to stay involved, so I went into a support mode. I joined the pep squad and helped organize activities that support our different sport teams and later was elected president of the pep squad.

Shawna attended church at Crossroads Cathedral in Oklahoma City. At the time, Joe had already attained a level of fame around the state for his athletic endeavors and was often sought to speak to youth groups, He had been previously been invited to come to Crossroads Cathedral to speak there, but never seemed to have the time from his busy travel schedule, which by then was taking him to Europe and all points beyond competing with the world's best vaulters.

As chance would have it, Joe was recovering from an injury and was on a temporary hiatus from active vaulting, so he decided to take the time to make the visit.

"I remember when Pastor Shaffer introduced Joe to our church. As he stood up, Joe looked mortified to be recognized before the group, " Shawna laughed.

After church, the youth pastor introduced Shawna to Joe. Later Shawna and Joe decided to head to Braum's for a Coke, and they seemed to immediately hit it off.

The rest, as they say, is history.

Shawna points out that Joe always wanted people to like him not because of his fame as a world-class athlete, but he simply wanted people to get to know and respect him as a person.

"When I first met Joe, his picture was on the front sports page of *The Oklahoman* for something like 30 straight days. It was funny but I still didn't know who he was because I didn't read the sports pages. I think Joe kind of liked the fact that I didn't know who he was or what he did," Shawna laughed.

The church introduction was in August, 1986. Joe proposed to Shawna two months later in October, and they got married in November. The couple observed their 30th wedding anniversary in November, 2016.

Joe and Shawna would go on to have the three athletic sons previously mentioned. Shawna would later join Joe in the coaching ranks and assisting Joe in the tasks and responsibilities of coaching a collegiate Division I track and field team. More on this later.

October 18-20, 1986 » Sao Paulo, Brazil

Despite his concern about not being in prime vaulting condition, Joe nevertheless traveled to South America to compete in a meet in Sao Paulo and ended up winning the meet as he cleared 18-10.

"I was in great running shape at that time, but just not in as good of vaulting shape as I wanted to be," Joe recalls of his efforts." I went down there and made 18-10 and almost broke the American record."

Again, as the meet in Germany, Joe remembers the trip more for something that did not occur on the runway.

"I had bought Shawna some jewelry as a gift while down in Brazil, but unfortunately the jewelry was stolen from our moving truck several years later while we were moving."

Joe had competed at this Sao Paulo meet for several years and recalls the time that Olympic sprint and long jump champion Carl Lewis was also competing.

"Carl was running the 100 meters and it was unbearably cold. He ran a really terrible time, for him anyway, and it was one of the few times that he got beat. The crowd who had come to the meet primarily to watch Carl run, got really upset at his disappointing performance and showed their collective displeasure by starting to throw oranges, apples and any other kind of fruit they could get their hands on," Joe recalled.

JOE DIAL AND SHAWNA BAILEY WERE MARRIED NOVEMBER 28, 1986 IN OKLAHOMA CITY.

Marriage to Shawna Bailey

From *The Oklahoman*; November 29, 1986:

A double ring ceremony uniting in marriage Daniel Joe Dial of Norman and Shawna Kathleen Bailey of Oklahoma City was held Friday evening, November 28, 1986, at the Crossroads Cathedral in Oklahoma City. Pastor Gary Bohanon officiated the exchange of vows at 7 p.m.

The bride is the daughter of Linda Beck of Oklahoma City and Doyle Hatcher of Wayne, and the bridegroom is the son of former Marlow residents Dean and Lena Dial of Tryon.

Traditional wedding music was provided by Mrs. Lori Folsom. Arrangements of flowers decorated the church altar and sanctuary.

Given in marriage by her father, the bride wore a formal wedding gown of white bridal satin and lace, featuring a pearl and lace-covered bodice accented by a dropped shoulder neckline. The gown was styled with a fitted waistline with a low bustle in back and a chapel-length train.

The bride's veil of silk illusion was adorned with a pearl drop at the side of the face. She carried a cascade of white roses.

Serving the bride as maid of honor was Mona Stark of Oklahoma City. She wore a tea-length gown of royal blue lace and carried a bouquet of royal blue and white carnations.

Flower girl was Jessica Gibson of Tulsa and ringbearer was Joshua Dial of Marlow.

Kirby Abney of Norman served as best man for the bridegroom. Ushers were Mike Gatlin and Steve Patterson, both of Stillwater.

A reception honoring the newlyweds was held following the ceremony at the Crossroads Cathedral.

Guest book hostess was Cindy Funk of Blanchard.

Serving as reception assistants were Brenda Davis and Robin Walker, both of Moore. The bride's table was draped with a white cloth, accented with blue ribbon and baby's breath and silver appointments. The table also held a traditionally decorated three-tiered white wedding cake.

After returning from a wedding trip to Hawaii, the newlyweds will reside in Norman.

December 5, 1986 » Mosier Indoor Practice Facility » University of Oklahoma » Norman, Oklahoma.

Joe made state history as he made the first 19 foot vault in the state of Oklahoma at the Mosier Indoor Practice Facility at the University of Oklahoma.

January 17, 1987 » Sunkist Invitational Meet » Los Angeles, California

This particular meet was the first opportunity for Shawna and Joe to travel to one of his meets as newlyweds, having just gotten married less than two months earlier.

Married life obviously agreed with Joe as he won the meet by clearing 18-4½. Meet officials then raised the bar to 19 feet, but according to Joe, "I tried to use a bigger pole and gripped higher than I ever have and I barely missed. It just wasn't there."

January, 1987 » Perth, Australia

Later that month, Joe was invited to travel to Australia where he competed in two meets "down under" in the city of Perth, the capital and the largest city in the Australian state of Western Australia.

The fourth most populous city in Australia with over two million residents, the city has an interesting connection with the United States. Perth gained fame as the "City of Lights" when its residents lit their house lights and streetlights for American astronaut John Glenn as he passed overhead while orbiting the earth in Friendship 7 back in 1962. Perth's residents repeated their act of American friendship when astronaut Glenn orbited again over the city in the Space Shuttle in 1998.

Joe's efforts in Perth resulted in winning both meets, as he made 17-8 in one meet and then 18-4½ in the other meet.

"Both meets were held in horrendously bad conditions. They had the pole vault set up to go only one way. So if the wind was blowing against you, it was bad. In both meets, the wind was blowing directly into our faces. It was just terrible," Joe explained.

While in Perth, Joe became acquainted with Ben Johnson, the Canadian sprinter who had won two bronze medals (100 meters and 4x100 meter relay) in the 1984 Olympics at Los Angeles. Johnson would later go on to establish world records in the 100 meters at the 1987 World Championships and the 1988 Olympics at Seoul, South Korea. However, he was later disqualified for doping and was forced to forfeit the Olympic title as well as relinquish both world records.

During an off-day from competition while in Perth, Joe was in the weight room and found himself working out beside Johnson, who was also working out on his off-day.

"I thought I was pretty strong at the time. I was lifting 300 pounds, did it twice and then 315 and did it twice. Ben was doing the sets with me. He hops in there and lifts it in a set of ten repeats. I thought, 'this guy is just playing with me. This guy is ten times stronger than me,'" Joe said.

"Then Ben goes over and squats 500 pounds in sets of ten like it's nothing for him. I had never seen a human being that strong," Joe said.

Joe was so impressed with Johnson's incredible feats of strength that he later decided to follow the sprinter's weight-lifting regimen in an effort to increase his strength on the runway and thus hopefully enable him to vault even higher. Little did he realize at the time that such a drastic change in his training routine would adversely impact his success in vaulting.

Four years later, their paths would also cross again. Joe was present at Johnson's first track meet after the sprinter's suspension for steroid use. It was in 1991 at the Hamilton Indoor Games in Canada. Johnson's comeback drew the largest crowd ever to attend an indoor Canadian track and field meet, as more than 17,000 enthusiastic and rabid fans squeezed into the arena anxious to witness their hero's comeback and hopeful return to the glory days.

With camera flash bulbs popping throughout the arena, Johnson slowly emerged from the tunnel into the crowded arena, all the while being cascaded with cheers and shouts of encouragement. In the uproar, Johnson spotted a friendly face in Joe and the two athletes proceeded to make small talk as the crowd enthusiastically welcomed the Canadian sprinter back into competition.

Johnson came over and sat next to Joe and asked, "How are you doing?"

"It's a little crazy, isn't it?" Joe asked.

"Yea, but it's all good. It's good to be back," replied Johnson.

Johnson did not disappoint his ardent fans in his comeback effort as he finished second in the 50 meter dash in an impressive 5.77 seconds.

There is an interesting side note regarding Joe's visit to Australia.

Joe's wife, Shawna, did not make the trip with him to Australia but stayed back in Oklahoma with her mother. While it is summer in Australia in January, of course it is the middle of winter in the States.

While Joe was enjoying the mild climate in Perth, the area around Oklahoma City was receiving in excess of two feet of snow, a record snowfall at the time.

Joe had recently purchased a Chevrolet Camaro, the model that has the large back glass. The sudden decrease in temperature brought on by the snowfall caused the back glass in Joe's Camaro to shatter resulting in a huge mess.

The familiar smell of "Icy-Hot"

One might question how Joe can remember all the minute details of all the meets in which he has participated. He can recall specific heights he cleared, as well as on which attempt at many, if not all, meets. He can recall vividly the misses he incurred and why; the specific heights cleared by his competitors; the unique weather and wind conditions; as well as many other details often not remembered, or even noticed, by others.

"I've always been able to remember lots of details. I can remember very clearly the first time I did certain things, like the first pole I got, whenever I hit a new benchmark (like 16 feet, 17 feet, 18 feet, etc.) and important jumps at the bigger meets, and things like that. When I get around a track meet, I get that smell of Icy-Hot (a heating liniment that track athletes would often apply to their legs to keep their leg muscles loose that possessed a very distinct smell). It brings me back to the day I first encountered that smell."

January 30, 1987 » Millrose Games » Madison Square Garden » New York City.

Joe seemed to be really hitting his stride with a series of impressive performances, and it was especially important that he vault well at such a prestigious meet as the Millrose Games, one of the longest running track meets in the country. Joe managed to clear 18-4¾, then went on to attempt 18-8, but was unable to make it.

Both Earl Bell and Joe each cleared 18-4¾, but Bell edged out Joe for the meet title due to fewer misses

But again, Joe has a recollection of an event from this meet that had nothing to do with track and field.

"This was the meet that Shawna kind of got lost. We stayed in the Waldorf-Astoria hotel right across the street from Madison Square Garden. I told her I would meet her after the meet at a particular spot. However, she came out a different door and we missed each other. Because she came out of the indoor meet, she didn't even have a coat. She had to walk all the way around the block around the hotel to get back to the arena. She ended up walking around those homeless guys on the street who had the little fires going in the steel barrels to keep warm — just like you see in the movies. They were saying all kinds of things to her. She was scared to death. But we finally found each other."

February 13, 1987 » Oklahoma Track Classic » The Myriad » Oklahoma City, Oklahoma

Joe returned to his "home indoor track" at the Myriad in downtown Oklahoma City as he jumped 18-8 at the Oklahoma Track Classic as he used "the biggest pole I had ever jumped on indoors."

"I was jumping great, but what messed me up was seeing Ben Johnson squatting all that weight (when Joe was in Australia). I just thought if it (lifting huge sums of weight) helps Ben, the world's fastest human at the time, then it would help me. I'm going to do that."

Joe started to follow Johnson's intense lifting workout as a guide as he drastically increased his lifting regimen, both in the amount of weight as well as the number of repetitions.

"I did that same lifting workout as he (Ben Johnson) did and then used that big pole. But it really messed me up. Instead of my normal workout that I had gotten used to and that worked for me, I tried something new and different. Not only did I increase the amount of weight, I did a lot more reps. I learned that I had messed, but it was too late. I was absolutely terrible. I had no explosion. I felt like I couldn't even run. I really didn't even come close to performing well the rest of that indoor season."

February 27, 1987 » TAC Indoor Championships » Madison Square Garden » New York City

Joe's extra efforts in his weightlifting workouts again took its toll as he admittedly did not perform well at this meet.

"I was terrible. I didn't do well at all here. My weight lifting really messed me up. I took full responsibility for what I had done. But I was determined not to have it mess me up for the outdoor season," Joe reasoned.

"Trying to do what Ben Johnson was doing in regard to weight-lifting was not right. I wasn't at that level. That might have been a part of his program, but it certainly wasn't a part of mine. I learned a valuable lesson."

THREE OF THE BEST POLE VAULTERS IN TRACK AND FIELD COMPETING AT THE 1987 TEXAS RELAYS: JOE DIAL, GREG DUPLANTIS; EDDIE LANGFORD (TEXAS RELAYS OFFICIAL) AND BILLY OLSON.

April 3, 1987 » Texas Relays » University of Texas » Austin, Texas

Joe jumped 18-2½ to capture second place behind Billy Olson in a close finish.

April 11, 1987 » OU Meet » University of Oklahoma » Norman, Oklahoma

Joe cleared 19-¼ to win this meet, but then unsuccessfully tried 19-5.

Taking the measurement into your own hands

April 18, 1987 » Kansas Relays » Memorial Stadium » University of Kansas » Lawrence, Kansas

Joe broke his American record, but not without some controversy and some drama from a most unlikely source — Joe Dial himself.

Joe soared 19-4¾ inches at the 1987 edition of the Kansas Relays as he broke his American record of 19-4¼.

Then the controversy arose.

After the record jump, Joe paced around the pit and runway for some 20 minutes while meet officials searched for a metric tape measure in order to make the record "official." After measuring, the officials then announced that Dial had only tied his old record.

Then the drama unfolded.

Joe and the officials got into what can be kindly described as a "heated argument" regarding the status of his jump.

The argument came to a head when Joe climbed atop the ladder himself with measuring tape in hand and measured the height.

"I'll measure it myself," he declared.

As he swayed in the warm spring breeze from his perch atop the ladder, he announced to everyone below that the record was indeed his. He also pointed out to officials and reporters standing around him that a metric tape measure does not have to be used to verify records.

"I've seen records set in London, Rome, Los Angeles, and they didn't use the metric tape measure," he said.

As Joe talked with reporters, a meet official approached him and said another re-measure had indeed given him the American record of 19-4¾. The official also pointed out a passage in the NCAA rule book which says a metric tape for measuring is required if a record is to stand.

According to the *Lawrence Journal-World*, Rob Miller, coordinator of officials for the Kansas Relays, said it was difficult getting the tape to an even spot on the crossbar as it swayed back and forth in the wind, and "there was a slight difference between measuring with the pole and the tape."

"But finally, it was a record with the tape," Miller said. "We had to measure with the tape. We would have had more egg on our face if we didn't measure with the tape."

After impatiently strolling around the pit area for about an hour awaiting a decision, Joe had grown cold and lost some of his competitive edge, — not to mention most of his adrenaline, but ultimately he decided to continue.

"I'm not sure what the problem even turned out to be. The meet officials measured the height before the jump as a new American record height. And I didn't even touch the bar on my jump. So how could it have changed?" Joel asked incredulously.

After being assured of the new American record, Joe followed up with three attempts at 19-9, which would have erased the world mark of 19-8½ by Sergey Bubka of the Soviet Union.

Joe barely brushed against the bar with his chest on his third try at the world record.

Joe was disappointed with what he called the needless delay. "All it did was to cost me the world record," Joe claimed. "If they had let me go jump again instead of having the delay, there is zero doubt in my mind that I would have broken the world record that day. Zero doubt! The conditions were perfect! I was so tight. My hip flexor started hurting me. I went down through the first time and just didn't feel as good."

Joe also disclosed that he was using new poles.

"They're getting better and better every week," he said. "I'm feeling really good about the world record. Hopefully, next week," he announced.

He also mentioned to reporters in an post-event interview that he was not disappointed in missing the Soviet's record.

"Not at all," Joe said. "I jumped higher today than I've ever jumped. I have to be happy."

April 25, 1987 » Mosier Indoor Facility » University of Oklahoma » Norman, Oklahoma

Competing unattached in a triangular meet with Oklahoma, Baylor and Texas Tech, the pole vault event was moved indoors to the Mosier Indoor Facility on the OU campus due to inclement weather.

Joe maintained his streak of 19 foot jumps as that turned out to be his winning height. Joe then had the bar moved up to the world record height of 19-9, but unfortunately did not clear it on any of his three attempts.

Joe had endured the rigors of a long meet on his way to the win. He started his competition at 17-6, which he cleared easily on his first attempt. But it took him two tries each on 18-0, 18-6 and 19-0. He even brushed the crossbar on his 19 foot clearance, but the bar slightly shook but managed to stay on.

"I tried 19-7 for the world record, but I was feeling my hamstring a little bit. I could just run up to a certain point. My hip flexor was also hurting. I could feel it pretty good at the Kansas Relays (the previous week) and it was still hurting. I decided to take some time off," Joe decided.

May 27, 1987 » USA-Mobil Championships » San Jose, California

Joe defeated Earl Bell in a dramatic jump-off and cleared 19-0¼ height to win the national pole vault title at the USA-Mobil Championships at San Jose, California.

By virtue of the victory, Dial earned a berth on the United States team for the second-ever World Championships, set for Rome, Italy in late August, and a possible shot at world record holder Sergey Bubka of the Soviet Union.

Both Dial and Bell cleared 18-4½ and 18-8¼ without a miss, and then both vaulters missed all three of their attempts at 19-0¼.

The bar was left at that height to begin the jump-off.

Dial then proceeded to clear the 19-0¼ height for the victory.

"I smoked that one," said Dial. "I barely brushed the bar, but Tim McMichael (OU vaulter) said I cleared it by six or eight inches."

Bell, a 31-year old pole vault veteran from Jonesboro, Arkansas, and a member of three U.S. Olympic teams, failed in his attempt as Joe became the U.S. national champion for the second time.

In addition to Joe and Earl Bell making the team to represent the USA at the World Championships, Billy Olson became the third member of the U.S. pole vault contingent.

A New American Record at 19-5¾: "The best jump in my life"

June 13, 1987 » Albuquerque, New Mexico

Joe continued his hot streak of outstanding performances, as he established a new American record at 19-5¾. But even though Joe would ultimately jump higher, ironically, he has always maintained that this was his single best jump he had ever experienced.

"This was easily the best single jump of my life. Forget about where the bar is at. I would have easily cleared 20 feet on this jump. Easily!!

"I made that so far over it was crazy. I killed it! It was just one of those jumps in which you put it all together," Joe recalled.

Joe continued the competition and asked that the bar be raised to 20 feet — a height that no person had yet conquered.

But with Joe setting his new American record, meet officials were exercising extreme caution in order to ensure that all the proper procedures were being followed in order to comply with the requirements of documenting the new record. A taller step-ladder had to be brought out along with a new tape measure, as well as additional officials. All this additional activity took precious time while Joe was anxiously awaiting his turn at a new milestone height.

"They were really taking a lot of time to make sure the record was broken. They had a lot of people measuring the bar just to make sure," Joe said.

"By the time the officials had completed their work, the wind had completely switched to a straight head wind. I knocked it (the crossbar) off all three times, but I never swung up and went with it. I even dropped down a pole with the wind being so bad. There was just no chance of making it.

"But that single jump was the "greatest feeling jump" I ever had. I just launched it," Joe said. "I amazed myself. There was so much daylight when I cleared that bar."

Another American Record at 19-6½

June 18, 1987 » OU Invitational Meet » University of Oklahoma » Norman, Oklahoma

Joe was certainly hitting his stride as this was his seventh outdoor meet of the season and the sixth consecutive meet in which he cleared at least 19 feet. After conducting a pole vault clinic the entire week at a track and field camp on the OU campus, the week's activities culminated in a track meet. Joe set a great example for his clinic students by establishing another new American record of 19-6½. In his last two meet meets over the course of just five days, he had set consecutive American records of 19-5¾ and 19-6½.

At that point in the season, no other American had gone as high as 19-1 outdoors. He was easily the hottest vaulter in America, if not the entire world.

It was obvious that Joe was at the top of his game with even more records to accumulate and new worlds to conquer.

September 2, 1987 » World Championships » Stadio Olimpico » Rome, Italy

Coming off his impressive streak of victories and rapidly gaining notoriety as America's best pole vaulter, Joe had set his sights on defeating Sergey Bubka at the World Championships. But just days prior to the meet, Tim Skitt, Joe's adopted son, was killed in a tragic hit and run accident. (See Part VIII — "A Painful Death").

"Everything went bad," was how Joe described his ordeal in still dealing with Tim's death while trying to compete on the world stage.

"I remember being there at the meet and having other athletes telling me how fast I looked going down the runway. I didn't realize at the time that I had lost ten pounds from what I would normally be jumping. I was well into the 140's (pounds). I just couldn't get those same poles to move. What I needed to do was to jump on my little warm-up pole. That was definitely a low, low point for me," Joe lamented.

"Then to make things worse, someone stole all my poles — the poles on which I had set all those records, " Joe sighed.

Meeting the Pope

Each of the national teams at the World Championships received three tickets that would allow a visit with Pope John Paul II at the Pope's summer cottage outside Rome while attending the meet.

During the meet. Joe had made friends with a coach from Bahrain. Bahrain's team members had already completed their competition and were making preparations to return home. The Bahrain coach would not be able to visit the Pope due to time constraints so he offered Joe his team's three tickets.

Joe readily accepted the offer and asked his roommate, who was a race walker on the USA team, and one of the race walker's friends to accompany him on the visit.

"We rode the bus to the Pope's cottage and, of course, we all wore our USA uniforms. We go in to listen to the Pope, and he was running about 30 minutes late. Finally, the Pope came out and delivered a really short sermon in 16 different languages. I can't even really remember what the sermon was about; I was just so impressed that he could deliver it in 16 different languages," Joe recalled.

When the Pope was finished with his sermon and as he started to walk among the visitors to greet them, he was immediately swarmed and surrounded by the crowd who craved the opportunity to simply touch him or his garment.

"People were flying up to him to get close and to touch him. It just reminded me of when Jesus would walk and the people would flock up to him just to touch him. Even with his body guards elbowing and pushing the crowds away in an effort to protect the Pope, people still lunged and reached for the Pope when he approached them."

Joe recalls that the Pope was approximately 25 yards away but noticed that the Pope appeared to be on a direct line to where Joe was standing.

"He's coming right to me," Joe thought to himself.

As the Pope approached Joe, who by now was standing up in his chair to obtain a better vantage point, Joe grabbed his camera to snap a quick picture. Then as the Pope inched even closer, Joe snapped another photo, but this one was almost directly in the Pope's face, gaining the Pontiff's full attention.

"He looked at me and reached his hand out for me to kiss his ring. Being caught entirely off guard, I just reached out, grabbed his hand, turned it over and shook it, and said, 'Hey, how're you doing, buddy?'"

Today, Joe laughs at himself as he reflects on his interaction with Pope John Paul II.

"For some reason, I just couldn't bring myself to kiss his ring. I really didn't try to disrespect him, so I thought the next best thing to do would be to shake his hand," Joe explained.

But in any event, there are not many citizens from Marlow, Oklahoma, who can proclaim that they actually enjoyed a face-to-face encounter with a Pope and shook his hand.

July 21, 1988 » U.S Olympic Trials » Indianapolis, Indiana

Still reeling from the pain brought on by the death of Tim Skitt (see Part VIII), Joe readily admits he was battling depression.

"His death just did something to me. I really didn't care. As crazy as it sounds, I really didn't have any motivation," Joe said.

Working hard for a couple of months and starting to use some of his largest poles seemed to alleviate some of the agony of losing a close and trusted friend.

"I'm thinking it's going to come around. It's going good," Joe felt.

In practice, Joe would often have one of his practice partners tap him on the back as he took off on the vault. On the last vault during a practice session a few months prior to the 1988 Trials, Joe asked a different practice partner for the tap.

But for some reason, as he started his lift-off of the runway, the partner, instead of tapping Joe on the back, hit him on the butt, "exploding" his sartorius muscle.

"It was one of the times that changed my whole life," Joe disclosed.

The injury was so severe and painful that Joe couldn't even think about vaulting for a month and a half, leaving just a month of valuable training to get back in shape and prepare for the Trials.

"I couldn't even think about vaulting for awhile," Joe recalled.

Once at the Olympic Trials in Indianapolis, Joe tried to maintain a positive attitude, but it was difficult to convince himself considering his lack of quality training.

"Deep down inside, I knew I was done," Joe explained.

Entering the competition at 17-3, Joe failed to clear his opening height.

His dream of emerging from the Olympic Trials with a top three finish and earning a spot on the U.S. Olympic had sadly come to a sudden halt. Again.

March 5, 1989 » World Indoor Championships » Budapest, Hungary

Perhaps the highlight of Joe's international travel and competition was when he won the bronze medal at the 1989 World Indoor Championships at Budapest, Hungary.

Joe had qualified for the World Indoor Championships and seemed to be in great shape, mentally and physically, and peaking seemingly at just the right time for the indoor season.

Consistency seemed to be Joe's hallmark and that trait was certainly on full display at this particular meet.

"I made 17-10½; 18-0½; 18-2½; 18-4½; 18-6½; 18-8¼ — all on my first attempt. I thought; 'I've got the lead, I might as well keep jumping.' I tried 18-10 and barely missed," Joe said.

Joe ultimately ended up placing third and taking home the bronze medal.

Even though it was third place, Joe's accomplishment represented a significant milestone as noted by Dwight Stones, a national track and field television analyst and two-time Olympic bronze medalist and former three-time world record holder in the men's high jump.

"Joe Dial has been consistent all year, and this was the first medal in a major championship since 1976 for an American pole vaulter," commented Stones.

Also while in Budapest, Joe enjoyed another unique experience, his very first cappuccino.

"This high jumper was telling me, 'Man, that cappuccino really helps you jump high; it will help your endurance," as Joe relates the conversation.

Always receptive to trying anything that could improve his performance, Joe was willing to experiment with change."I thought, OK, I'll try it." But unfortunately, Joe did not experience the expected boost as he was told.

But as is the case in many instances, hindsight is always 20-20.

"Looking back at that, it was a mistake to try something totally new and unknown like that. It could have really messed me up," Joe revealed.

Paying it forward

In November 1989, Joe donated $1,000 to Marlow High School. Joe had always been grateful for the opportunities that Marlow High School had provided him in getting started in track and field, and he wanted to show his appreciation with the gift.

Unwelcome news from the doctor

Once the year 1990 arrived, Joe discovered the year was slowly evolving into a "bad" year for a variety of reasons.

The downturn in fortune started when Joe initially came down with knee trouble.

"In 1990, my knee started hurting. I didn't really know why. During the indoor season, I was vaulting pretty normal, usually around 18-6 to 18-7. But I was getting injections in my knee almost weekly. Once in the outdoor season, I continued with the injections. I just got to where I wasn't jumping very good. I couldn't train correctly. I ended up getting surgery on my knee.

"At the time of my knee surgery, they (the doctors) said that it would be one of two situations. If what they thought was the case, I'd likely be back 100% in 10 days or so. Or in the more unlikely case, that once there were in surgery and discover more damage that what they initially suspected, it would require extensive surgery and would require a much longer period of recuperation and more intensive rehab time. After surgery, I wore a knee brace and it was killing me. After about a week, I still could hardly move. I thought I must be getting soft. I finally took the brace off and simply told myself that I have to toughen it up. But I could barely move. I called the doctor's office up and said, 'Hey, something is wrong. It's been 10 days and I can't even hardly move. You said I would back 100% in about 10 days.'"

The doctor then delivered some unwelcome news. "Oh my god, you don't know? I had to do the more extensive procedure. Your recovery time will be about nine months."

Joe later learned the doctor had gone in during the surgery and discovered there was considerably more damage than originally anticipated which would require more than a simple scope procedure, which was what was originally expected and what Joe was expecting.

It was a classic example of a giant miscommunication snafu.

"The doctors probably told me that at the time, but I was under the anesthetic and didn't remember being told anything like that. I really didn't hear anything like that. When my knee failed to improve in 10 days like they originally told me, I just thought I was being soft and being a sissy."

Once Joe realized the extent of his surgery, he was forced to have a complete change of plans.

"With having major surgery on my knee, I was therefore unable to work. Without being able to work, we had no income. We went nine months without any income to speak of. I had lost just about everything by then. You couldn't get any lower. Everyone we knew who would see our situation, would simply ask, 'What happened?'"

Luckily, when times had been better earlier, Joe had invested in rental properties and had purchased several rental houses. These houses came in handy as Joe found himself being required to sell them off in order to provide finances for his family. The family would move from house to house as they were being sold off. Finally, down to the final house after all the others had been sold off, Joe and his family found themselves living in what he considered the worst house of the entire bunch.

Ever the eternal optimist, Joe still managed to stay positive.

"Even though we couldn't have gotten any lower, we were still happy. We had to do the dishes outside where there was a faucet. There was no running water inside," Joe explained.

The house wasn't the only substandard issue with which the family had to contend.

"We had to jump start Shawna's vehicle each day to get it started. She learned to park on a hill so the car would roll, then she would jump in and pop the clutch to get it going."

With no funds for entertainment, Joe recalls a rather unique activity to help pass the time.

"We had no television for entertainment. But we had a b-b gun and would shoot mice for entertainment.

"You can't imagine how bad it was at the time. We went from having lots and lots of money and driving nice cars to having absolutely nothing."

But soon things would start changing for the better and the outlook on life was turning positive.

Oklahoma Missionary Baptist College

When Joe left Oklahoma State after using up his eligibility back in 1985, he had always expressed the desire to take some Bible classes just for the fun of it.

Then in late 1990, an official from Oklahoma Missionary Baptist College, which was located in Joe's hometown of Marlow, called Joe and informed him that that he needed only 26 hours in order to graduate. The official also indicated that Joe could complete the course work in one semester with the caveat that it would not be easy carrying that number of hours.

"Man, what a great opportunity to graduate. I just have to pass the 26 hours," Joe thought to himself.

Starting course work during the 1991 spring semester. Joe took several home-study classes while others were regular classes.

"All I did that semester was work out, go to class and then come home and study," Joe explains. "We lived in a little trailer that we set on my brother's lot there in Marlow."

Joe's ties with the Oklahoma Missionary Baptist College go back a long ways historically.

The College was originally affiliated with the Fifth Street Baptist Church in Marlow, the church that Joe attended as a youngster.

"My granddad, Herbert Ward, had helped the college previously on numerous occasions, even to the extent of mortgaging his house in order to raise funds to help the college make it through some financial hard times. He was a really nice man," Joe said.

"It was a really big deal for me to graduate. I actually got my degree in Christian Education. A few years later, the school closed down," Joe explained.

During that semester of study, Joe enjoyed the camaraderie of working out with a former teammate.

"My old high school quarterback, Bobby Shannon, would work out with me, and we would lift weights. He was my lifting partner. Then I would go out to the Marlow track and do my running."

Obviously the hard work paid off as he ended up making the 1991 U.S. Team for the World Championships held in Tokyo.

"I made 18-6½, but there was a nasty cross-wind. It was really bad day," Joe said.

He then traveled to Europe for a series of meets that summer and was enjoying some solid and consistent performances.

"1991 was turning out to be a good year. I was competing really well in Europe. I was jumping 18-4, 18-8 at just about every meet. Even a few times at 18-10. I was almost up to 19 feet at about every meet. I was making good money. I felt like I was back on my game. "

Then disaster hit. In late October, Joe discovered he had ruptured two discs in his neck.

"I didn't actually know what the problem was. I kept thinking it was just a crick in my neck. As I was trying to lift weights, my arms would almost become paralyzed. Then I knew something was really bad."

Surgery was then scheduled for November, 1991. To repair the ruptured discs, the surgeons, in an intricate and complicated procedure, removed some bone from Joe's hip and utilized bone fragments to fuse the ruptured discs. The doctors told Joe that such a procedure would require a lengthy recovery and recuperative process. But with the 1992 Olympic Trials at New Orleans coming up in just seven short months, time was a luxury that Joe did not possess.

June 21, 1992 » U.S. Olympic Trials » Tad Gormley Stadium » New Orleans, Louisiana

Joe's misfortunes at Olympic Trials continued, as he failed to make the qualifying height at the 1992 Trials held in Tad Gormley Stadium in New Orleans.

Prior to the Trials, Joe's two ruptured discs in his neck cast a dark gloom over continuing his career. After his doctors grafted a portion of his hip bone to fuse the vertebrae, a lengthy recovery time was required. But the necessary time to heal and recuperate left precious little time to train and regain the highly competitive edge he needed to get back to his younger form and make a serious run at a spot on the United States Olympic team.

Then Joe's streak of unfortunate events surfaced again. With a portion of the Trials set to be televised live, meet officials had little room for altering their scheduled start time.

Due to the events prior to the pole vault taking longer than anticipated, the meet officials were forced to squeeze down the time for the vaulters to prepare their warm-ups and run-throughs.

"The officials came to us vaulters and informed us that some event, I think it was either the javelin or discus, was taking longer than anticipated. Because of certain time constraints and the set time established for the televised portion of the meet, we would each get only one run-through prior to the competition in order for the event to coincide with the television schedule," Joe recalled.

"I had never been to a meet in which we received only one opportunity for a run-through. Usually all I needed was about three run-throughs. The biggest meet of the year and we get only one run-through? I had to quickly think as to how exactly I wanted to use my one and only run-through. Do I want to run-through in order to make sure I have my steps down or do I want to just plant my pole and see how it goes?

Joe decided to use his one and only run-through to plant. Without the opportunity to run-through in order to ensure his steps were down, Joe took off on down the runway. As he approached the box and then fully stretched to get to the box, he severely pulled his left hamstring.

Realizing that he likely had only one jump left, he decided to pass until the bar got higher and take his chances in the hope that one successful vault might hopefully earn him a spot among the top three finishers and claim a roster spot on the Olympic team.

"I decided to wait and get in the competition at 18-8. I then asked for an injection of xylocaine as I knew it was my only chance to get a jump in. It took me forever for me to talk them (the team doctors) into giving me the injection. The doctors initially did not want to do it. I argued, and then pleaded with them, 'my career is likely over here anyway if I don't do good, so it really doesn't matter,'" Joe reasoned.

After the apparently convincing pleas from Joe, the doctors finally relented. Right before Joe's next attempt, he received the injection to help lessen the pain.

Alas, Joe gallantly attempted the vault. He actually cleared the crossbar but hit it on the way down.

By the time Joe's turn for his second attempt came around, the effects of the initial injection had worn off.

So Joe asked for another injection since he had nothing to lose at this time.

"They said no way. You won't find another doctor who will give you anymore," Joe recalled as the response to his request.

With his hamstring almost totally useless, the meet, as well as the season, was over for Joe.

After the meet, Joe explained what he was experiencing.

"It was almost like running down the runway with one leg. I could hardly feel my leg. What made it even worse was it was my take-off leg. It was just a total nightmare," he lamented.

As Joe reflected on the recent events, he surmised it was simply another year wasted and another lost opportunity to make the Olympic team.

"If I hadn't suffered the neck injury, things would have been much different. That injury threw a huge wrench in my plans. Who knows what might have happened if I hadn't missed all that practice and training because of the injury?

"After that, I was really disgusted. I figured that I was done. I packed it up. I started seeking for what God had in store for me," Joe recalls.

After the frustration, pain and disappointment of not making the Olympic team again, Joe did not compete for a couple of years.

"I figured I was totally done vaulting," he said.

Facing reality

Anxious to get to the next step in his life and realizing the need to generate an income in order to provide for his family, Joe had contemplated as what his next move would be. Time was of the essence. He could not be choosy. He had already decided to take the first job that came along. Through the grapevine, he had heard of a roofing job that was based in Dallas. Moving there and taking the job was a real awakening. Once relocated to Dallas, he found himself living with nine Hispanic co-workers in one house. There was no furniture, no creature comforts or no beds, just bodies sleeping on the floor. As to his actual workload, since he was one of the stronger guys on the roofing crew, his job was to throw the bundles of shingles up to the men working on the roof.

"The work was hard, miserable, and came with low pay. It was not quite what I had envisioned. After a couple of weeks of late and often incorrect pay, poor working conditions and other issues, I quit that job," Joe said.

Leaving Dallas and moving to Oklahoma City, Joe started mowing lawns which then quickly expanded into a lawn service. Through hard work, many satisfied customers and a great work ethic, Joe soon found himself operating a profitable business that grew into a customer base that included over 70 Circle K convenience stores that was bringing in about $4,000 of business per month.

Joe's crew? It was just Joe and his son, Timmy.

The work was steady, the pay was good and since Joe's primary client was a successful corporate customer, he could depend upon timely payment and not have to worry about late — or bouncing — checks.

But fate would soon intervene and opportunities for Joe to get back into the sport he loved presented themselves. Serving as an assistant track coach at Tulsa Union High School, specializing in the two events with which he was most familiar and most proficient — pole vault and long jump — got his coaching blood circulating which proved to serve as a springboard to move up the coaching ladder.

In 1993, Joe accepted an offer to become an assistant track coach at Oral Roberts University. Then in 1994, he was offered the head coaching position. (See Part IX. Coaching Career.)

Once back full-time in the track and field environment, Joe discovered his competitive juices again flowing. Coaching at ORU offered Joe the perfect opportunity to train again.

Joe worked out, lifted weights and ran with his ORU athletes. He soon began to realize that the workouts made him faster, stronger and in better physical condition than he had ever been during his long track and field career.

"I do absolutely love the sport," Joe said. "There's always another inch to get, and there is always something you can do to help make yourself better. So I thought I might as well grab a vaulting pole and see what I can do."

Enjoying the sessions, Joe gave some thought to making a comeback and one last attempt to qualify for the 1996 Olympic Team. Joe set his sights on the 1996 Olympic Trials at Atlanta.

As in anything Joe did, he did it full-speed, head-on and without reservation. After some time, he started back on the road to competing again.

Joe traveled to Europe on another summer tour as he competed in a pair of meets over the next two weeks in Europe. Joe soon found his stride and was again vaulting in grand style.

May 30, 1995 » Dijon, France

Joe ended up placing sixth in a meet in Dijon, France, as he cleared 18 feet, 8¼ inches which qualified him for the U.S. Nationals.

"I was feeling really good at this meet," Joe recalled.

June 6, 1995 » Rome, Italy

Joe and a friend, Bill Paine, spent a day sightseeing in Rome and decided to visit the Vatican.

The pair walked several blocks to the Vatican and once there encountered a number of stairs. Wanting to take in the whole experience, the two walked up to what seemed to be "never-ending" sets of stairs.

"We walked up to the top. When we finally made it all the way up, my legs were quivering. Our legs were shot. And we had the meet the next day.

"At the meet, I couldn't even run down the runway to save my life, my legs were still so sore. I no-heighted at this meet. I got booed. Loudly. On my third and final attempt, I missed and the 30,000 some-odd fans whistled and booed me mercilessly. It was devastating," Joe recalled.

June 15, 1995 » All-Comers Meet » Oklahoma State University » Stillwater, Oklahoma

Joe dialed back the pages of history as he won an All-Comers meet at Oklahoma State University by clearing 19-4¼. What was almost as remarkable was the fact that he cleared the height on his first attempt.

The win at that height was also significant for several reasons:

- It was the best mark in the United States so far this year.
- It was the third best vault in the world so far this year.
- It was the fourth best vault of all-time for Joe.
- It was highest vault by Joe since 1989.

Joe easily cleared 18-6 on his first attempt and cleared 19-0¼ on his second attempt on the way to clearing 19-4¼.

Also factoring into his winning effort was the fact that it was achieved despite the rainy and cold conditions. Conditions were so adverse, that several other vaulters opted to pass on attempts or to scratch themselves out of the competition entirely.

June 26, 1995 » U.S. National Meet » Hornet Stadium » California State University » Sacramento, California

Joe finished fourth at 18-10¼ at the U.S. National Meet, which automatically qualified him for his fifth Olympic Trials.

An interesting and unique milestone was announced at this meet in which Joe shared with one of the best-known Olympic athletes of all time — Carl Lewis.

"During the meet, they announced on the PA system and Carl and I were the only athletes competing at the 1995 U.S. National Meet that had also participated in the 1981 U.S. National Meet, Joe explained.

Joe even recalled watching Lewis run the 100 meter dash.

"The sprinters ran into a really strong head wind. I was sitting right on the side watching it all. Hershel Walker (the 1982 Heisman Trophy winner and 15 year pro football veteran) beat Carl. It was one of the few times that Carl Lewis got beat in the 100 meters," Joe recalled.

Competing at the top of your game and at a national level in such a demanding sport as pole vaulting spanning a period of 14 years is truly an amazing accomplishment and a testament to Joe's dedication and longevity.

June 8, 1996 » AAU Meet » Jenks High School » Jenks, Oklahoma

Joe prepared for the U.S. Olympic Trials with fellow vaulter Mike Holloway at an AAU Youth Meet at Jenks, Oklahoma.

"I've jumped three times in these meets this spring," Joe said. "I guess that means I've practiced three times. I wouldn't go to the Trials if I didn't think I could make the team. I know I can do these heights. I've done them many times. If the good Lord wants me, I'll make it. If not, there's a reason. I'll go on coaching and love it."

June 14, 1996 » U.S. Olympic Trials » Centennial Olympic Stadium » Atlanta, Georgia

Going into his fifth Olympic Trials, Joe felt confident. In possibly the best shape of his career, the 33 year old had defied Father Time by working harder than ever to get into the physical condition that is demanded of world-class athletes.

"I was finally perfectly healthy. So I thought I'd have my best shot ever," Joe said. "I knew the only thing that could hurt me would be a straight head wind. I can't stand jumping into a head wind."

Joe instantly knew he was going to have a tough road to hoe when he lined up on the runway for his first vault in the qualifying round, and he felt the wind hit him squarely in the face.

"I'm not a power vaulter. A head wind knocks my speed down and speed is what compensates for my lack of size. By living in the state of Oklahoma, I got used to vaulting in the wind. But not everyone knows how to jump with a tail wind."

Joe related that there were two pole vault runways in Atlanta and they were about 40 feet apart.

One runway was fine, but the other runway was facing an opening in the stadium concourse through which delivery trucks would enter and leave the stadium. The wind was whipping right through the opening directly into the faces of the vaulters.

Of course, the competition was scheduled to take place on the runway with the head wind.

Despite Joe's request to meet officials to switch to the runway unaffected by the wind, his plea fell on deaf ears and the competitors were forced to jump into the head wind.

Being the competitor that he is, Joe decided to make the best of a bad situation.

Grabbing a smaller pole, Joe cleared his initial height of 18 feet,½ inch, but then missed at his three attempts at 18-4½, failing to advance to the finals.

"Being the smallest vaulter at the Trials, the wind impacted me a lot greater. I was the shortest and the lightest vaulter, and it hurt when I had to go down to such a smaller pole. Basically, when you are dealing with jumping into a head wind, it depends on how big and how strong you are."

That statement was proven absolutely true as evidenced by the results. Whoever said size doesn't matter had obviously never pole vaulted.

Lawrence Johnson of Tennessee won the Trials as he cleared 19-1/4. Johnson happens to be a chiseled 6 foot, 1 inch, 190 pound specimen that could fight through the wind compared to Dial's 5-8, 158 pound stature.

Despite the disappointment of failing to make the Olympic team, Joe said after the competition that he wouldn't rule out another attempt to come back in 2000 for one more shot at his Olympic dream.

"In-Betweeners"

For whatever reason, there are some track and field athletes who compete at the top level in their respective event during most of their career except when it comes to Olympic years. Often the lack of Olympic year success may involve injuries. Or perhaps a case of bad luck can be the cause. Or perhaps the blame should fall on the issue of serendipity and the fickleness of such a highly technical and detailed demanding sport as pole vaulting.

Track and field veterans commonly refer to those fellow athletes who are normally highly regarded in their event but seem to never "get over the hump" in Olympic years as "in-betweeners."

Joe claims he could be classified as an "in-betweener." Having qualified for five Olympic Track and Field Trials (1980, 1984, 1988, 1992 and 1996), but yet never making an Olympic team, despite his American and World records, could be considered the ultimate "in-betweener." (Joe was officially an alternate on the 1984 team). But competing in five Olympic Trials as a pole vaulter is a record in itself. Well, actually that ties a record. Joe and fellow vaulter Earl Bell each competed in five Olympic Trials — the most of any American pole vaulter in Olympic history.

Bell competed in the U.S. Olympic Track and Field Trials in 1976, 1980, 1984, 1988 and 1992.

Japan beckons for one final international competition

After the 1996 Olympic Trials, Joe figured his career was over from active competition.

"I figured I was through jumping for good. I was tired and wanted to concentrate all my efforts on my coaching," he explained.

But out of the blue, Joe received a call from a Japanese meet promoter inquiring if he would be interested in traveling to Japan for an exhibition.

"They called me up and asked if I would jump in Japan. They would pay all my expenses and pay me $5,000," Joe recalled.

Joe, believing he was not adequately in shape to perform up to his expectations, was not quite sold on the proposition and was reluctant to accept the otherwise enticing offer.

"But I haven't even worked out in six months. I'm done jumping," was Joe's reply to the promoter.

"Joe, they don't care what you can jump. They just want to see you jump one more time," countered the promoter.

After some consideration of an "offer that was too good to refuse," Joe accepted and traveled to Japan where he jumped 17-4½, an impressive performance for a 34 year old who had been inactive and had not practiced in some six months.

Hanging up the poles for good

January 24, 1997 » John Lance Arena » Pittsburg State University » Pittsburg, Kansas

Joe's last indoor competition was at Pittsburg State University as he competed unattached. Local track and field fans were excited about the opportunity of a lifetime to watch an American record holder (and former world record holder) in action. Joe did not disappoint the fans as he cleared 17-7. Perhaps that height was not up to Joe's usual expectations, but to the fans that witnessed his performance that night, it didn't matter.

Pittsburg State Coach Russ Jewett, who was an outstanding track athlete in his own right in his college days at Pittsburg State, recalls Joe's last indoor competition. Jewett was a three-time conference champion hurdler and an All-American decathlete in 1982, placing second at the NAIA Outdoor National Championships competing for the Gorillas, so he possesses a full appreciation of the rigors of the pole vault. His recollection follows:

"I do remember that meet in 1997 that we hosted and Joe came to vault. I remember that we had quite a few vaulters and he started vaulting after everyone else was already out of the competition. By then the rest of the events were all concluded, but nobody left the building. Most everyone headed up to the mezzanine level to watch Joe. He got a big slow-clap from the crowd each attempt and lots of applause and cheering when he made a jump. Then a big collective groan came over when he missed his last attempt (it was 18-0 or higher). It was pretty cool having the American record-holder in the building and putting on a great show," Jewett said.

The 1997 meet was not Joe's only appearance at Lance Arena on the

Pittsburg State campus, which is approximately 200 miles northeast of Stillwater.

"I actually vaulted many times at Pittsburg State through the years. It was a small facility but I enjoyed competing there," Joe said.

Jewett also tells of the time that Joe set the arena record back in 1983.

"Joe actually set the Lance Arena record in the pole vault in 1983 at 18-0. I was a senior on the Pitt State team that year, and I didn't really watch him vault much that day. Back then, we had a pretty small pole vault pit that wasn't necessarily built for 18-foot vaulting. I remember talking with Joe a few years later about that day, and he told me that when he landed in the pit after his first jump, it took the wind out of him a little. So on his subsequent vaults, he landed with his arms and legs spread straight to dissipate the force when he hit that small and shallow pit."

May 3, 1997 » Abilene Christian University » Abilene, Texas

Approaching the end of his career as an active vaulter, Joe had already sensed that his vaulting days would soon come to an end.

At the time, Coach Dial had taken his Oral Roberts University track team to Abilene Christian University for a track meet and he decided to compete one last time. Even at age 34, Joe was still physically capable of keeping up, and even defeating, athletes 15-16 years his junior. But no matter how good of physical condition or mental sharpness he possessed, the realization that his competitive days would soon be over could not escape his thoughts. Giving up one's life activity and passion after almost three decades is not an easy task.

"I truly knew that this was it. There was no doubt in my mind that this would be the last time I would ever compete," Joe reflected. "It was really, really emotional for me."

"I made 17-6½, and then tried 18-0½. I missed twice and then on my last attempt, I felt really good, had a great run and take-off and just hit the bar on the way up," Joe recalled.

"I must admit I got pretty teary-eyed after that. I knew it was my last time to jump."

PART VII

EPIC BATTLES WITH BILLY

Friendly and easily approachable, Joe readily made friends with most other vaulters with his down home manner and easy-going personality. Even some of the top foreign vaulters such as Sergey Bubka from the Soviet Union found Joe to be a friend, ready to help and advise whenever assistance was needed.

Joe, normally a fairly laid-back and mild-mannered athlete, would find himself evolving into a fierce competitor once he set foot on the runway. A perfectionist in technique and highly detailed on the proper execution in all phases of the pole vault, Joe was all business whenever he had a vaulting pole in his hands.

Joe was very adept at shutting out all distractions, whether they emanated from the crowd, from other competitors, or internally within himself. But there was one fellow athlete with whom Joe seemed to be often at odds for one reason or another.

His name was Billy Olson.

In the February 7, 1983, issue of *Sports Illustrated,* Olson was described as a troublemaker with a "seemingly dim future, traveling with a fast crowd." While attending Abilene, Texas High School, Billy played golf and was fairly proficient on the links. It was only when a friend introduced him to the pole vault the summer between his sophomore and junior years that Billy first began to take athletics seriously.

"I had been a total nobody all my life," Olson said in the article. "My dad said I was a bum and I probably was. It was just that I was always so small. In ninth grade I was 5'6" and 90 pounds. When I graduated I was 6'2" and 135, which wasn't much better."

But despite the small size, Olson had broken the Texas state high school record in the vault by clearing 15'10." However, later Olson did add some weight to his lanky frame

Four years older than Joe, Olson broke the world indoor pole vault record a total of 11 times during a four-year period from January, 1982 to February, 1986. Seven of those records were set in a compressed sixteen month time frame. Until Sergey Bubka came along in the mid 1980's, an argument could be made that Olson was one of, if not the top, vaulter in the world at the time.

While Olson and Joe each possessed several characteristics in common, an abiding passion for track and field, immense talent and an insatiable desire to succeed in the sport of pole vaulting, there were some obvious differences. The primary one was in size. In their heyday, Olson was a strapping 6 foot, 2 inches and 160 pounds compared to Joe at a mere 5 foot, 9 inches and 148 pounds.

Joe was always considered small for a world-class pole vaulter, where the majority of the premier vaulters are six foot plus in height. Being on the small side, Joe seemed to be often fighting certain pre-conceived notions and ill-founded generalities, such as "you're too short to grip the pole high enough"; "you're too small to bend the pole as much as necessary"; or "you're too small to vault into even a small wind."

With their disparity in size, among other differences, Billy and Joe, could be likened to oil and water. There seemed to be no love lost between the two world-class vaulters at various times through the years.

Take that time in Dallas back in the spring of 1985 when Joe and Billy got into a shoving match on the runway at a meet at SMU. Olson and Mike Tully were there competing and Joe was there as a spectator to simply watch the action.

Tully ambled over to the stands where Joe was sitting and congratulated Joe for his prior achievements, including setting a new American record while Olson went over to confront Joe and proceeded to question his ability.

Olson had implied that Dial's record vault of 19-2¼ in Norman earlier that year was accomplished only due to the "friendly" conditions and that Joe would not be able to repeat such a comparable accomplishment outside of his home state. Olson challenged Joe to get dressed and immediately compete on the spot.

Here's how the exchange between the two vaulters transpired as reported in the *New York Times* June 2, 1985:

> Olson: "Get your stuff on, Dial!"
> Dial: "I'm not jumping. I don't have anything to prove."
> Olson: "You've got a lot to prove with all of your bogus heights in your backyard."
> Dial: "Billy, you better stop that, or I'm going to push this pole down your throat."

Olson continued his taunting which incited Joe to the point that Joe left his seat, charged the field and pushed Olson off the runway.

Olson: "What's the matter with you?"

Joe: "I'm just tired of you mouthing off."

At about that time, an Oklahoma State coach intervened and restrained Joe from further attacks on Olson.

Joe later reflected on the confrontation.

"That's not my personality. I made the first contact, but he made the first mouth. I think he wanted me to jump in front of them, and I think last week when I made 18-8, I proved it. They say I can only jump with a big tailwind."

Afterwards, Olson offered his perspective of the situation as reported in the *Chicago Tribune*.

"He didn't push me off the runway. I don't like this at all, but I think I could have handled Joe Dial pretty easily."

Olson continued, "He's a little hot-headed. I've lost a little respect for him as a person. He obviously doesn't know how to take care of himself. I think his problem is in his own mind. He never has gotten the publicity he deserves, and he thinks we've called him a big bogus head. I've never said that, ever."

Olson related to the *Chicago Tribune* that Dial also threatened to "bop him over the head" with a broken piece of pole three weeks after Olson told him he had plenty to prove.

"He got on my bad side," said Dial.

Olson said he was just trying to egg him on to jump in the meet at Dallas against Tully and Olson. Dial countered that he was there only to watch as a spectator.

"He (Joe) said he had nothing to prove and I said, 'Sure you do. Anybody can set records. You have to do it against me and Tully," Olson recalled. "We were led to believe he was going to compete."

Later at the NCAA National Outdoor Championship meet at the University of Texas, Joe claimed his second national collegiate outdoor title with a jump of 18-6. Joe then passed at 18-9¼ and instead attempted 19 feet, but failed on all three attempts. Had he attempted 18-9¼ and successfully made that height, he would have broken Olson's stadium record of 18-8¼.

"If I had thought of that, I would have gone for it," Joe said with a sly grin.

"Everyone says I'm too little. I don't know when it's going to stop. I guess I'll have to break the world record before they say, 'Well, maybe he's all right.'"

In spite of Joe doing that very thing — breaking the world record — Olson was still casting doubts on Joe's abilities.

When Joe established a new indoor world record of 19-4¾ in Columbia, Missouri, Billy could only offer a sarcastic remark, "Why doesn't he come out and do these things where we can see them?"

Olson insinuated that Dial pulled out of a meet in Dallas due to a pulled hamstring, but then showed up in Missouri where he set the world record.

Joe then offered his side of the situation. "I hadn't practiced in two weeks. I'm not going to go to a meet where I have to start high. I wanted to go to a meet in Missouri where I could start low. Apparently, I was all right. I wasn't ducking anyone."

Joe went on to explain that he considered it "totally stupid" for Olson to accuse him of ducking competition indoors, because he could have cashed in on appearance fees in Dallas. Instead, Joe chose to pay his own way to Missouri. "I'm in the sport to jump high, If the money comes, great," added Joe.

"The trouble with Americans is they go crazy indoors to make money, and they run around like chickens with their heads cut off to jump in every meet. That's what happens to Billy every year. He gets rich indoors and doesn't have to jump outdoors," Joe said in a quote in the *Chicago Tribune*.

For another example of the apparent bad blood existing in their relationship, consider Olson's comment at the 1985 USA-Mobil National Track and Field Championships held at the Los Angeles Memorial Coliseum.

"I told him to his face when he made 18-4 that was about as good as he was going to get," said Olson.

Even other fellow vaulters seem to question Olson's integrity.

Dave Volz, former vaulter from the University of Indiana and frequent competitor of both Olson and Joe, offered a somewhat blunt observation of Olson to a *Chicago Tribune* reporter prior to the 1986 Bally Invitational Meet at the Rosemont Horizon in Chicago, at which Olson was scheduled to compete, but instead was a no-show.

"He cheats. No wonder he's set all those records," Volz told the *Chicago Tribune* referring to Olson.

Volz later accused Olson of getting extra jumps when he (Olson) set the indoor world record February 8, 1986. That mark eclipsed Joe's world indoor record which was set just a week earlier on February 1, 1986.

"Olson decided after two misses that the standards were wrong, so they started the competition over," Volz declared in a *Chicago Tribune* article.

Soviet vaulter Sergey Bubka likewise was apparently not a big fan of Olson's either.

In referring to Olson being a no-show at a Chicago meet, Bubka noted that the rivalry between the two of them will likely resume elsewhere.

The *Chicago Tribune* reported this nugget about the Bubka-Olson rivalry: "And an authentic rivalry it seems to be. Bubka apparently doesn't like Olson, not that it makes him unique. Olson has the reputation of ducking big meets."

"I don't think he will jump any higher because of his personal qualities and techniques," Bubka said referring to Olson through a translator.

While Joe often stood out due to his smaller size as compared to others in the sport, Joe's long-time friend and pole vault competitor, Earl Bell, offered a unique perspective as to another trait in which Joe stood out from the crowd and is often the most easily identifiable vaulter at any meet.

"Joe always smells like a grease monkey," said Bell.

Here's the reason behind that statement.

While other vaulters attempt to improve their grip on the pole by utilizing two-sided tape or perhaps chalk or even lighter fluid (which makes the adhesive on the tape gummy and more sticky), Joe improved his grip on the pole by using a rather unorthodox aid — gasket sealer.

But Olson expressed another opinion as to why Joe stood out from the rest of the field.

"Joe's a little bitty skinny old kid," Olson described his competitor in the February 7, 1983, *Sports Illustrated* issue. "Maybe 5'8", 5'9". Doesn't have a muscle. Doesn't know what a muscle is."

But as in many instances, age and experience will often help to counteract any problems and issues brought on by the lack of the same. Such was the case with Joe and Billy. Despite their intense competitive natures that brought them to the level of contentiousness, physical altercations and the many instances of verbal sparring, the two athletes seemed to mellow somewhat through the years.

Their respect for each other gradually evolved into a friendship that exists even today. The two vaulters were teammates at the 1989 Indoor World Championships.

"As teammates, we actually looked after each other and were willing to help the other one to become a better vaulter," Joe explained. "That was something lacking earlier in our relationship."

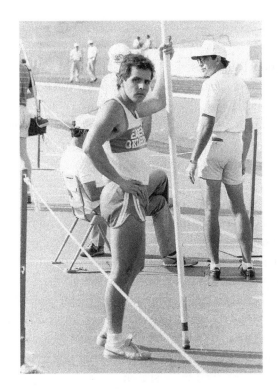

TIM SKITT COMPETING IN THE POLE VAULT FOR EASTERN OKLAHOMA STATE
COLLEGE. TIM WAS A THREE-TIME STATE CHAMPION IN THE POLE VAULT.
SINCE TIM WAS IN THE SEVENTH GRADE, JOE LOOKED AFTER TIM AND
MENTORED HIM. JOE WAS LATER APPOINTED TIM'S LEGAL GUARDIAN. TIM
WAS TRAGICALLY KILLED IN A BIZARRE HIT-AND-RUN ACCIDENT IN 1987.

PART VIII

A PAINFUL DEATH

Tim Skitt — promising pole vaulter

Joe was the epitome of the "small-town boy does good" sentiment and seemingly was the pride and joy of Marlow. Many of the younger boys in town would look up to Joe as he was becoming well known throughout the state and the country for his pole vaulting prowess.

One of these youngsters who admired Joe was Tim Skitt.

Joe first became acquainted with Tim when Joe was a senior at Marlow High School and Tim was just a seventh grader.

The high school track team was assisting in running the junior high track meet and Joe, of course, was overseeing the pole vault event. Joe noticed that a large group of kids had gathered around Tim. Joe asked some of the kids what was going on and was told that Tim's mother had died that morning. Tim, in an attempt to get his mind off his mother's death, had come out to pole vault as originally planned in an attempt to escape the reality of his mother's passing.

Tim went on to clear nine feet, one inch that fateful day, which ironically tied the seventh grade record that Joe had established some five years earlier when Joe was a seventh grader.

"From that day on, I watched out for him and made sure he was taken care of. He was in a rough situation. My heart just went out to him," Joe explained.

Tim was keenly interested in pole vaulting and Joe took an interest in Tim. Joe made sure Tim had things most kids that age would have, like a bike, and would make sure Tim had the right clothes to wear.

With Tim's mother's passing and Tim's father not around since Tim was seven years old, Tim seemed to be simply searching for guidance and some semblance of a family relationship. Fortunately, Joe appeared in Tim's life to help fill that void. Joe and Tim became close friends through the years with Joe sharing advice not only on pole vaulting, but on life matters as well. Joe was looking after Tim in a "big brother" role. Joe decided to ask his parents, who at the time were living in Perkins, Oklahoma, if Tim could move in for his junior and senior years of high school. Joe's parents had met Tim several times and readily agreed to take him in.

The relationship between Joe and Tim grew deeper as Joe would look out for Tim's best interests. The connection between the two grew to the extent that Joe took the unique step to be named Tim's legal guardian. Joe completed the legal process in Payne County District Court and the guardianship became official in June, 1985.

Tim was following in Joe's footsteps as an outstanding pole vaulter in his own right. Tim was a three-time state champion in the event. He was the 1983 Class 2A state champion at Marlow with a vault of 13-9. In 1985, he repeated as Class 2A state champion when he competed for Perkins-Tryon as he recorded a jump of 14-0. This was followed by a Class B state championship in 1986 while at Bowlegs High School when he cleared 13-3.

Tim, much like Joe, was also an outstanding football player who could run a 40 yard dash in 4.4 seconds and, for a defensive player, seemed to possess a knack to know exactly where the ball was and be involved in almost every play.

With Tim leading his team, Bowlegs made the state football playoffs his senior year.

"They were great and were a lot of fun to watch. I'd try to go back every Friday night to catch his game," Joe said.

Tim was selected to play in the All-State Eight-Man football game for the West squad and turned in an outstanding performance as he led his team in tackles.

Tim had also earned a track scholarship to Eastern Oklahoma State College in Wilburton, Oklahoma, and was anxiously looking forward to his sophomore year. He had recorded a personal best of 16 feet, 1¼ inches in the pole vault during his freshman year. His star was shining and his future was indeed bright.

All this ended tragically on the morning of August 23, 1987, when Tim was found dead four miles north of McAlester on U.S. Highway 69 after apparently being hit by a vehicle.

Joe explained that Tim had been on a blind double date Saturday night and was walking from his date's home, north of McAlester, to his car in McAlester when he was struck.

"His friend had left him at the girl's house in the country, and he didn't want to stay, so he left to get his car," Dial said later that Sunday.

"The Highway Patrol came out to the accident scene and there was no chance of survival. It's really unbelievable," Joe lamented.

The Oklahoma Highway Patrol officer investigating the accident, David Rycrof, reported that Skitt had been hit twice, apparently by two different vehicles. The officer indicated that Tim was walking on the highway but said what exactly he was doing or why would be merely speculation. The vehicle that hit Tim did not stop.

After the first vehicle hit Tim, he was lying in the road when two passersby stopped and attempted to slow down the passing traffic. But it was late at night and apparently drivers were apprehensive about stopping for two men who were trying to slow people down. While the men were trying the slow down the passing vehicles, another vehicle ran over Tim and also refused to stop.

"We have no witnesses, no vehicle tag number to go on, not anything to go on at all. A situation like this is very difficult," a spokesman for the Oklahoma Highway Patrol said at the time.

Officials estimate the accident occurred about 2 a.m. "I got a call about 2:10 a.m. and I got here as quickly as I could," the officer said. "It probably took me 15 to 20 minutes to get here. I would say it probably happened around 2 a.m. because a lady who drove by and saw him drove to McAlester and immediately called us," the officer said.

Dial recounted how he had obtained legal guardianship of Tim when he was a sophomore in high school.

"I brought him to Perkins to stay with my parents and me after his mother passed away. I started looking after him. He tied my seventh grade pole vaulting record (9 feet, one inch) that day and I coached him from then on," Joe said.

Joe described Tim as a popular kid and a Christian who never caused a bit of trouble.

To this day, the mystery of Tim's tragic hit-and-run death remains unsolved. No one was ever charged with the crime.

Death's aftermath

A mere ten days after Tim's death, Joe was scheduled to compete in the World Championships to be held in Rome, Italy.

But in retrospect, Joe readily admits that he was in no condition, at least mentally, to compete in the biggest meet in which he would compete that year.

"After Tim's death, I was so messed up in the head. I was in absolutely no condition to compete. I couldn't concentrate. I couldn't focus, " Joe explained.

Unable to generate the requisite attention his event required and lacking his normal level of concentration, Joe failed to clear the opening height.

Despite gallantly competing with an enormously heavy heart, Joe suffered even more. Nike, who had been one of Joe's primary sponsors, subsequently dropped its sponsorship of Joe after his subpar performance.

As a direct result of losing his sponsorship, Joe was forced to compete in more meets than he would have otherwise if he retained his sponsorship in an effort to make up for the monetary difference. He went from competing in 18 meets the previous year to competing in 38 meets, a dramatic increase that ultimately would contribute to breaking down his body.

"You just get used to a certain kind of lifestyle," said Joe, who had built a house in Norman, where he was serving as an assistant track coach at the University of Oklahoma.

As a consequence of competing in more meets, Joe ran the risk of becoming more susceptible to injuries. The increased wear and tear on his 26 year old body gradually started to take its toll. His body, beaten down by the stress that pole vaulting inflicts, resulted in frequent injuries that required several surgeries on his knees, on a disc in his neck, and then later in his lower back.

His aspirations as a world-class vaulter seemed to be coming to an end.

But yet the oncoming year of 1988 seemed to be his best opportunity to make the U.S. Olympic team.

"If I was going to make the team, 1988 would have been the year," Joe explained. "I left the sport knowing I hadn't jumped my best."

PART IX

SPREADING THE FAITH

Joe and his wife Shawna, currently an assistant coach, are one of a very few husband and wife coaching teams in NCAA Division I in any sport. The fact that they share coaching duties at a Christ-centered university provides them the unique opportunity to help shape and influence the lives of many college-age young adults, athletes and non-athletes alike.

Founded to educate the whole person — spirit, mind and body — Oral Roberts University has students from all 50 states as well from some 90 international countries. The university's stated Vision is as follows:

Oral Roberts University is a charismatic university, founded in the fires of evangelism and upon the unchanging precepts of the Bible. The university was founded as a result of the evangelist Oral Roberts' obeying God's mandate to build a university on God's authority and the Holy Spirit.

God's commission to Oral Roberts was to:

Raise up your students to hear My voice, to go where My light is dim. where My voice is heard small and My healing power is not known, even to the uttermost bounds of the earth. Their work will exceed yours, and in this I am well pleased.

The University's mission is:

To build Holy Spirit-empowered leaders through whole person education to impact the world with God's healing.

Even at the tender age of nine, Joe vividly remembers the day he was saved at Trinity Baptist Church in Texas City, Texas, where his family was living at the time. The family later moved to Marlow, Oklahoma.

"I remember my mother's brother, Gene Ray, had come down that Sunday and preached at the church. He had served as a missionary in Costa Rica. He did an altar call and I went down there and felt in my heart it was the proper thing to do. I've always been conscious of that commitment that I made so long ago. Even all the way through high school and college into the present, it's always been a focus that's kept me on an even keel. Life can be stressful at times so you have to have something to fall back on. My faith has always been that solid foundation for me to rely on.

"I was active in the Fellowship of Christian Athletes in high school at Marlow under Coach Ken Lane. I was also a youth pastor at a small non-denominational church in Tryon, Oklahoma, for a period of about six months during my sophomore year at OSU. Tim Skitt, the young man for whom I later became guardian, was in that group as well. (See Part VIII — A Painful Death.). It was just a small group of about ten kids. My junior year at OSU I had a lot of Bible studies at my apartment in Stillwater," Joe explained.

Joe and Shawna also conducted Bible studies for junior college students when Joe was coaching at NEO A&M in Miami, Oklahoma.

"We served as dorm parents and we lived in a small apartment at the bottom of the residence hall," Shawna recalls. "We did lots of Bible studies for the kids."

The Dials' witness and service with young people continued as they moved on to Oral Roberts University in Tulsa, Oklahoma, and Joe moved on up to the head coaching position for both men's and women's track teams.

"As a husband and wife coaching team, we try to live the life and provide good examples for our athletes and students," Joe commented.

Shawna explains how she and Joe counseled a specific former university athlete early in their ORU tenure and cites the example of how the situation evolved with positive and beneficial results.

"We had one athlete from years ago who actually came to us after he had graduated. He was a good kid who went to school, did everything he was supposed to, and went on to graduate. We ran into him several years later and he told us, 'I just wanted to tell you guys that I was raised around the church and heard a lot of preaching through the years, but I watched you guys over the time that I was here and you were living what you were selling. What you told us and what you did were not two different things. I just wanted you two to know that you played a huge part in me getting saved after I graduated from college,'" Shawna related.

"That was overwhelming to hear, and it was obviously great to hear, but many times you don't get that feedback. You may never know how and to what extent you might have impacted a student's life," Shawna said.

Joe explained how in some situations, and that as difficult it may be to fully comprehend, failure may often be a proper first step in helping a student ultimately achieve their life's objectives.

"As much as my dad loved me, he used to let me fail. I think that actually can be a good thing in certain situations. Sometimes it may best to let people fail so they can become stronger from the experience," Joe opined.

One other prime example of how the Dials reached out to help others involved two young victims from Hurricane Katrina that hit the Gulf Coast in August, 2005.

Shawna tells the story:

"When Katrina hit New Orleans and the Gulf area, all the schools and universities there just shut down. Many of the college kids got shipped to Houston and wherever and were simply stranded. Most of them had no idea what to do or what was going to happen to them.

"There were two girls from Zimbabwe, Africa, attending college in New Orleans on track scholarships. Once their school was closed, they were sent to Houston on a bus and simply got stuck in Houston. They didn't know anybody and had no idea what their next step should be. They were pretty much on their own. Being from Zimbabwe, they had no idea what to do."

Shawna and Joe still don't know who told these girls this but a mutual acquaintance in Houston apparently gave them Joe's phone number and told them to call Joe and to inquire if he could possibly help. So they did just that.

Joe's initial response was that he would try to do what he could simply in order to help the two stranded athletes.

"We've never experienced quite anything like this, and it was a whole new situation for all of us, but I wanted to help simply as a person, not necessarily as a coach," Joe explained.

With the Gulf Coast devastated and the area colleges and universities not knowing when, or if, they would re-open, all the impacted athletes were granted total releases, thereby being free to transfer to any school of their choice and becoming immediately eligible without incurring any penalties of sitting out a year as is normally the case when transferring.

As fate would have it, Oral Roberts University had two available scholarships. It was decided that those scholarships would be awarded to the two girls from Zimbabwe.

Joe, later citing divine guidance, called the girls back with news that would ultimately impact the two in ways that no one could reasonably expect.

"I'll take you both. If you can get a bus ticket to Tulsa, we'll give you a scholarship and you can move into our dorms right way on be on our track team," Joe told them.

The rest as they say is history.

After an interim semester at Louisiana State University, the two young ladies ultimately scraped up sufficient money to purchase two one-way bus tickets to Tulsa where they were met and brought to the ORU campus at 81st Street and Lewis in Tulsa. Not knowing a soul either at ORU or in the City of Tulsa, the two young ladies were welcomed into the ORU family and became a part of the women's track team in time for the spring semester and a new track season.

"They both became great runners for us. They both graduated from ORU and both continued with their education. Today, they both are doctors. One actually just moved back to Tulsa. What a wonderful contribution to their family and to be able to make such an important difference in their families' lives. And to think, it just got tossed into our laps. Who knows what would have happened if Joe had not taken that call and offered to help the girls recover from their predicament?" Shawna asked.

Joe and Shawna also were involved in a personal missions trip to assist children in the South American country of Paraguay.

"The first day we met President William Wilson, ORU president, and he told us about an orphanage in Paraguay and that the kids living there run track as an activity," Joe recalled.

President Wilson's daughter, Sara Morton, and her husband Shaun served as directors of Hogar El Camino, a Christian home for abandoned children and the New Path Christian School. "Hogar El Camino" means "The Path" Children's Home.

President Wilson remarked about how exciting it would be if one of the children from the Paraguay home would someday attend Oral Roberts and participate on the University's track and field team.

Shawna Dial pointed out to President Wilson that one of the University's former athletes, Cami Parelli, was from Paraguay and that she holds eight national track and field records in her native country. A recent Oral Roberts University graduate who competed in the hepthathlon for ORU, Parelli is now residing back in Paraguay.

"She is the premier athlete in Paraguay. She is in television commercials and everything," Joe noted.

Joe also explained that he and Shawna contacted Parelli in Paraguay and assisted in coordinating her traveling to the orphanage where she helped the children in their track sessions, providing tips on running, and improving their technique.

After learning of the children's delight and enjoyment in learning and participating in track and field activities, Shawna asked Joe why couldn't they make a trip to Paraguay themselves and assist the children in their track and field activities first-hand?

In no time, Joe had touched base with some of his friends in the track and field business including Gill Athletics, who manufacturers track and field equipment, and asked if they would donate some equipment.

Soon Joe and Shawna had accumulated a variety of track and field equipment, including starting blocks, hurdles, relay batons, and stop watches that soon found their way to Paraguay along with Joe and Shawna in the summer of 2015.

"We stayed for five days and we had a great time. The kids ran on a dirt track that surrounded a grass soccer field. The kids loved doing track. We put the hurdles up and set out the starting blocks. The kids were on cloud nine. They had been using starting blocks that were literally made of a piece of wood and a big nail. When they got these new blocks, they couldn't believe it. They stayed out practicing in the dark that first day because they were so excited," Joe explained.

"We ate at a different house every night with all the little kids. We got so much fulfillment from helping the little kids. They are so much in need down there," Joe said.

Another charitable endeavor involved a trip to Taiwan that Joe made in 1989. Competing in the last meet of his season, Joe decided to bequeath his vaulting poles to the local Taiwanese track and field athletes who were lacking an adequate supply of poles. Joe had no idea as to who, how or when any Taiwanese vaulter would benefit from Joe's gift.

Fast forward to the year 2014.

Some twenty-five years later, Joe received a Facebook message from Hung En Hsu, a Taiwanese pole vaulter from that era, who had been a beneficiary of Joe's earlier gift of the poles. Now the National Pole Vault Coach for Taiwan, Hung had searched out and located Joe on Facebook and thanked him for the poles.

Hung later sent his son, Jimmy, also a pole vaulter, over to the States where Jimmy trained under Joe for three weeks.

Apparently, Jimmy was a quick learner under Joe's tutelage.

"While he was here, he was able to increase his height from 14-8 to 15-6," Joe said.

The Dials also credit the Green Family for providing the stable on-campus environment that fosters not only learning in the classroom but excellence on the athletic fields of competition as well.

"The Green Family has just done a tremendous job — just incredible — of restoring the university and setting it up for success. It's tough to compete in all the sports right now, but it's definitely better here than it's been for a long time," Joe explained.

Mart Green is the founder and Chief Executive Officer of Mardel Christian and Educational Supply and an heir to the Hobby Lobby family of companies which was founded by Mart's father, David Green.

The Greens pledged a $70 million gift to Oral Roberts University in November 2007, an amount sufficient to retire much of the university's debt. Mart Green became the new Chairman of the Board of Trustees at ORU, a position in which he served from January 2008 to April 2014.

PART X

SHARING THE KNOWLEDGE

Joe featured in GQ Magazine

Joe appeared in the May, 1988, issue of *Gentlemen's Quarterly* Magazine. The issue highlighted "Total Summer Fitness" as illustrated by several of the top American athletes who had their sights on participating in the 1988 Olympic Games in Seoul, South Korea.

Joe and the other athletes featured in the article share with readers how they train for the different events, as well as how they condition their bodies for the intense competition they put themselves through in their pursuit for an Olympic gold medal.

An interesting side note is that Joe had heard unofficially that he was slated to be on the cover of this particular issue. However, Olympic gold medal diver Greg Louganis hit his head on a diving board while in a competition and then became the cover subject for the May 1988, issue, knocking Joe off the cover.

The Table of Contents of the magazine teases the article, "Total Summer Fitness" with the following:

How do they do it? If you want to better your personal best, heed the workout wisdom of four top-form Olympians, each at the top of their game: Terry Schroeder (water polo), Joe Dial (pole vault), Karch Kiraly (volleyball); and Dan Haden (gymnastics).

The article on Joe in its entirety follows:

Joe Dial

Joe Dial is living proof that a talent for pole vaulting can be considered hereditary. His eldest brother, older by twelve years, was state champion in 1969, and his dad, Dean, who is also his coach, would have been one too most likely — if only he'd not had that car accident on the way to the state regionals. At that, Dean still long jumped — with a cast on his broken arm — and came in second.

"My dad and I know more about the vault than anyone," Joe Dial contends. He's been known to get a little contentious about the subject at times. At the NCAA meet in Dallas back in 1985, for example, he got into a scuffle with another premier vaulter, Billy Olson (who is about forty pounds heavier), right after Dial had set a new American record. But this was nothing compared with the fights Dial has had off the track trying to get his six or so seventeen-foot fiberglass poles onto different types of transportation.

"It's incredible," Dial laments, "The airlines always tell you the poles can't go on, and, of course, they always do. You just have to talk them into it."

In fact, after Dial set the current American record — nineteen feet six and a half inches — at the World Championships in Rome last summer, he had to abandon the poles he's used and has yet to get them back. "They're just settin' over there."

The amazing thing about the 25-year-old Dial is his complete unflappability. Partially it's the result of being in a sport where "you either do it or you don't."

When asked who his main competition will be at Seoul, he answers, "Oh, I don't know. Probably the French guys. I could care less who the competition is." Everybody, though knows the man to beat is Sergey Bubka of the Soviet Union, the world-record holder at nineteen feet nine and a half inches."

Aware of the vagaries of his sport, Dial is first concentrating on making the American team, the final three who go to the Olympics. "With the pole vault, you never know," he says. "But even when I'm jumping my best, I feel I can beat anybody, even Bubka."

Maybe it was all oil gushers in Marlow, Oklahoma, that inspired Joe Dial and family. Joe was jumping six hours a day in his front yard when he was still in grade school and just going higher until he made the 1984 Olympic team as an alternate (although he did not compete).

He's been, as he puts it, "the best ever since."

Nowadays, he trains and coaches at the University of Oklahoma in Norman; spends a lot of time with his wife of a year and a half, Shawna (they met in church in Oklahoma City), and their 8-month-old son, Timmy Joe; goes to meets; and does endorsements "to make some money."

It hasn't been all lofty times for Dial, though. His and Shawna's adopted son died suddenly last year, right after Dial set the American record. So he's had more than his fair share of his ups and downs, but in his family, there's no choice but to dial the bar a little higher.

A Vaulter's Bag

Every athlete has his tricks of the trade. For Dial, it's the tool bag. Before he begins jumping, he always marks precisely where he wants to grasp the pole. Then he wraps tape — sticky side up — around that area, for a solid grip. For an even better hold, Dial gives the tape a few blasts of high-tack spray.

When Dial needs to have both feet planted firmly on the ground, he wears Zoom Ultras, Nike's new shoes for track and field. The shoes are designed for distance running, but, as Dial found out, they're "great for pole vaulting." The shoes' spikes are good for traction and for gripping synthetic tracks. They have built-in air units for extra cushioning.

The High and the Mighty

You have to train to be in top physical shape, and running and lifting weights is the bulk of it," says Joe Dial. "When I'm training hard, I work out five to six days a week, one to four hours a day, running, lifting and jumping."

Dial focuses at different points in his training on his legs, upper body and stamina — then he puts it all together.

"I concentrate on endurance early in the season by running about 300 yards at an even pace, Then I focus on quickness and power by cutting my reps down when weight lifting and by doing short sprints."

Like most athletes, Dial varies his weight workout every day.

"One way to do that is to work the lower body one day and the upper body the next. Or do pushes one day — like a bench press, where you're pushing the weight away from your body. Then pulls the next — bicep curls, where you pull the weight towards you."

How do you know if you're in great pole vaulting shape? 'You feel real good running down the runway — strong and fast," says Dial.

"It's really a pole vault high when it all comes together, and you can just put a pole in your hand and it's easy to jump. You get a sense of confidence. When I'm in good pole vaulting shape, I know when I step on the runway that I'm going to jump over nineteen feet. I'm at my best."

One key: Always maintain the body weight at which you jump best. You can become fatigued easily if you're overweight and tire even more if you're too light.

"If I drop below my normal body weight, 150 pounds, I get into trouble" says Dial. "Then it doesn't take too long for me to peak out."

Weight Training

After ten to fifteen jumps, Dial hits the weight room for forty-five minutes to two hours.

You can't do it all in one day," he says. "So on Monday and Thursday, I do upper body, and on Tuesday and Friday, I do lower body. All this in one day would take about four or five hours."

Even though pole vaulting is the best way for Dial to tone his gut, he still does about fifty sit-ups every other day.

"Your abdominals are the stabilizers of your body," he says.

"If your stomach is strong, the rest of your body is usually strong, and you can coordinate everything a lot better."

The Hamstring Stretch

"If you stretch before warming up," says Dial, "you are more prone to injury, such as a muscle tear or strain.

"Before you take the big leap, run, jog or bicycle for ten minutes to raise your body temperature. Then carefully stretch.

"I concentrate on stretching out my hamstrings because they're usually the easiest to strain. Any injury can happen, but usually the hamstrings are the tendons that would put you out for a long time."

With Back Benefits

Stretching the hamstrings and hip flexors keeps the pelvis from tilting forward and putting extra stress on the lower back area. Stretching and strengthening the abdominal muscles is a must. Faster than other muscle groups, stomach muscles tend to become soft and slack as the years go by, putting strain on the lower back.

After stretching, Dial does high knee kicks, running in place quickly while lifting his knees as high as he can, to get his body prepared for a run.

Oklahoma All-Century Track and Field Team

In the summer of 1999, *The Oklahoman* newspaper selected an Oklahoma All-Century high school track team, as well as a post-high school team. Joe was selected as the pole vaulter for each team, the only athlete so recognized as a member of both teams.

The pole vault event seemed to be Oklahoma's premier track and field event with Joe and J.D. Martin, who both were world champions and NCAA Champions multiple times. In addition, the State of Oklahoma also produced three other NCAA pole vault champions, Tim McMichael, Jim Graham and Frank Potts.

Risky business

Pole vaulting can be a dangerous sport and is definitely not for the faint of heart. Joe sustained a number of injuries through the years he competed. Several of the injuries still cause him pain even today.

A quick recap of his major injuries:

• Two broken toes on right foot. Joe had ventured into taking karate lessons in an effort to increase his flexibility which is of primary importance to a pole vaulter. During one sparring session, Joe noticed his small toe on his right foot was angled out at 90 degrees. Another time, another toe was broken when running across a room and he hit his foot into a bed frame.

• Fallen arches on both feet. Through the thousands, if not the millions, of steps Joe has taken through the years, fallen arches are often a natural result of such wear and tear.

• Dislocated right ankle — Joe suffered this dislocation back during his high school days during a meet at Duncan High School when he landed awkwardly in the vaulting pit. After an extremely painful initial period immediately following the accident, the injury amazingly cleared up the next day and it has never affected him since even though the ankle bone protrudes from the side of his foot. Doctors have told him the bone simply "froze" in its present position after the dislocation and should cause no further problems.

• Stress fracture in right leg. The constant pressure and pounding from the years of training and competing would often result in stress fractures, especially towards the end of a long season. Usually, a little rest and time-off would heal this ailment.

• Surgeries on both knees, including partial reconstruction of his left knee. This particular injury was previously described in an earlier section of the book. In summary, what Joe anticipated to be a somewhat minor surgical procedure with a 10-day recovery period, actually turned into a major operation with an expected nine-month recovery period, which Joe reduced down to six months.

• Tendon tear above left knee. After setting the American record of 19-4¼ in 1986, Joe then attempted 19-7 and he suffered a tendon tear. "It was a really bad tear," Joe said."It took two full months to recover."

• Eight hamstring pulls in left leg. With the left leg being Joe's "take-off leg" in vaulting, it always incurred an enormous amount of stress and pressure.

• Severe quad pull in left leg. In 1988, a teammate assisting Joe in practice pushed him in the hips rather than in the back resulting a serious quad pull that required a couple of months for recovery.

• A bone was cut out of his hip because the bone was needed for neck surgery. "My hip hurt forever and I couldn't even run for a long time." With this particular surgery taking place in late 1991, Joe had precious little time for a full recovery in order to prepare for the 1992 Olympic Trials. But four months after surgery, Joe cleared 19 feet.

• Ruptured and herniated disks contributed to six back surgeries and one neck surgery. Joe explained that vaulting places massive pressure on the back so this condition is often a necessary evil of the sport.

• Torn rotator cuff in right shoulder. With the enormous amount of pressure exerted on the right shoulder during the take-off, this is a frequent injury.

• Torn tendon in right elbow. A tremendous amount of stress and tension is placed on the right elbow by right-handed pole vaulters. Something as basic as shaking hands still causes Joe pain to this day.

• Torn tendon in right index finger. Joe suffered this injury during a meet in Sao Paulo, Brazil. The old standby of applying tape was the remedy.

• Broken left wrist. This resulted from a fall during the ninth grade basketball season. Anxious to return to the basketball court with his teammates, Joe removed the cast after four days and used a splint instead. The one game that Joe sat out was the team's lone loss that season.

• Possible concussions. Dropping 19 feet from the sky can be inherently dangerous.

OSU's Top Ten athletes of all time

In 2004, *Daily Oklahoman* sports columnists John Rohde and Berry Tramel assembled their list of the top 10 careers from athletes who attended OSU. Here is what they determined along with a brief description of each:

1. John Smith: Six-time world champion wrestler.

2. Barry Sanders: Put his face on the NFL's Mount Rushmore.

3. Joe Dial: Pole vault world record holder.

4. Allie Reynolds: Best pitcher on the New York Yankees' greatest dynasty.

5. Michele Smith: One of the world's best softball pitchers for a decade.

6. Thurman Thomas: Only slightly behind in Sanders in NFL production.

7. J.W. Mashburn: Olympic gold-medal sprinter.

8. Bob Kurland: Pioneer giant in basketball.

9. Bob Tway: PGA champion.

10. Leslie O'Neal: Potential NFL Hall of Famer.

Good Samaritan

This anonymous "Letter to the Editor" appeared in the *Tulsa World* in 2008:

"Thanks for help in the sun"

"I would like to thank the kind man who helped me when I ran out of gasoline in the hot midday sun on South Elwood. The man got my AAA card, went back to his home, called them, came back with his van, brought me a bottle of water and let me sit in his air-conditioned van until AAA arrived.

He was the track coach at ORU. Thank you."

When asked about the details, Joe recalls that this incident involved an elderly gentleman but in his always humble nature, Joe merely explains it as "no big deal."

"It's nothing that anyone else wouldn't have done on a hot day," he claims.

Still has his fans

Even today, some twenty years after his last competition and over thirty years after his collegiate days, fans still recognize Joe and often stop him and engage in conversation.

"When I go to a high school track meet, I hardly ever get up to go somewhere, even to the rest room. Invariably, people will stop me and want to talk about my pole vaulting. It seems it takes me forever to get around.

"When I do walk somewhere at a meet, I just try to keep my head down and walk quickly," Joe adds.

Perhaps it is someone who Joe hasn't seen in 15 years who simply wants to catch up with Joe, or a fan who watched Joe vault at some big meet in the past, or even someone who competed against Joe in high school. He has encountered all these types. But when recognized, Joe is glad to accommodate the people.

While being bothered or interrupted perhaps may be a nuisance at times, Joe doesn't mind, but rather, he looks at the bright side.

"It's good for recruiting," Joe said as he smiled.

PART XI

COACHING CAREER

"The satisfaction from coaching is just as good or even better than competing. Setting world records is really no different than winning conference championships. It all produces the same thrill."

— **JOE DIAL** REFLECTING ON THE
COMPARISON OF COACHING
AND COMPETING.

UNIVERSITY OF OKLAHOMA; NORMAN, OKLAHOMA

An old friend and mentor calls

In 1985 Joe started serving as an assistant track coach at the University of Oklahoma under head track coach J.D. Martin and he served in that position for three years. Joe's primary duties during this stint included coaching the Sooner pole vaulters. In the third season, his duties expanded to coaching the long jumpers, primarily helping the jumpers improve their technique on their runway approach. Recruiting also was on Joe's list of responsibilities. Joe's level of personal success in pole vaulting played an instrumental role in his helping encourage vaulters to come to the University of Oklahoma.

Terry Womack, who jumped 17-10½ when he was previously at OSU, transferred to OU at the same time that Joe came on board at OU.

"After arriving at OU, Terry jumped 18-1 and was named a two-time All-American," Joe recalled.

Jeff Hanoch, who pole vaulted 18-1, Tim McMichaels and Perry Hottel also greatly benefited from Joe's expertise as well. All four vaulters advanced to compete at NCAA Outdoor Championship meets under Joe's guidance.

"As I started to do more in the coaching profession, I realized that I really wanted to expand my role as a track coach. I wanted to have the opportunity to coach more than just a couple of events," Joe explained.

He would soon receive that opportunity.

NEO A&M COLLEGE; MIAMI, OKLAHOMA

Gaining valuable experience in all aspects

The 1988-89 academic year was a milestone year in Joe's life from the coaching perspective. It was the year that Joe first gained experience as a coach over an entire collegiate team in his quest to expand his coaching abilities.

Joe accepted the position of assistant track coach at Northeastern Oklahoma A&M College and moved to Miami, Oklahoma, in far northeastern Oklahoma.

"I went there to learn and to be able to help coach all the events. I thought it would definitely benefit me to gain the experience of learning and coaching all the events. I felt that we were successful as we had several athletes who did well on the national level," Joe explained.

Among those athletes from NEO A&M gaining national recognition were Mike Hines who won the National Junior Collegiate Athletic Association pole vault title with a jump of 17 feet, 10½ inches, breaking the national junior college record. Another one of his pole vaulters, Todd Brockoff, placed third, and a long jumper and the 4x400 meter relay team also placed high in the national competition.

In addition to his coaching responsibilities, Joe and his wife Shawna served as dorm parents during their one year stay at NEO A&M.

"Shawna was just 19 years old at the time. She was actually younger than several of the students that she was looking after," Joe laughed.

But perhaps the coaching-related experience Joe gained off the track and pole vault runways was even more valuable from a long-term perspective.

"I had a great relationship with all the kids. We (Shawna and Joe) started a Bible study for the kids that was well attended," Joe explained.

But Joe eventually found that the head track coach was somewhat difficult with which to work. The environment could be described as "toxic" at times and not particularly conducive to the proper development of young, impressionable athletes. Disrespecting his athletes, name-calling, and discipline issues brought on by the head coach were just some of the issues Joe had to face from his position as assistant coach.

With Joe being the sole assistant coach on the track and field staff, it was up to Joe to smooth over the rocky relationships that often existed between the head coach and the athletes.

"I think that experience really helped prepare me for all types of situations that I might find in the coaching profession. Looking back at it now, I think it really helped me grow as a coach," Joe explained.

After the academic year at NEO A&M was completed, Joe and Shawna moved back to Oklahoma City where they lived until the fall of 1992 when they moved to Tulsa.

TULSA UNION HIGH SCHOOL; TULSA, OKLAHOMA

Called on by an "Angel of Light"

Discouraged after his performance at the 1992 Olympic Trials, frustrated with a succession of what seemed like a streak of bad luck and incurring a seemingly endless rash of injuries, Joe seriously entertained thoughts of leaving the sport which he loved so much.

Still seeking to better himself for his family's benefit, Joe was exploring all possible options.

Joe had a friend who was living in Tulsa who was operating a lawn care service.

Joe had helped this friend previously by giving him six months free rent at one of his rental houses. The friend reciprocated by providing Joe's family free rent for a period of time until they could get back on their feet. The friend, whose lawn business had greatly grown more than he could adequately handle, offered Joe the opportunity to mow and care for one of their major accounts, Taco Bueno, a chain of Mexican fast food restaurants.

Once settled in Tulsa, Joe and Shawna's son Tim attended Tulsa Union Junior High and was quite an impressive athlete in his own right. Participating in football, basketball and, of course, track, Tim excelled in all three sports. On the track team, he was — what else — a pole vaulter.

Joe especially enjoyed teaching Tim the intricacies of pole vaulting and took great pride in witnessing how much Tim improved under his guidance.

Joe's impressive level of knowledge and his coaching efforts were soon noticed by others as well.

In the spring of 1993, Tulsa Union High School head track coach Terry Collins asked Joe if he would like to help out as an assistant track coach on the high school level, and Joe quickly accepted the offer. Joe soon found himself in charge of coaching athletes in the two events that were very personal to him — the vaulters and long jumpers.

"Coach Collins was an angel of light for me because I was out of coaching, which I realized was my passion. At that particular time in my life, I just didn't see a way I was going to get back in coaching. That is, until Coach Collins called me," Joe explained.

ORAL ROBERTS UNIVERSITY; TULSA, OKLAHOMA

Getting a foot in the door at ORU

As in many situations in the coaching profession, it is a matter of being in the right place at the right time.

"The summer of 1993, Bruce Dial, my nephew from Missouri ended up being ranked the number one high school pole vaulter in the country. I had coached him in the past and he wanted me to continue coaching him," Joe explained.

"About that time, the head track coach at Oral Roberts University, Claude Roumain, whom I would see and talk to at many of the summer track meets, told me if I could get my nephew to ORU, they would get him a scholarship. I also would be able to coach the field events, and the university would provide housing for my family."

Joe agreed to the part-time coaching assignment while still maintaining his lucrative lawn business.

Then in February, 1994, Bob Brooks, the ORU Athletic Director, called Joe and informed him that with Coach Roumain leaving ORU, the head track coach position was his.

As in many similar situations when taking over a program, there were some issues that were of concern to Joe that required his attention and which he needed to address. Joe initially agreed to fulfill the position for three months until the end of the spring semester, just to ensure that he would be a good fit for the job.

"I served the three months, resolving the issues that had initially concerned me and rediscovered that coaching was extremely fun. Now, 24 years later, I am still here. I found dealing with the kids was the best aspect of the job. Plus we had a good team. We experienced a lot of success," Joe explained.

What made Joe's level of success remarkable was the fact that he was the sole track and field coach overseeing a total of seventy-some Division I collegiate athletes, male and female. Perhaps what aided Joe in connecting so successfully with his athletes could be attributed to his youthfulness at the time, being only 31 years old when he became head coach.

"I was the youngest head track coach in Division I at the time," Joe explained.

"We had lots of good athletes. But many of the athletes at that time didn't know what was required from them in order to compete on that level. I had to show them how to compete. I ran with them. I lifted weights with them. I worked out with them. They saw firsthand how committed I was. Once they saw how hard I worked and how committed I was to our program, that help them develop a stronger work ethic and drew us closer as a team," Joe explained.

This change in the team's overall culture and philosophy would soon pay handsome dividends as the Oral Roberts University men's and women's track teams, under the guidance of Coach Dial, would begin to dominate the sport of track and field in their conference. As evidence of the influence and leadership Coach Dial brought to his squads, the Golden Eagles collected a number of conference championships. Six men's indoor titles, one men's outdoor title, six women's indoor titles and two women's outdoor titles, plus two titles in women's cross country were accumulated.

The conference coaches also recognized the importance of Coach Dial's contributions as he was awarded a number of Conference Coach of the Year Awards as well. Seven men's indoor track awards, five women's indoor and two women's outdoor Coach of the Year Awards all spoke to Coach Dial's dedication to making his teams they best they could be.

Coaching help is on the way

Early in his ORU coaching career, Joe was a truly a one-man coaching staff for a NCAA Division I men's and women's track and field program. With the demand of performing the necessary administrative duties, completing and submitting the required paperwork and reports, checking and monitoring the academic progress of his student-athletes, making travel arrangements and reservations for his teams as they competed around the Midwestern United States as well as completing arrangements for recruiting visits, Joe was being pulled in so many different directions that his time to actually coach track and field was slowly shrinking.

Something had to be done.

Enter Shawna Dial.

She decided to come into the office whenever she needed to help relieve some of the load on Joe's shoulders.

"I took over all the administrative duties of the head coaching job strictly as a volunteer for two years," Shawna explained.

After those two years of serving as an unpaid volunteer, one of the university's assistant athletic directors took notice of Shawna's contributions to the track team.

"This is not right that you're doing all this work for nothing. Others are getting paid for doing this type of work," the assistant AD noted of Shawna's efforts.

A small $2,000 stipend was available and given to Shawna for her work in the track and field program.

That arrangement continued for a few years until such time as the amount of work and time required to fulfill the responsibilities dictated that the position be upgraded to a full-time position in 1994.

Shawna describes why she appreciates coaching at ORU: "One of things that has been a blessing to be here at ORU is family. Family didn't have to be on the outside of your job here. Family can be a part of your job. For example, if I had to go to a track meet, our boys could go with us. Or if Joe had a meet someplace for ORU and Tommy had a track meet, I would be free to go with Tommy to watch him. It's allowed us a lot of flexibility to raise our boys."

Joe shares his recruiting philosophy

As anyone connected to sports is well aware, recruiting is the life blood of any collegiate athletic program. Successful recruiting can take many stances depending upon the particular sport involved, the geographic area, the available budget, the specific needs of the team and perhaps most critical of all, the coach's philosophy and objectives in recruiting.

Joe, being a veteran of almost 40 years of national and international track and field experience, has some definite objectives when he recruits track and field athletes to Oral Roberts University.

"I kind of approach recruiting with one of the primary considerations being age. I look at their age. For an example, if a kid is running 10.7 seconds in the 100 meters, but he is graduating from high school and he is only 17 years old, I'm thinking there is a lot of potential in that kid versus recruiting a kid running the same 10.7 seconds but who is 19 years old.

That was the case of Virgil Mattox (former ORU sprinter who placed third in the 100 meters at the 1999 NCAA Track & Field Championships).

"Everybody was looking at him, but very few were offering anything. I checked his age, his weight and size, his physical condition and body type, and I just knew he would be a great athlete. So I got him here and from age 17 to 18 and from 18 to 19, he just matured physically into a man. He went from being in the top 500 in the U.S. in the high school 100 meters to the top three in the nation at the NCAA Championships. He ran a 10.12 in the 100 meters," Coach Dial explained.

It was the same way with Andretti Bain and Jeffery Gibson, two world-class athletes who hailed from the Bahamas and whom both were recruited to Oral Roberts University by Coach Dial. (Bain won the 400 meters at both the 2008 NCAA Indoor and Outdoor Championships and went on to help lead his native Bahamas team to a silver medal in the men's 4x400 meter relay at the 2008 Beijing Olympic Games. Gibson competed in the 2016 Rio de Janeiro Olympics in the 400 meter hurdles.)

"They (Bain and Gibson) were both 17 years old when they got here. With that young age and then I looked at their frame. A real slender, almost skinny, kid at age 17, can really improve in just a few years.

"I saw Jack Whitt (ORU pole vaulter who went on to capture the 2012 NCAA outdoor pole vault championship) vault 14-6 at a track meet during his senior year in high school. I decided then he was my guy. I saw all his potential —his approach down the runway, his pole plant, and his body control. I just knew at some point this guy is going to be great," Joe explained.

"When Joe offered Jack a full scholarship everyone said he was crazy," Shawna interjected.

During the recruiting process, Jack's father had emailed Coach Dial regarding Jack. After asking the ORU Athletics compliance official if it would be permissible to reply and getting such approval, Coach Dial responded.

"So I emailed Jack's father back and this is what I wrote: 'This is what I see with Jack: I could turn him into a NCAA pole vault champion and a world-class pole vaulter.'"

Jack's father retained that particular email through the years.

"After Jack won the NCAA title, graduated from ORU and signed a contract with Nike, Jack's father sent that email back to me and told me, 'I guess you did see the potential,'" Coach Dial related.

"I guess you could say my coaching philosophy is kind of a combination of the coaches I have had. I have had some really great coaches from grade school, then high school and then from Coach Tate from Oklahoma State. He was just a master at communications. He could get you excited about your event and any meet," Joe added.

Uncanny ability for total recall

Anyone who knows Joe is aware of his unusual ability to remember events and details to an infinite degree, especially as they relate to track and field. That particular skill, along with his penchant to totally recall and replay events mentally, proves to be especially useful in the coaching environment.

"One thing that is extremely interesting that I have noticed about Joe is his uncanny ability to replay something in his mind," his wife Shawna explains.

"When he pole vaulted, it was like he could watch himself after the jump. Another thing that he has mentioned to me was that when he was pole vaulting, everything seemed to slow down for him. It was easier for him to make any adjustments while up in the air. It would actually happen really fast, but in his mind it was happening a lot slower," she added.

"I think the more you do stuff, the more repetition you do, everything starts slowing down for you," Joe said.

As a coach, the ability to mentally replay events is extremely important. For example, while coaching a pole vaulter from the sidelines, Joe says he can see the whole jump, then re-watch it in his mind, and then he is able to discuss with the athlete and provide suggestions or tips for improvement.

"Another interesting item is that every time Joe stepped on a runway to vault, especially at the University of Oklahoma where he had so much success as a vaulter on that particular runway, people always expected him to break the American record. He could jump 19 feet and people would ask what's wrong? People seemed to get accustomed to his high degree of success and always expected a record performance from him," Shawna explains.

"If he had a bad meet, which didn't happen very often, he would be extremely quiet on the way home. Early on when I was new to the whole aspect of pole vaulting, I would try to talk to him and tell him that everything was ok. But he was always so quiet. I finally learned to be quiet and just let him sit there. Obviously what he was doing was replaying the whole meet in his head. Once he figured out what he did wrong, he would simply turn around and say, 'I now know what I have to fix.' And then everything would be back to normal. I learned to let him have his quiet time so he could replay everything in his mind," Shawna adds.

Another uncanny trait of Joe's is his incredible talent to totally recall virtually every small detail of just about every jump he has ever attempted. The meet location, height, the specific weather conditions, wind speed and direction, the pole size, where he gripped the pole, how he felt physically, how many attempts he had, who the other competitors were and the heights they missed and when they were eliminated are filed away in Joe's mind and can be instantly recalled as though it is stored in a computerized data base. He has possessed this unique skill as far back as his high school meets and considering the hundreds of meets and the thousands of vaults he has performed, the ability of such total and complete recall is remarkable.

A look to the future

Imagine trying to recruit three or four star-rated football players to a Division I collegiate program that didn't have its own football stadium and was forced to play all their games on the road. Or imagine attempting to entice basketball players to commit to play at a university without a home court on campus.

That is exactly the scenario that Coach Dial faced as head track and field coach at Oral Roberts University for 24 years. Without an on-campus track facility, Coach Dial and his Golden Eagle team members would often make the four-mile trek to Jenks High School in order to train on their track.

But starting with the 2017-2018 academic year, that hurdle should be cleared as the ONEOK Sports Complex, including an all-weather, eight-lane, state-of-the-art track, will be completed and open for competition.

The University's first ever on-campus track facility besides offering the opportunity to conduct home meets, also played a significant role in recruiting.

In April 2017, with the conclusion of the spring signing period and as

SHAWNA AND JOE DIAL ADMIRING THE RECENTLY INSTALLED SURFACE OF THE NEW TRACK. LANE MARKINGS WERE STILL TO BE ADDED.

the track construction was nearing completion, Coach Dial was ecstatic at the prospects he had signed and credited a significant part of the recruiting success to the excitement accompanying the installation of the new track.

"The construction of our new track facility is not even complete yet, but it is already making a positive impact for our program," said Joe. "This has to be the finest overall recruiting class that we've had during my time at ORU."

Not only did the prospect of the new track attracted new incoming recruits, the promise of the gleaming new facility caused several top athletes to redshirt the current season in anticipation of completing their ORU careers on one of the finest new tracks in the country.

The group of track athletes who will enjoy the privilege of breaking in the new facility include several junior college All-Americans, nationally ranked high school athletes and a pair of sprinters who have won medals in international competition, as well as descendants from former outstanding ORU track and field athletes.

Conference Championships

Coach Dial has enjoyed a phenomenal level of coaching success during his career at Oral Roberts University. He has coached his Golden Eagle teams to eighteen conference championships: two in women's cross country; seven in men's indoor track and one in men's outdoor track; and six in women's indoor track and two in women's outdoor track. A recap of the conference championships that Joe's teams have captured:

WOMEN'S CROSS COUNTRY (2)

2005

2006

MEN'S INDOOR TRACK (7)

1997–1998

1998–1999

2000–2001

2001–2002

2002–2003

2004–2005

2005–2006

MEN'S OUTDOOR TRACK (1)

2003

WOMEN'S INDOOR TRACK (6)

1999–2000

2000–01 (Co–Champions)

2001–2002

2004–2005

2005–2006

2006–2007

WOMEN'S OUTDOOR TRACK

2002

2006

In addition to all those conference championships, several coaching honors have come to Coach Dial as well. A summary of coaching honors he has received while serving as head coach at ORU:

MEN'S INDOOR TRACK – CONFERENCE COACH OF THE YEAR (7)

1997–1998
1998–1999
2000–2001
2002–2003
2004–2005
2005–2006
2007–2008

WOMEN'S INDOOR TRACK – CONFERENCE COACH OF THE YEAR (5)

1999–2000
2000–2001
2004–2005
2005–2006
2006–2007

WOMEN'S OUTDOOR TRACK – CONFERENCE COACH OF THE YEAR (2)

2002
2006

Joe was named the U.S. Track and Field and Cross Country Coaches Association (USTFCCCA) 2006 Midwest Region Men's Coach of the Year for the outdoor season, after leading the Golden Eagles to a ranking as high as 16th in the USTFCCCA Division I poll.

Joe has also coached 48 Golden Eagle All-Americans during his coaching stint at ORU with those athletes earning All-American honors in almost 30 different events.

Among the more prominent athletes Coach Dial has mentored through his tenure at ORU are Garth Robinson, who was ORU's first Olympic medalist and Andretti Bain. Robinson, from Jamaica, ran a leg on his nation's 4x400 meter relay team in the 1996 Atlanta Olympics and claimed a bronze medal. He was the first collegian to qualify for three events at an NCAA Indoor Championship meet. Bain, from Nassau, Bahamas, helped his native Bahamas capture the silver medal in the 4x400 meter relay at the

2008 Beijing Olympics. He also claimed a gold medal for the Bahamas in the 2007 Pan American Games in Rio de Janeiro also by running a leg on the 4x400 meter relay. Bain was also the first-ever NCAA National Champion in the history of the university in any sport by capturing first place in the 400 meters in both the 2008 NCAA Indoor and Outdoor Championships. Bain, a four-time All-American also placed eighth in the 400 meters and ran a leg on the 4x400 meter relay team who placed seventh at the 2007 NCAA Indoor Championships. He captured eleven conference championships in four years at ORU.

Jack Whitt is another NCAA track champion developed under Coach Dial's tutelage. A pole vaulter, Whitt benefited immensely from Coach Dial's guidance and mentoring. Whitt, from Norman, Oklahoma, was the 2012 NCAA Outdoor Champion as he cleared 18 feet, 6.5 inches. He was also the runner-up in the 2012 NCAA Indoor Championship Meet. Whitt also claimed the runner-up spot in the 2011 NCAA Outdoor Championship Meet and finished sixth in the 2010 NCAA Indoor Championships. He holds ORU school records in both the indoor and outdoor pole vault events as well as the Summit League Championships record and Southland Conference indoor and outdoor records.

ORU middle distance runner Prince Mumba claimed second place in the 800 meter run at the 2006 NCAA Indoor Championship as well as third place at the 2006 NCAA Outdoor Championships. He also captured ten conference championships during his ORU career. Mumba qualified for the 2012 Olympics in London representing his native Zambia and was honored by being selected as his country's flag bearer. Also at the 2006 NCAA Outdoor Championships, Diana Chelimo took eighth place in the 800 meter run.

ORU sprinter Marvin Bonde took fifth place in the 200 meters at the 2009 NCAA Indoor Championships while Rachel Talbert placed sixth in the discus at the 2008 NCAA Outdoor Championships and captured third in 2010. Shaun Smith placed in the 800 meter run at three different championship meets: eighth place at the 2007 NCAA Indoor Championships; sixth place at the 2007 NCAA Outdoor Championships and sixth place at the 2008 NCAA Indoor Championship Meet.

Marsha Dawkins, a 400-meter runner from ORU, claimed fourth place at the 2003 NCAA Indoor Championships and sixth in the 2003 NCAA Outdoor Championships in that event.

Coach Dial helped his niece, Dena Dial, take seventh place in the pole vault at the 2000 NCAA Indoor Championships and to fifth place at the 2000 NCAA Outdoor Championships as well as qualifying for the 2000 Summer Olympic Track & Field Trials.

Another ORU athlete coached by Coach Dial to qualify for the 2000 Summer Olympic Trials was Virgil Mattox who also finished third in the 100 meters at the 1999 NCAA Outdoor Championships.

Coach Dial also helped ORU pole vaulter Ben Chisum place eighth at the 1999 NCAA Indoor Championships.

PART XII

HALLS OF FAME

A testament to Joe's prominence and standing in the pole vaulting world is the fact that he has been inducted into six different halls of fame.

GOLDEN SOUTH CLASSIC HALL OF FAME

The Golden South Classic Track Meet is one of the most prestigious high school track meets held in the country. It regularly attracts the top high school track and field athletes in the country to Florida to compete.

In May 1981, Joe was invited to compete as he was coming off his fourth consecutive state title. Joe and his vaulting friend, Greg Duplantis from Lafayette, Louisiana, staged a classic battle as they entertained a crowd of approximately 3,000 fans.

The two vaulters did not disappoint. The competition ended as both Joe and Greg cleared 17-4. But with Joe having fewer misses, he was declared the winner.

Not satisfied, both Joe and Greg continued their competition and each attempted 17-10½. If cleared, that height would have been a new national high school record. Joe came to closer as he nearly cleared that height but nicked the crossbar with his hand on the way down.

In recognition of his outstanding and memorable performance, Joe was inducted into the Golden South Classic Hall of Fame in 1986.

OKLAHOMA STATE UNIVERSITY HALL OF HONOR

Joe was inducted into the Oklahoma State University Hall of Honor with the Class of 2002 along with Clinette Jordan (women's basketball); Joe McDaniel (wrestling); Pat Smith (wrestling); Scott Verplank (golf); and John Ward (football and wrestling).

He was nominated for the honor by O-Club Letterwinners Association.

At the induction ceremony, Joe explained his induction into the Oklahoma State University Hall of Honor would be somewhat bittersweet.

Joe would have dearly loved to share his time in the limelight with his father, Dean Dial, who had coached him throughout his career, first at

Marlow High School, then at OSU and later during Joe's professional career. But declining health issues prevented Mr. Dial from attending.

"He's in pretty bad shape. He has trouble breathing (without an oxygen tube)," said Joe.

"He's not doing very good. It's real sad, and it's going to be hard to get up and talk about it because he's the reason that I got as far as I did. There was nobody else."

Joe pole vaulted to four straight state titles at Marlow High School and set a national high school record of 17 feet, 9½ inches during his senior year in 1981 that stood for 18 years.

He was one of the most decorated track athletes in OSU history. Counting indoor and outdoor seasons, he won six Big Eight and four NCAA titles from 1982 through 1985 and won All-American honors seven times.

All this success came under the tutelage of his father, who was a pretty fair pole vaulter himself back in the 1950's.

The younger Dial first started pole vaulting at age five with a broken pole handed down by his older brother Rex's high school coach (Rex Dial won a state championship in pole vaulting in 1969).

"We wore out a lot of picture tubes watching tapes of other pole vaulters," Joe said. 'If there was a good guy he heard about in Louisiana or Kansas, we'd just hop in the car and go there. He wanted me competing against the best in the nation."

Dean Dial continued working with his son when Joe went to OSU in 1981 because then-Cowboy coach Ralph Tate wanted it that way, Dean Dial also coached OSU's other vaulters, and in 1984 Joe Dial and Eric Forney finished first and third in the NCAA Outdoor Championship Meet.

KANSAS RELAYS HALL OF FAME

Since 1923 the Kansas Relays has given track and field fans some amazing stories, and this Hall of Fame is meant to give those stories and the athletes who made them, a vehicle to be remembered for years to come. Individuals are judged only on their impact on the event regardless of their successes in the sport other than this Kansas event held each April. Each class of the Hall of Fame is selected by the vote of alumni, the media, and the Kansas Relays' Greater Relays Committee. Any athlete, coach, official, sponsor or individual associated with the event is eligible for selection. Joe was inducted into the Kansas Relays Hall of Fame, Class of 2007.

As only a high school junior from Marlow, Oklahoma, in 1980, Joe set a national high school record in the pole vault at the Kansas Relays as he cleared 17-5¼. At that meet, he was also named as the Meet's Outstanding Performer, the first time in the history of the Kansas Relays that a high school athlete received such an award.

In 1985, Joe captured a double victory as he won the Collegiate Division with a vault of 18-5 and also the Open Division by clearing 18-8. He also captured his second award for being named the Meet's Outstanding Performer.

In 1987, Joe again won the Open Division of the Relays when he cleared 19-4¾, breaking his own American record in the process.

NATIONAL POLE VAULTING HALL OF FAME

Joe was inducted into the National Pole Vaulting Hall of Fame in 2011 along with fellow pole vaulters Sabin Carr, Nick Hysong, Dan Ripley and Kellie Suttle.

In 1927 Sabin Carr was the first person ever to vault 14 feet both indoors and outdoors. Nick Hysong was the 2000 Sydney Olympic Gold Medalist as he set an Olympic record with a vault of 19-4¼ (5.90 meters). Dan Ripley broke his first world record at 18-1 (5.51 meters) in 1975. He finished his career with several more world records and all-time best of 18-9¼ (5.72 meters). Kellie Suttle was a member of the 2000 and 2004 Olympic teams and in 2001 was the second woman in history to jump 15 feet.

The National Pole Vaulting Hall of Fame is located in Reno, Nevada, and the annual induction ceremonies are held in conjunction with the Reno Pole Vault Summit which attracts hundreds of high school, collegiate and professional pole vaulters from around the world.

NATIONAL HIGH SCHOOL HALL OF FAME

Joe was inducted into the National High School Hall of Fame on July 2, 2017 at Providence, Rhode Island.

The National High School Hall of Fame was started in 1982 by the National Federation of State High School Associations to honor high school athletes, coaches, contest officials, administrators, performing arts coaches/directors and others for their extraordinary achievements and accomplishments in high school sports and performing arts programs. This year's class increased the number of individuals in the Hall of Fame to 458. Inductees are chosen after a two-level selection process involving a screening committee composed of active high school state association administrators, coaches and officials, and a final selection committee composed of coaches, former athletes, state association officials, media representatives and educational leaders. Nominations were made through NFHS member associations.

Joe's biography in the ceremony's program describes his accomplishments:

> Joe Dial was one of the top pole vaulters in high school history during his days at Marlow (Oklahoma) High School in the early 1980s. As a senior in 1981, Dial broke the state and national record with a vault of 17-9½, which stood as the national high school record for 18 years. Although the performance was outside of high school competition, Dial became the first high school athlete to clear 18 feet in the pole vault, and eventually cleared 18-1¼ before concluding his high school career. In addition to his record-setting performance, Dial claimed the state title in the long jump with a 23-5½ effort.
>
> Prior to his record-setting outdoor season as a senior, Dial broke the national record indoors at 17-4½ after eclipsing the mark several times as a junior. In his junior season outdoors, Dial recorded a national best of 17-5¼ at the famed Kansas Relays and was the youngest athlete invited to the 1980 Olympic Trials.
>
> While Dial excelled nationally in the pole vault during his junior and senior years, he dominated the event throughout his four years at Marlow High School as he won the Oklahoma Secondary School Activities Association state title four consecutive years.
>
> Dial was the recipient of numerous honors during his high school days. He was selected to the *Track & Field News* High School All-American team in 1980 and 1981, and was *Track & Field News* High School Athlete of the Year in 1981. He was also named Athlete of the Meet (including high school, college and open divisions) at the 1980 Kansas Relays, was inducted into the Golden South Track Meet Hall of Fame and was the Hertz #1 Award Winner in 1980 and 1981.
>
> Dial's success continued at the next level, where he was a four-time NCAA pole vault champion while competing at Oklahoma State University and was the first collegiate pole vaulter to clear 19 feet. He broke the Big Eight Conference record in 1985 with a vault of 19-1½ and later was inducted into the Oklahoma State University Hall of Fame.
>
> Dial held the American pole vault record for nine years (1985-84), breaking his own record nine times during that span, and was the world record-holder in the event in 1986. His highest vault was 19-6½. he won the bronze medal at the 1989 World Championships in Budapest, Hungary, and, in 2011, he was inducted into the Pole Vault Hall of Fame.
>
> After concluding his career as a participant, Dial joined the athletic department staff

at Oral Roberts University in Tulsa, Oklahoma, in 1993. He became head coach of the men's and women's cross country and track and field teams in 1994 and just completed his 24th season as the Golden Eagles' coach. He has had 70 NCAA championship qualifiers, along with five who advanced to Olympic Trials competition.

Dial was born October 26, 1962, in Marlow, Oklahoma, and currently resides in Tulsa, Oklahoma, where he serves as men's and women's cross country and track and field coach at Oral Roberts University.

The 11 inductees of the 2017 Class included four former high school athletes, five top coaches, one official and one administrator.

In addition to Joe, the athletes included Bobby Richardson (baseball and basketball standout at Edmunds High School in Sumter, South Carolina and former New York Yankee star); Lisa Fernandez (outstanding softball pitcher at St. Joseph's High School in Lakewood, California) and Melissa West (a three-sport standout, basketball, softball and soccer, at Franklin Academy in Malone, New York.

The other two members of the 2017 class are Bill Laude (sports official from Frankfort, Illinois) and Rick Wulkow (an administrator with the Iowa High School Athletic Association).

Joe joins some elite company from the state of Oklahoma. Previous inductees from the Sooner State include Bertha Teague (1983); Johnny Bench (1986); Bill Blackburn (1990); J.C. Watts (2002); John Smith (2004) and Kenny Monday (2011).

MEMBERS OF THE OKLAHOMA SPORTS HALL OF FAME, CLASS OF 2016, MEET PRIOR TO THE INDUCTION CEREMONY ON AUGUST 1, 2016. LEFT TO RIGHT: SCOTT VERPLANK (GOLF); JIMMY HOUSTON (FISHING); BRIAN BOSWORTH (FOOTBALL) AND JOE DIAL (TRACK AND FIELD).

OKLAHOMA SPORTS HALL OF FAME

Joe was inducted into the Oklahoma Sports Hall of Fame, Class 2016, on August 1, 2016. The 2016 Class was representative of a true cross section of Oklahoma sports heroes. Included were Brian Bosworth and Leon Heath, both former OU Sooner football players who went on to play in the National Football League; Scott Verplank, former OSU, PGA Tour and Champions Tour golfer; Jimmy Houston, bass fisherman; and Bob Barry, Jr., Oklahoma City sportscaster.

The expressed mission of the Oklahoma Sports Hall of Fame is "to encourage excellence through sports, academics, health and fitness; preserving our sports heritage while building pride in Oklahoma in the spirit of Jim Thorpe." The stated principle of the Hall of Fame is" encouraging and recognizing excellent character in people who demonstrate this through participation in sports.

At the Oklahoma Sports Hall of Fame Awards banquet held at the Windstar Casino, Joe was presented by Steve Patterson, his high school and college teammate and life-long friend.

The following is Steve's presentation of Joe:

First of all, I would like to say that we drew the short stick in having to follow Jimmy on this induction as well as Mr. Holder and Mr. Castiglione. I am just a high school track coach of 29 years but the one thing I can say is that Joe and I have been friends since elementary school and I would just like to thank him for giving me the honor to be a part of this induction.

Like I said, I have known him basically my entire life. In Marlow, Oklahoma, Joe is affectionately known as "Jumpin' Joe Dial" and that's without the "g" on the end. That's "jumpin'" as in Oklahoman. He's always been the town hero. He's got the sign outside town that says "Home of Joe Dial." He's always been one that the people of Marlow have aspired to. It's like Jimmy said — you have to have a passion. I've been coaching and teaching for 29 years this coming year, and I've never seen anyone have more passion for what they did than Joe Dial. He got that passion from his father, Dean Dial, who was his coach and gave him that passion for pole vaulting.

I can remember Joe, his dad and my dad, when we were in elementary school would get us in the car and say,"C'mon, boys, we're going to the track."

They would take us to the track and we would have their own little decathlon meet, but of course, it would only be Joe and I competing.

They would say, "What do you think we should run now?" "Well, let's run the 100." So we would run the 100. They would give us a little bit of a break. Then we would go ahead and do a different event.

Now our memories may be a little different. He would probably say he won more than I did. But I know one thing. When it came to the pole vault, there was no competition in that particular event. And the reason I can say that, because I witnessed Joe as he was growing up from the small town of Marlow, he had a passion for pole vaulting. He had a passion and a vision for greatness that we all aspire to as we were growing up in our school.

He was the one that shed light to people that were growing up in Marlow at the time. Sam Hinke, who was the general manager for the Philadelphia 76ers, was in a class below ours. Barry Hinson, who is now a coach at Southern Illinois, was a long-time coach with Bill Self at Kansas. Keith Patterson, who is a defensive coordinator at Arizona State University. The list goes on and on of people from that small town that are Marlow born and bred, so to speak.

*A lot of that had to do with Joe Dial. I think he started that passion.
I can remember Joe back in the day. I think half the people in Marlow
thought, what is this guy doing? He would practice all day. Now when
I say all day, I mean from sunup to sundown. And after sundown, I can
remember his dad and his brothers would get the cars out and they would
shine the headlights on the runway and he would vault.*

*This is something he did over and over throughout his junior high school
years all the way into his high school years. I can remember sitting in a
class with Joe and the question was: "what do you want to do when you
grow up?"*

*Joe told the teacher, "I want to be an Olympic champion." And the
teacher kind of scoffed at Joe. Joe was a sophomore in high school and he
said, "I want to be an Olympic champion." And the teacher says, "No,
let's get realistic.*

*I'll never forget what Joe said. He goes, "You mark my words. I'm going
to be an Olympic champion."*

*Joe never became an Olympic champion, so to speak. But he was an
Olympic champion to all of us. He was a junior in high school when he
went to his first Olympic trials. He went to five Olympic trials all together.*

*Like the video said, he was four-time state champion in the pole vault.
He was a great athlete; he ran on all of our relays. He was also voted Track
& Field News High School Athlete of the Year. The video stated that he
was a four-time NCAA champion. He was the first collegiate vaulter to
jump 19 feet at the time. He is also inducted into the OSU Sports Hall of
Fame. He's a professional athlete, we've already gone through that. He
jumped 19-6 as a professional athlete and was the first American to do
that. He was a bronze medalist at Budapest, Hungary. I think the story
he has told was a guy from Hungary was one of the favorites to medal. As
Joe came in, he had people throwing beer on him, spitting on him and
yelling at him and things like that and he thought he was back in Stephens
County (audience laughter).*

*But after his athletic days were over, Joe focused his attention on
coaching. Conveying that passion to the kids on his team, as well hundreds
of kids that he had the chance to influence at his camps that he runs every
day. He runs them all throughout the year and into the summer. It's not
about the money for him. It's about helping them to reach their goals and
to continue to strive for the things that they want in their lives. He can be
that shining light.*

One thing that I will say about my friend Joe. We have been life-long friends and I treasure that. You have someone that you have gone from grade school with all the way through college. We were roommates in college and after that, you know you have a good friend. I would like to thank Joe for his friendship over the years and allowing me to do this.

I would like to say this. I would like to add this one thing that I'm sure Joe would agree that at the pinnacle of his best accomplishment was marrying his wife Shawna of thirty years. She's the perfect assistant. Of course, she is his assistant track coach at ORU and his loving wife. His three boys are such that he, above all things, would put them above any accomplishment that he got at any track meet throughout his career.

At this time, it is my honor to present for induction into the Oklahoma Sports Hall of Fame Mr. Joe Dial.

Joe graciously accepted the honor and delivered his induction speech, the text of which follows:

Well, if I had to pole vault in front of all you guys, I'd be zero nervous. I've vaulted in front of a crowd of 50,000 people in Rome and it didn't even bother me. I didn't even notice they were there. I will be the worst speaker tonight.

I want to thank so many for this honor tonight. Like Jimmy (Houston) said, you can't get to this spot without help. And Lord, I've had plenty of it. I want to thank the Oklahoma Sports Hall of Fame Committee for voting me in. It's a huge honor to me. I want to thank all my family and friends who are here tonight. Thank you very much.

I'd like to tell a quick story. I don't think I'm as long-winded as Jimmy Houston. Gina, Bob Barry's wife, I told her awhile back that I was going to tell this story. I haven't told it to her yet.

In 1986, Bob Barry, Jr. called me and asked me if I would take part in a fund-raiser in Florida called the Goofy Games. I said sure, no problem. I had just broken the American record in El Paso and then I flew out to Florida and we meet up. We had this relay that we had to run. It was a 4 by 1. Each one ran 100 yards, but you had to wear goggles and flippers and carry a bucket of water. I don't know if you had ever ran with flippers before, they are sticking out this far, it is very difficult.

We had this lady who had won a contest to be on our team. She ran the first leg and she did ok. Then Leslie O'Neal was on the second leg. Everybody remembers him as a football player and he did great on the back stretch.

Then Bob Barry, Jr. gets it. He is running around. I remember looking at him with those goggles. He is just laughing and smiling but he's trying as hard as he can. It's really hard to run in flippers. Either you got to get your knees really high or just kind of go like a penguin and that is what he choose to do.

The whole time he is telling me that the guy from the Green Bay Packers who is running the anchor leg was the fastest guy in the NFL. I was actually more fired up to run against this guy than pole vault my American record the week before. My college coach, he never let me run. I was thinking I could be fast. I'd ran a 4.27 40 with five guys clocking me so this is my chance. I'm going to show this guy I can do it. But the problem is I've got flippers on. By the time Bob Barry gets everything off and I put it on, he is just screaming at me," Go get him, Joe!"

I tightened them (the flippers) up since I don't think he tightened them up from Leslie O'Neal. They were just huge. That's probably why he was running like that. So I tightened them up and the first step I almost fell on my face cause my flipper was dragging. But that was the last bad step I had.

Bob Barry, Jr. said to "Go get him" and that is what I did. I remember running that dude down and we won and we were so fired up after that. Gina, I thought you would enjoy that.

I got to travel all over the world many times pole vaulting coming from a small town of Marlow, Oklahoma. I started traveling when I was 17 years old and I retired at the age of 34. So for 17 years, I would grab my poles and go vault some place in the world.

I could tell you many stories all night long of where I went and what I did. I could tell you about the time I was 17 years old running from guys in the streets of Paris right in the middle of the night. Of course, I was only a junior in high school when they invited me to Paris. You don't tell your mom you're running from guys. I couldn't sleep so I was out wandering.

Or the time two guys were chasing me in the streets of Amsterdam. Or the time Pope John Paul II walked up to me and wanted me to kiss his ring. Or the time a bus full of people in Budapest, Hungary wanted to beat me up because my poles had fell off the rack and knocked one of them out. Or being on the awards stand after winning a medal at the World's Championships or the time I competed in eight track meets in five different *countries with only two days of rest. Or the few times I've been with O.J. Simpson — who's going to bring that up? Or the time I sat in the seat that Adolf Hitler sat in at the 1936 Olympics in Berlin to watch Jesse Owens win four god medals.*

But I can't talk about pole vaulting without . . . (pause) . . . without talking about my dad. He showed me how to pole vault when I was five years old. And was my coach my entire career. He never made me go pole vault. I went because I loved to. He was disabled from several back surgeries so he had all the time to go work with me.

And Steve wasn't kidding when he said after breakfast we'd go pole vault till lunch to dinner and after dinner all the way to dark. If it was cold, we would knock the ice out of the box and we'd shine the headlights on. We a had a little Chevy Chevette I'd warm up in and then hop out and go vault real quick.

But one amazing man. He changed the way poles are made today. I'd come home and he'd have a light down inside my pole. I'd say, "What are you doing, dad?" He' said, "I'm figuring out how they made these poles."

And boy did he. When you see them pole vaulting in the Olympics the next few weeks, know that me and my dad had a few things to do with what they are using. I felt like a test pilot when the pole companies would send me new poles to try out with me and my dad's new ideas.

My mom and dad taught me the importance of being a Christian. Not by words, but by example and by the willingness to help others. My whole family is like this. My brother, Jimmy, has volunteered at Marlow and they never asked for any pay. My family has the kindest heart because of my mom and dad. Thanks, mom.

I wish I could stand up here and tell you how great of an athlete I was, but I would be lying. Having a great family and friends' support and by the grace of God is the only reason I was a great pole vaulter.

Thank you for this honor.

APPENDIX

JOE DIAL'S POLE VAULTING CAREER HIGHLIGHTS
(RECORDS, CHAMPIONSHIPS AND SIGNIFICANT EVENTS)

DATE	EVENT	LOCATION	HEIGHT
May 5, 1978	Oklahoma Class 2A State Meet Championship	Midwest City, OK	13-6
May 4, 1979	Oklahoma Class 2A State Meet Championship	Moore, OK	14-6
Jan. 18, 1980	Set National High School Indoor Record	Oklahoma City, OK	16-7.25
Jan. 26, 1980	First H.S Athlete to clear 17 feet indoors	Oklahoma City, OK	17-0
Mar. 7, 1980	State of Texas record	Graham, Texas	16-10
Mar 21, 1980	State of Oklahoma outdoor record	Dickson, OK	16-2.75
April 1, 1980	State of Oklahoma outdoor record	Duncan, OK	16-8.75
April 5, 1980	State of Oklahoma outdoor record	Konawa, OK	17-0
April 12, 1980	Tied State Oklahoma outdoor record	Marlow, OK	17-0
April 19, 1980	Set National H.S record – Kansas Relays	Lawrence, KS	17-5.25
May 2, 1980	Oklahoma Class 2A State Meet Championship	Oklahoma City, OK	17-1
Jan. 16, 1981	National H.S. Indoor Record	Oklahoma City, OK	17-4
Feb. 28, 1981	National H.S. Indoor Record	Oklahoma City, OK	17-4.5
April 3, 1981	National H.S. Outdoor Record	Oklahoma City, OK	17-9.5
May 9, 1981	Oklahoma Class 2A State Meet Championship	Oklahoma City, OK	15-6
May 9, 1981	OK Class 2A State Meet Championship (LJ)	Oklahoma City, OK	23-5.5
June 27, 1981	National H.S. Outdoor Record	Norman, OK	17-11
Aug. 11, 1981	National H.S. Outdoor Record	Stillwater, OK	18-0.25
Aug. 25, 1981	National H.S. Outdoor Record	Stillwater, OK	18-1.25
Feb. 27, 1982	Big 8 Indoor Meet Championship	Lincoln, NE	18-0.5
March 6, 1982	Set NCAA Freshmen Record	Boulder, CO	18-3
April 17, 1982	Kansas Relays Championship	Lawrence, KS	17-0
May 1, 1982	Big 8 Outdoor Record	Stillwater, OK	18-4.5
	New NCAA Freshmen Record		
May 15, 1982	Big 8 Outdoor Meet Championship	Norman, OK	18-0.5
Jan. 8, 1983	State of New Hampshire Indoor Record	Hanover, NH	18-2
	First athlete to clear 18 feet in New England		
Jan. 29, 1983	Career-to-date best	Oklahoma City, OK	18-4.75
Feb. 26, 1983	Big 8 Indoor Meet Championship	Lincoln, NE	18-0

DATE	EVENT	LOCATION	HEIGHT
April 9, 1983	Career-to-date best	Stillwater, OK	18-5.25
Jan. 7, 1984	Career-to-date best	Albuquerque, NM	18-6
Jan. 21, 1984	Tied Career-to-date best	Oklahoma City, OK	18-6
Feb. 25, 1984	Big 8 Indoor Meet Championship	Lincoln, NE	18-0
Mar. 10, 1984	NCAA Indoor Meet Championship	Syracuse, NY	18-0
May 14, 1984	Big 8 Outdoor Meet Championship	Lincoln, NE	18-0
June 2, 1984	NCAA Outdoor Meet Championship	Eugene, OR	18-2.5
Feb. 9, 1985	NCAA Indoor Record	Fayetteville, AR	18-7.625
Feb. 23, 1985	Big 8 Indoor Meet Championship	Lincoln, NE	18-0
Mar, 2, 1985	NCAA Indoor Record	Boulder, CO	18-7.75
Mar. 9, 1985	NCAA Indoor Meet Championship	Syracuse, NY	18-6
April 20, 1985	Kansas Relays Championship	Lawrence, KS	18-8
May 3, 1985	Career-to-date best	Norman, OK	18-9
May 12, 1985	Big 8 Outdoor Meet Championship New American Record First Collegian to clear 19 feet	Manhattan, KS	19-1.5
May 19, 1985	American Record	Norman, OK	19-2.5
May 30, 1985	NCAA Outdoor Meet Championship	Austin, TX	18-6
July 13, 1985	U.S A. Track & Field Championship	Indianapolis, IN	18-9.25
July 27, 1985	Won U.S.A.-Germany Duel Meet	West Germany	17-4
Feb. 1, 1986	Indoor World Record	Columbia, MO	19-4.75
Apr. 12, 1986	Outdoor American Record	Norman, OK	19-2.75
Apr. 20, 1985	Outdoor American Record	El Paso, TX	19-3.5
Apr. 25, 1985	Outdoor American Record	Norman, OK	19-4.25
Feb. 22, 1986	San Diego Invitational	San Diego, CA	19-0.25
Oct. 20, 1986	Won South American Meet	Sao Paulo, Brazil	18-10
Dec. 5, 1986	First 19-foot vault in State of Oklahoma	Norman, OK	19-0
Jan. 5, 1987	Won Australian Meet	Perth, Australia	17-8
Jan. 10, 1987	Won Australian Meet	Perth, Australia	18-4
Jan. 30, 1987	Tied for Millrose Games title (Earl Bell won on fewer misses)	New York City, NY	18-4.75
April 18, 1987	American Record	Lawrence, KS	19-4.75
May 27, 1987	Won U.S.A. – Mobil Meet Championship	San Jose, CA	19-0.25
June 13, 1987	American Record	Albuquerque, NM	19-5.75
June 18, 1987	American Record	Norman, OK	19-6.5
March 5, 1989	IAAF World Indoor Champ. – Bronze Medal	Budapest, Hungary	18-8.25

MAJOR RECORDS

NATIONAL AGE GROUP RECORDS

RECORD	HEIGHT
AAU 14-15 Age Group Record	14-8
Age 15 –Age Group Record	14-9
Age 16 – Age Group Record	16-2.25
Age 17 – Age Group Record	17-4.75
Age 18 – Age Group Record	18-1.25
Age 19 – Age Group Record	18-4.5
Age 20 – Age Group Record	18-5.25

HIGH SCHOOL RECORDS

National Sophomore Class Record	16-2.25
National Junior Class Record	17-5.25
National Senior Class Record	18-1.25
State of Oklahoma H.S. Indoor Record	17-4.50
National High School Indoor record	17-4.50
State of Oklahoma H.S. Outdoor Record	17-9.50
National High School Outdoor Record	18-1.25
Kansas Relays Record	17-5.25
Four-time Class 2A State Champion	
First high school pole vaulter to clear 18 feet	

COLLEGIATE RECORDS

NCAA Freshmen Record – Indoor	18-3
NCAA Freshmen Record – Outdoor	18-4.5
Big Eight Conference Indoor Record	18-0
Big Eight Conference Outdoor Record	19-1.5
NCAA Indoor Record	18-7.75
First collegiate pole vaulter to clear	19 feet

AMERICAN RECORDS (OUTDOOR)

May 12, 1985 Manhattan, Kansas	19-1.50
May 19, 1985 Norman, Oklahoma	19-2.50
April 12, 1986 Norman, Oklahoma	19-2.75
April 20, 1986 El Paso, Texas	19-3.50
April 25, 1986 Norman, Oklahoma	19-4.25
April 18, 1987 Lawrence, Kansas	19-4.75
June 13, 1987 Albuquerque, N.M.	19-5.75
June 18, 1987 Norman, Oklahoma	19-6.50

AMERICAN RECORDS (INDOOR)

RECORD	HEIGHT
February 1, 1986 Columbia, Missouri1	19-4.75

WORLD INDOOR RECORD:

RECORD	HEIGHT
February 1, 1986 Columbia, Missouri	19-4.75

POLE VAULT RANKINGS

TRACK & FIELD NEWS — WORLD RANKINGS

YEAR	RANK
1984	10th
1985	7th
1986	8th
1987	9th

TRACK & FIELD NEWS — U.S. RANKINGS

YEAR	U.S. RANKING
1981	8th
1982	10th
1983	8th
1984	3rd
1985	1st
1986	3rd
1987	4th
1988	10th
1989	3rd
1991	5th
1995	10th

AWARDS AND HONORS

National High School All-American Track Team, 1980

State of Oklahoma High School Pole Vault Champion – 4 years; 1978-1981

National High School Indoor Track Athlete of the Year, 1980 and 1981

Track & Field News National High School Outdoor Track Athlete of the Year; 1981

Hertz Number 1 Award — Best High School Athlete in the State; 1980 and 1981

Kansas Relays Outstanding Performer Award (first high school athlete to win award), 1980

Jim Thorpe Award; Oklahoma's Most Outstanding Athlete, 1981

Big 8 Conference Indoor Champion; 4 years; 1982, 1983, 1984 and 1985

Big 8 Conference Outdoor Champion; 3 years, 1982, 1984 and 1985

Kansas Relays Outstanding Performer Award; 1985

Big 8 Conference Outdoor Track MVP; 1985

Big 8 Conference Male Athlete of the Year; 1985

NCAA National Indoor Champion; 2 years, 1984 and 1985

NCAA National Outdoor Champion; 2 years, 1984 and 1985

NCAA All-American Indoor Track and Field; 4 years: 1982, 1983, 1984 and 1985

NCAA All-American Outdoor Track and Field; 3 years: 1983, 1984 and 1985

Bronze Medalist; Indoor World Championships; Budapest, Hungary, 1989

Member of U.S.A. Team for World Championships: 1987 (Rome); 1989 (Budapest); 1991 (Tokyo)

U.S.A. OLYMPIC TRACK & FIELD

U.S.A. Olympic Track & Field Trials Qualifier; 1980, 1984, 1988, 1992 and 1996

U.S.A. Olympic Team Alternate, 1984

HALLS OF FAME

Golden South Classic Hall of Fame

Oklahoma State University Hall of Honor

Kansas Relays Hall of Fame

National Pole Vault Hall of Fame

National High School Hall of Fame

Oklahoma Sports Hall of Fame

SOURCES

INTERVIEWS:

Joe Dial

Shawna Dial, Joe's wife and ORU assistant track coach

Lena Dial, Joe's mother

Darvis Cole, former Marlow High School track coach

Phyllis Cole, wife of Darvis Cole

Gary Boxley, former Marlow High School track coach

J.D. Martin, former University of Oklahoma track coach

Steve Patterson, friend and teammate at Marlow High School and
     Oklahoma State University and former assistant coach at ORU

Russ Jewett, head track and field coach, Pittsburg State University

NEWSPAPERS:

The Oklahoman

Chicago Tribune

Duncan Banner

Ardmore Daily Ardmoreite

Jenks Journal

Lawrence Journal-World

Lawton Constitution

Lawton Morning Press

Manhattan Mercury

Marlow Review

Meeker News

New York Times

Norman Transcript

Topeka Capital-Journal

Tulsa World

Wewoka Times

Wichita Eagle and Beacon

Wichita Falls Record-News

Wichita Falls Times

PUBLICATIONS:

The Sporting News

Sports Illustrated

Track & Field News

Gentlemen's Quarterly

ACKNOWLEDGMENTS

Thanks to the following individuals who assisted in bringing Joe's story into print.

Shawna Dial

Lena Dial

Bonney & Bob Clark

Ryan Folmar, ORU Baseball Coach

Blake Freeland, ORU Sports Information Department

Steve Patterson

Darvis Cole

Phyllis Cole

Gary Boxley

J.D. Martin

Russ Jewett

Todd Brooks, Editor, *Marlow Review*

Don Ligon

Kerry Sachetta

Carl Brune

Billy Olson

Andretti Bain

Garth Brooks

Jack Whitt

Jeff Hartwig

Oksana Boyko

Sergey Bubka

Kurt Eaton

Kristi Eaton

Jan Eaton

A special thanks to Lena Dial and Shawna Dial for their dedication in compiling the scrapbooks through the years documenting Joe's accomplishments. Their efforts provided invaluable resources for this book.

CPSIA information can be obtained
at www.ICGtesting.com
Printed in the USA
BVHW032143180820
586769BV00004B/8/J